Sir Arthur Sullivan

Sir Arthur Sullivan

PERCY M. YOUNG

LONDON
J. M. DENT & SONS LTD

First published 1971

Copyright © by Percy M. Young, 1971

Made in Great Britain
at the
Aldine Press · Letchworth · Herts
for
J. M. DENT & SONS LTD
Aldine House · Bedford Street · London

ISBN 0 460 03934 2

Preface

A study of Arthur Sullivan is also a study of Victorian England, of which in one sense he was the embodiment. To appreciate him as a great Victorian, however, it is first necessary to relieve him of the inferiority implicitly imposed by the fact of his generally being regarded as the junior member of a particular partnership. Sullivan himself was far from pleased merely to be thought of as Gilbert's coadjutor; if he was to merit consideration, he thought, then it should be on account of his all-round accomplishments. He wished to be counted among composers and not merely among composers of operettas.

As far as his posthumous reputation was concerned Sullivan made the error of achieving success according to the tenets of the popular Victorian philosophy of self-help. He was born poor and became rich. He moved, in stages, from Bolwell Street, Lambeth, to an exclusive address in Westminster, and in so doing accumulated names in his Visitors' Book that represented the ultimate in social achievement. Sullivan walked among princes and earned the envy of those who did not. He was a familiar figure on the race-course and in the casino. He lived almost as luxuriously as Wagner, though not at other people's expense. But he was tolerant and generous, and a good friend.

Sullivan was created by the circumstances of his age. His music caught its opulence and vulgarity, its sentimentality and inclination towards moral evasion, but also its vitality and drive. In his operettas Sullivan helped to sustain that sense of self-mockery that was the most valuable ingredient in the British tradition. He was well qualified to do this, for although he was a notable figure on the Victorian scene he was an outsider. The volatility of his genius and the sharpness of his perception he owed to his forefathers, of whom none were English.

This was a many-sided man, outwardly gay but assailed by inner doubts and fears, often giving the appearance of indolence but

v

continually oppressed by distressful ill-health. The chameleon
qualities of the man are the qualities also of his music. Here I have
tried to gather together all the relevant facts and am grateful to
those, separately acknowledged, who have put material at my disposal. The resulting portrait, I hope, shows the man as he was and
his music as it is.

PERCY M. YOUNG.

Windsor, Ontario.
15th April 1971.

Contents

Illustrations

Music Examples

Unless otherwise stated examples are taken from Sullivan's works

Acknowledgments

Mr Leslie Baily; Peabody Conservatory, Baltimore; Mrs Ruth M. Bleecker, and the Boston (Mass.) Public Library; City Archivist, Bruges; Mr Charles Moore, and the American Conservatory of Music, Chicago; Miss Bridget D'Oyly Carte; Professor Philip Cranmer; Mr Jonson Dyer, and Chappell and Co. Ltd; Dr Walter Eisen; Mrs Phyllis Francillon; Mr Martin Hall, and Boosey and Hawkes Ltd; Murhardsche Bibliothek der Stadt Kassel und Landesbibliothek; Leeds City Libraries; Dr K. McCrone; Frau Herta Schetelich, Musikbibliothek der Stadt Leipzig; Frau M. Walter, Museum für Geschichte der Stadt Leipzig; Borough Librarian, Luton; Public Record Office of Northern Ireland, Belfast; Library and Museum of the Performing Arts, The New York Public Library at Lincoln Center, New York; Professor Dr Piet Nuten, Royal Conservatorium of Music, Antwerp; Rev. M. E. C. Pumphrey, St Michael's Church, Chester Square, London S.W.1; Sir Eric Riches, M.S., F.R.C.S.; Royal Academy of Music, London N.W.1; Royal Military School of Music, Kneller Hall, Twickenham; Charles Russell and Co.; Museum Carolino Augusteum, Salzburg; Mrs Marjorie P. Schofield; Mrs Irene Seccombe, and the Cambridge University Musical Society; Sotheby and Co.; Mr Albert A. Truelove.

1

Chapel Royal Chorister

In a characteristically trenchant essay—on 'The True-Born Englishman'—Daniel Defoe observed that: '. . . speaking of Englishmen ab Origine, we are really all Foreigners ourselves.' The paradox of Arthur Sullivan is that while he appears on the roll of national worthies as a typical Englishman (or, at least, as a typical English composer) he was, *ab origine*, 'all foreigner'. He had no English blood in his veins.

In the Victorian era an Irishman—a special type of foreigner—was not infrequently considered as a kind of second-class Englishman. If, however, he achieved eminence in, or in the service of, England, he was not only up-graded but his Irish antecedents were even regarded as marks of merit. English Romanticism often depended on a gentle disturbance of distant Celtic backwaters. Sullivan, part Irish, but also part Italian and possibly part Jewish, became a legend in his lifetime, and after his death the legend was enlarged.

> His father . . . had selected music as a profession when it was discovered that the paternal acres which he would in ordinary circumstances have inherited as an Irish squire had all been lost to the family.[1]

The name Sullivan (or O'Sullivan) was not only Irish but also, however remotely, noble in origin. The legendary founder of the clan was Oliol Ollum, a King of Munster in the second century, who was himself descended, so it was said, from Heber Fionn, one of the sons of Milesius. In the seventeenth century the principal O'Sullivan, a squire in Cork, omitted the prefix from his name, begot much progeny and left a large number of Sullivans about the south of Ireland. Some were passably rich, most were wretchedly poor. Of the latter some became soldiers in the British Army with a greater or lesser show of willingness. Among those who were unwilling was one of the obscurer Sullivans, Thomas, a native of Kerryshane, Tralee, in County Cork. Thomas, who was born in

1785, served in the 57th Regiment of Foot throughout the Peninsular Wars. Transferred to the 66th Foot and having attained the rank of sergeant, he was among those deputed to guard the exiled Napoleon on St Helena. In 1821 Sergeant Sullivan was invalided from the army. Nine years later he became a pensioner of the Royal Chelsea Hospital, where he died in 1838. His widow became a matron at the Duke of York's School in Chelsea.

Three of Sergeant Sullivan's children attained respectability in later life. A daughter, Elizabeth, became a nun and was said to have ended her life in Bruges as mother superior of a convent.[2] One son, Thomas, became a musician. The other son, John, who was trained as a printer, outlived both his brother and his brother's sons and was present at the funeral of Sir Arthur Sullivan in 1900.

Born in 1805, the year of the Battle of Austerlitz, Thomas learned to play a number of musical instruments at the Duke of York's School, and on the recommendation of the bandmaster he was in due course taken on as an instructor at the Royal Military College, Sandhurst. While here he met Mary Clementina Coghlan (b. 1811) whom he married in 1838—the year of his father's death. Mary was of Italian extraction and it appears that she retained, or at least was loth wholly to lose contact with, the faith of her forefathers (see page 54). That she was partly Jewish is suggested in *The Jewish Year Book* of 1896, by an entry which no one ever seems to have disputed.[3] At the time of her marriage Mary was helping to teach the inmates of a young ladies' seminary.

The better to support his bride, Sullivan went to London and joined the orchestra of the Royal Surrey Theatre as clarinettist. This theatre, garishly appointed, had had a long and varied history. Originally known as the Royal Circus, it had a tradition of equestrian displays, melodramas and pantomimes. Under the management of R. W. Elliston (1774–1831), operas were occasionally staged in the 1820s. Elliston died in 1831, and when Thomas Sullivan joined the theatre orchestra the manager was Mrs Frances Davidge (hence 'Davidge's Royal Surrey Theatre'), whose tastes were catholic and whose attitudes were permissive.

Not long after Sullivan's arrival early in 1839, he was required to play in 'musicals' based on Dickens—*Oliver Twist* and *Nicholas Nickleby*—which were respectively coupled with a pantomime, *Harlequin and the Enchanted Figs*, and a 'nautical burletta' *Blue Jackets*. Even then the Queen's Navy was a popular subject for comic opera, and in March 1839 *The Female Midshipman* (preceded by Auber's overture *Le cheval de bronze*) was played. Taking into account the public demand for the spectacular, Mrs Davidge invested large sums of money in the transformation scenes which naturally belonged to romantic and fairy pieces. In 1843 *Harlequin Puck, or The Elfin Changeling and the Enchanted Statue* (advertised as being based on Shakespeare, Spenser and Chaucer), with music by the regular conductor George Stansbury, was played. In its blend of the supernatural and the topical this piece may be seen to have anticipated *Iolanthe*. One tableau, 'Victoria Tavern and Parliament Skittle Ground', depicted terrain made familiar in the later work, while another gave a poignant Gilbertian touch to satire. This was entitled 'A Call for the Income Tax—Have you no pity for my family?— An awkward reply'. The tradition of *The Beggar's Opera* (played at the Royal Surrey in Thomas Sullivan's time in 1842) was maintained by a succession of historical-realistic thrillers. Hogarth provided the basis for *The Lure of Mammon* (1839) and *Village Tragedy* (1840) —a 'moving amplification' of the *Harlot's Progress*—while *Jack Sheppard*, with a dioramic 'Procession from the Old Bailey to Tyburn' (music by J. M. Jolly), was also performed in 1840.

Mrs Davidge promoted 'grand opera' when works within this genre could be made to appear as belonging to the true Royal Surrey tradition. Her audiences were intent on having their fun (in various directions), but also appreciated a little culture as long as this was well disguised. When occasional operas were staged, there were few pretensions to uplift. For their performance Mrs Davidge augmented her own resources by introducing guest-stars (as also orchestral players and chorus singers) from Covent Garden and Drury Lane. In May 1839 Michael Balfe sang the role of Count Rudolph in Bellini's *Somnambula* and of Caspar in *Der Freischütz*. During the same brief season Donizetti's *L'Elisir d'amore* and Auber's *Fra Diavolo* were given. A year later John Barnett's *Mountain Sylph* (1834) was included in the brief season of opera. In 1845 Edward Loder was guest composer and conductor at the Surrey Theatre, and his *Fair Maid of Perth* was performed there. At about the same time Samuel Beazley's *Ivanhoe*, with music by John Parry, was also given—but with as little success as Arthur Sullivan's 'grand opera' on the same subject half a century later. Nor were the more distant paths of English music untrodden. In 1846 *Macbeth* was played, 'with the whole of Locke's music'.

Mrs Davidge was not unaware of the fact that audience comfort and acoustical excellence were matters to be taken into account. In 1842 the management could proclaim that this

> . . . Popular Place of Amusement . . . [has been] made to resume its Former Elegant and very Commodious Form, care having been taken, in its re-construction, to seize upon every available improvement that could add to the comfort of the Audience: A New Orchestra has been raised on an ingeniously constructed Sounding-Board, to facilitate the diffusion of the Sound . . .

Thomas Sullivan's life at least was interesting and his experience wide. When he took on his job at the theatre he also took a house in south London: 8 Bolwell Street, Lambeth. Earning a guinea a week, Sullivan paid a large part of his wages in rent.[4]

In 1839 a son, Frederic, was born to the Sullivans, and on 13th May 1842 a second son, Arthur, arrived. Registered on 24th June with one Christian name, he was given another—Seymour—at the time of his christening. In later life he discovered that the resulting conjunction of initials was an embarrassment and he eventually came to prefer the form of his name that had been first recorded with the Registrar of Births and Deaths.

The family at first lived in Lambeth in respectable poverty—respectability being attained by Mrs Sullivan's making use of her convent education and going out to teach. Thomas, always on the look-out for means of bettering himself and his family's prospects, was finally able to remove himself from the drudgery of the theatre in 1845, for in that year he returned as Bandmaster to Sandhurst, where he remained for twelve years. In 1857 his reputation for versatility—he was competent as a string, wood-wind and brass teacher—gained for him the coveted post of Professor of Brass Instruments at the Military School of Music, Kneller Hall. His duties were general as well as particular, and included the arrangement of music for military ensemble as well as the actual conducting of the ensemble. It was against this kind of background that the gifts of Sullivan's second son began to blossom.

> The band my father conducted was small, but very good, for he was an excellent musician. I was intensely interested in all that the band did, and learned to play every wind instrument,

with which I formed not merely a passing acquaintance, but a real, life-long, intimate friendship. I gradually learned the peculiarities of each, and found out where it was strong and where it was weak; what it could do, and what it was unable to do. In this way I learned in the best possible way how to write for an orchestra. The oboe and bassoon were the only instruments I was never very proficient on, though I could play them both a little.[5]

In those days it was rare in England for a small boy to be exposed to music in this way—so that he could subconsciously absorb the distinctive qualities of instrumental sonorities—and at the same time to undergo a rigorous training in fundamental techniques. In the environment in which he was nurtured Arthur Sullivan developed early ambitions, of which the most important to him was that he should become a chorister of the Chapel Royal at St James's Palace. The direct route to musical greatness in England was by way of the music of the Anglican liturgy, and to achieve eminence necessitated a strict training as a chorister in a cathedral foundation, or (as was the Chapel Royal) one of similar standing.

Thomas Sullivan was not at all sure that he wished his precocious younger son eventually to follow a musical career, having himself suffered disappointment and disillusion in his profession, and did not immediately respond to Arthur's importunities. Arthur was satisfactorily settled as a boarder in a young gentlemen's academy in Bayswater kept by one William Gordon Flees, where, it was confidently anticipated, he would be adequately prepared for a steady, if unspectacular, future in some safe profession. But the boy, already well informed musically, had a beautiful singing voice. This developed outstandingly, so that by the time Arthur was nine or so it was clear that he should at least be given a chance to gain admission to the Chapel Royal. A friendly clergyman, Rev. Percy Smith, wrote to Thomas Helmore (1811–90), Master of the Children, on 23rd March 1852. On 8th April Helmore replied that he would hear the boy even though he was above the normal probationer's age. It appears that Helmore was strongly advised to admit Sullivan to the choir by Sir George Smart (1776–1867).

Smart, himself an old Chapel Royal boy, was at that time the most influential, and in some respects the most interesting, musician in England. He had sung in the choir of the first great Handel Commemoration in 1784, had played the drums for Josef Haydn, and had been acquainted with Weber (who died at Smart's home in London) and with Mendelssohn. The first conductor in England to have a national—as distinct from a metropolitan—reputation, Smart was a frequent director at the great provincial festivals. He gave first English performances of works by Beethoven, Weber and Mendelssohn, and was a founder member of the Philharmonic Society. In editing madrigals by Gibbons, and Handel's *Dettingen Te Deum*, he helped to stimulate early musicological enthusiasm. Smart was Composer to the Chapel Royal (he succeeded Thomas Attwood in 1838) and produced a sizable portfolio of works for royal occasions, as well as a miscellany of songs and glees, that were as quickly forgotten as they had been composed. His was a dominant personality, and his word was law. But he was generous to the young, and where he detected talent he sought to encourage it. Arthur Sullivan was fortunate to enjoy Smart's favour from the outset, and to have access to his influence at the most critical stage of his apprenticeship to music.

It was in (June?) 1855 that Smart showed his generosity to Sullivan in a remarkable manner—by personally conducting a performance of the boy's anthem *Sing unto the Lord* (of which the manuscript was later given by Sullivan to W. H. Cummings) at the Chapel Royal. This work not only gained the approval of the Prince Consort, but (according to François Cellier, a fellow-chorister) also anticipated 'the refrain' of *H.M.S. Pinafore*.

The ancient office of Master of the Children of the Chapel Royal had once been filled by some of the most eminent names in English music. Since the time of Bernard Gates (Handel's friend) the quality of the Masters had declined, and Helmore, who was appointed in 1846, was no more than an averagely good choir-master of limited aims. The last Master also to be designated 'violist', Helmore was also the first priest to hold the office since the Reformation. He was an experienced teacher, having been Precentor and Vice-Principal of St Mark's College, Chelsea, and a firm disciplinarian. He had a loud voice and a heavy hand, and his pupils feared both.

Helmore was interested in musical pedagogy, plain-song and hymnology, in which branches of scholarship he published a number of works. In 1853, in association with J. M. Neale, he issued a useful collection of *Carols for Christmastide*, and two years later a similar collection for Eastertide. He also had a minor talent for painting, and sometimes displayed examples of his work at the Summer Exhibitions of the Royal Academy. He lived at 6 Cheyne Walk, Chelsea, where his choir-boys lived under his care. As a result of this arrangement the boys saw a good deal of him—sometimes more than was wished. Nothing if not conscientious, Helmore supervised their general as well as their musical studies and insisted on high standards in both.[6] In accordance with the prevailing pedagogic principles of the period there was a strong syntactical foundation to learning. Sullivan found the laws of the grammar of harmony and counterpoint less intractable than those of Latin, so that his excellence in one faculty helped to mitigate the severity of the beatings he earned for his indifferent performances in the other. He was otherwise favoured because of his voice—which drew frequent compliments from the eminent worshippers of the Chapel Royal—and his appearance. He was a good-looking boy.

There were many events in the life of the royal family which required the seal of divine authority, and the presence of the Chapel Royal choristers. Christenings, confirmations, weddings and funerals occurred with some regularity and were often held in the chapel of Buckingham Palace. On 28th June 1853 Sullivan was taken to the Palace together with his fellow-singers, to provide 'sacred music' for the baptism of Prince Leopold, Queen Victoria's youngest son and later known as the Duke of Albany.[7] For an impressionable boy it was a memorable introduction to the fantasy of royal ceremonial. For the first time in his life he saw the Yeomen of the Guard engaged in a major operation, deployed 'in the Great Hall of the Palace, in the Passages leading from the Lower Dining Room and the approach to the Chapel, and upon the Grand Staircase'. He saw all the high officers of Church and State, from the Archbishop of Canterbury to the Master of the Buckhounds. He saw the King of Hanover and the Prince of Prussia—the infant prince's sponsors—as well as a dozen other German princelings. And his was the awful responsibility of singing the solo in the anthem specially composed for the occasion by Michael Costa (1808–84), *Suffer the little children*.

For this exercise he gained the approval of Costa and a bonus of ten shillings from the Prince Consort. Singing solos was, indeed, to prove a highly profitable occupation. The Duke of Wellington (whose musical taste centred on the compositions of his father, the Earl of Mornington) also once gave him ten shillings. This would seem to have been the statutory token of goodwill, for when the Bishop of London (also Dean of the Chapel) wished to mark his appreciation he also handed over half a sovereign. In doing so the Bishop was, in fact, guilty of underpayment; for on that occasion Sullivan had not only sung in, but also composed, the anthem.

It is to Helmore's credit that when he discovered Sullivan's early bent towards composition he encouraged it. Characteristically he suggested a regular routine and wrote to Mrs Sullivan that Arthur should do a weekly stint of exercises, songs and/or anthems. He also enjoyed his pupil's assistance in the harmonization of psalm- and hymn-tunes for various of his publications. While he was still a chorister at least two of Sullivan's anthems were performed in the Chapel. In 1855 he published his first work, *O Israel*, which had been composed while on holiday in Devonshire. He dedicated it to Mrs C. V. Bridg[e]man, mother of a fellow-chorister with whom he was staying at the time.

Sullivan was taking himself seriously as a composer and collected his best work into a manuscript book, of which the title-page was inscribed, 'Arthur Sullivan May 3rd 1855'.[8] In addition to *O Israel* (dated 1st September 1855) this contained: a setting of Psalm 103 for four unaccompanied voices (1856); a madrigal for four voices (26th March 1857); a Scherzo for piano solo (17th April 1857); and a *Capriccio No. 2* (unfinished, April 1857). The madrigal carried an additional note by the composer: 'Written whilst lying outside the bed one night undressed and in deadly fear lest Mr. Helmore should come in—A.S.S.' The habit of working late at night carried on throughout life. Sullivan also collected into this music-book contrapuntal exercises and the trio from *The Martyrdom of St Polycarp* by Sir Frederick Gore Ouseley (1825–89). Presented to the University of Oxford as a doctoral exercise in 1854, this oratorio aroused more interest among the musical (even more among the unmusical) than its few merits should have allowed. Ouseley, of aristocratic lineage, had impeccable social references. He was also rich, and able to hire a choir to sing his oratorio at Oxford. Sullivan was among the choristers engaged, as he was on another Ouseley occasion in the autumn of 1856.

On 26th September the chapel of St Michael's College, Tenbury (founded by Ouseley for the maintenance of a 'Cathedral service'), was consecrated. For this occasion a large choir—from the Chapels Royal at St James's and Windsor, and the cathedrals of Oxford, Exeter, Worcester, Gloucester and Hereford—was assembled. Helmore, who knew Ouseley as a fellow-member of the council of the Musical Institute, and Worcestershire because he had himself been born and brought up at Kidderminster, sang among the tenors. Sullivan led the trebles in a Service in D by Benjamin Rogers and anthems by Boyce and Goss. It is not surprising that at that time he had a high regard for Ouseley, from whose greatest work he not only copied the trio (a direct crib from *Elijah*), but also recommended the March to his father for the Kneller Hall band. There being no printed parts available he obligingly copied out a set (according to legend he wrote this music out from memory) for the use of the military musicians.

On 10th June 1855 Queen Victoria opened the Crystal Palace— to be a focal point of British musical culture for many years to come —and the music came under Costa's direction. At that time he was the principal virtuoso conductor in England and, being Italian, was considered the most proper undertaker of music for national occasions. The 'Hallelujah' chorus from *Messiah* was sung by a choir of 1,500, supported by an orchestra that included 200 brass players. (The soloist in the national anthem was Clara Novello, whose final high B flat was so affecting that all the policemen present defied convention and standing orders by removing their helmets.) The Crystal Palace was to occupy an important place in Arthur Sullivan's life, and as a boy he visited it frequently. On 2nd July 1855, for example, he replied to an invitation from a Mr Gray saying that he was 'an invalid at home', but hoped to be able to go to the Crystal Palace on Friday, and asking where he should meet Gray. The Crystal Palace soon became a natural home for oratorio, and the Chapel Royal boys, who were frequently hired out to maintain the reputation of Handel, soon found themselves singing there. Sullivan was a member of the chorus for the Handel Festival of 1857 (a tryout for the Centennial Festival of 1859). What he particularly remembered from that period, however, was his first hearing of Jenny Lind. Thirty years later, in a letter to Otto Goldschmidt after Jenny Lind's death, he wrote:

> My memory carries me back thirty one years, when as a boy in the Chapel Royal I received the greatest & most lasting impression of . . . my life; when, singing at your concert, I heard her for the first time, and was taken notice of & praised by her. She it was who made me think that music was divine. . . .

In addition to his other commitments Costa had been conductor of the Philharmonic Society. In 1854 he resigned this appointment after some dissension and was replaced for a season by Richard Wagner. If Wagner's own works met with general disapproval, the fact that he was willing to conduct home-grown symphonies—by Cipriani Potter and Charles Lucas—was an encouragement to some of the young to believe that prospects for a native composer were not quite hopeless. Then and later Wagner exerted some influence on the young Sullivan, but in 1855 his importance in England declined as William Sterndale Bennett (1816–75), very much the rising light in musical affairs in England, took over the Philharmonic.

Bennett undertook the direction of the Philharmonic concerts with enthusiasm. After a year or two his enthusiasm diminished. He came to the rostrum, as Hanslick noted in 1862,[9] palpably tired from teaching, bored, and always under the handicap of never having more than a single rehearsal. In the end this meant playing safe, and abjuring new works in favour of the hardy annuals. In his first year, however, Bennett gave increased space in the programmes to modern German music—to Spohr, Mendelssohn and Schumann. At the sixth concert of the 1856–7 season Schumann's *Paradise and the Peri*, with Jenny Lind as principal soloist, was given its first English performance. The libretto was based on part of Thomas Moore's *Lalla Rookh*, a work which within a year or two was also to inspire Sullivan. The chief Philharmonic novelty of 1857 was the E minor Piano Concerto of Anton Rubinstein (1829–94). J. W. Davison, of *The Times*, did not much like Rubinstein; nor did Sullivan, who described Rubinstein as one who 'had a lot of clap-trap about him, whose own composition, lacking in even two bars of harmony or melody, is a disgrace to the Philharmonic'.[10]

As was becoming apparent from the general trend of Philharmonic programmes, German influence was intensifying. The belief that Germany was the greatest of musical countries derived in large measure from the virtual beatification of Mendelssohn in England. One result of this was that, after Mendelssohn's death, his friends in Leipzig proposed the institution of scholarships in his memory, to be tenable in Leipzig. A London committee was set up to consider this project, consisting of Smart, Karl Klingemann,[11] and E. Buxton, a member of the publishing house of Ewer and Co. The first intention, to make it possible for a British student to study in Leipzig, was not immediately fulfilled,[12] but in 1856 the accumulated funds were drawn on to provide a Mendelssohn Scholarship at the Royal Academy of Music in London.

The competition to determine the first holder of the scholarship took place in June 1856. The result left Sullivan and Joseph Barnby (1838–96) sharing first place. Barnby, formerly a chorister in York Minster, had the advantage of having already studied at the Academy for two years. At the second trial, however, on 28th June, Sullivan was preferred, and on 22nd September, while still retaining his place in the Chapel Royal, he took up his scholarship.[13]

The records of the Royal Academy indicate that he was recommended by 'Mr. Goss'. His teachers in the first place were Arthur O'Leary (1834–1919)—an Irishman from Tralee who had studied in Leipzig where he had got to know Mendelssohn and the Schumanns—and Bennett. He also had lessons with Frederick Jewson (1823–91), a Scottish pianist and composer, and with his sponsor John Goss, the then paragon of Anglican musical virtue, who at the end of 1856 was appointed to succeed William Knyvett (1779–1856) as Composer to the Chapel Royal.[14] This meant that Sullivan, who learned harmony from Goss at the Academy, met him in two capacities.

As his first royal occasion occurred soon after his admission to the Chapel Royal, so Sullivan's last such occasion came just before he gave up his place in the Chapel, at the end of his first year at the Academy. On 16th June 1857 the baptism of Princess Beatrice took place at Buckingham Palace. The ceremonial was as colourful, the crowned heads as plentiful, the Yeomen of the Guard as ubiquitous, the Master of the Buckhounds as active, as at the christening of Prince Leopold. Arthur Sullivan was impressed by Court and Society as a boy. He developed and retained the manners and attitudes of a courtier.

Early impressions, as suggested in this connection, have a lasting influence. In the autumn of 1857 there were others which also made a lasting mark. His brother Fred was of a livelier disposition than Arthur, and his inability to take life seriously ultimately proved unhelpful to his career as an architect. He was, in fact, never quite good enough in any faculty to enjoy an easy life. But his great interest in the theatre was an early incentive to Arthur. In the autumn of 1857 Fred Sullivan became a member of a newly founded dramatic society which had its headquarters in Pimlico. Requiring a supporting team of musicians at minimal cost, the society turned to Fred's brilliant brother. Arthur duly undertook the responsibility and collected an ensemble of twenty-six players (all Academy students), which he himself conducted. For a time all went well. But the Duke of Westminster, who owned Pimlico and a good deal of several other parts of London, exercised his prerogative as landlord and banned dramatic activities on his territory. Thus the Pimlico Dramatic Society was short-lived.[15] Nonetheless, it furnished Arthur Sullivan with early opportunity to practice music in a theatrical setting. It was at about this time that he busied himself with a Shakespearian overture, though it is improbable that the subject, *Timon of Athens*, was one with which he became acquainted at the Pimlico Dramatic Society.

Sullivan composed with some regularity at the Academy, and the end of his career there was marked by the public performance of the Overture in D minor which he dedicated to Goss. This work was played at the Academy on 13th July 1858, four days before Sullivan's leaving it. Among other works, the programme contained:

> . . . 2 movements from symphony in G minor, by Mr. J. B. Turner (pupil of Mr. G. A. Macfarren), which gives evidence of originality and considerable orchestral skill; and an overture by Mr. Sullivan (pupil of Mr. J. Goss), the young gentleman who gained the Mendelssohn scholarship. . . .[16]

By the time the notice of this concert appeared the 'young gentleman' was packing his bags and preparing to go to Germany. A clause in the constitution of the Mendelssohn Scholarship which made study abroad for a year possible, was brought into effect for the first time for the benefit of Arthur Sullivan.

NOTES TO CHAPTER ONE

1. Obituary of Sir Arthur Sullivan, in *The Manchester Guardian*, 23rd November 1900.
2. *See* H. Sullivan and N. Flower, *Sir Arthur Sullivan, His Life, Letters and Diaries*, 2nd edn., London, 1950, p. 5, fn. 1. According to the City Archives of Bruges, however, Elizabeth Sullivan did not die in the city, nor was her name ever recorded among the resident foreigners. The records of the 'English Convent' do not show that she was ever a member of that house, nor is she to be traced in the episcopal records. There were Sullivans (and O'Sullivans) in Bruges. On 5th March 1867, Michael Sullivan 'sans profession . . . né & domicilié à Cork . . . résidant à Bruges', aged 24, died. On

1st December 1884, Daniel O'Sullivan (*aet.* 14), son of Daniel O'Sullivan and also born in Cork, died at 11 rue Adrian Willaert.

3. Joseph Righy, an Italian, married Mary Louisa Frances Lawrence. Their second child, Mary Louisa Margaret, married (firstly) James Cog[h]lan, and Mary Clementina Coghlan was the second child of this marriage. After the death of Mary Clementina's father, her mother married (secondly) Robert Foy. (*The Jewish Year Book, 5657*, London, 1896.) In a list of 'Jewish celebrities of the nineteenth century', first compiled in 1885, Sullivan is shown as having had one Jewish parent (p. 125). On Sullivan's origins *see also* quotation from Francillon in Note 4, Chapter 2 below.

4. In 1901 the gross value of the property was still, as in Sullivan's time, £28; the rateable value, £23. On 20th July 1901 a memorial plaque, subscribed for by the Incorporated Society of Musicians, was unveiled.

5. Autobiographical fragment, quoted in *Birmingham Mail*, 23rd November 1900.

6. 'His duty is to preside not only over the Musical, but over the general, and above all the moral and Christian education of the Children . . . [and] he provides an Usher or Assistants . . . [and] instruction in reading, writing, Arithmetic, Geography, History, and the Rudiments of Latin as well as Music. . . .' From the report of a commission appointed to consider the Chapel Royal, signed by the Bishop of London on 3rd July 1860, and recorded in the Cheque Book of the Chapel. Public Records Office, P.R.O. 28 (1).

The same report showed that the organists (2), composers (2) and Gentlemen (16), who worked in two shifts, with 2 altos, 3 tenors and 3 basses in each, each earned £58 per annum. The organ-blower's stipend was £16. The Master was allowed £577 (plus £32, the salary of 'violist a sinecure'), out of which he had to maintain the boys in his home. According to *Crockford's Clerical Directory* (1860) Helmore's personal stipend as Master was £77, to which his appointment as Priest in Ordinary added £100.

7. See 'The Chapel Royal Days of Arthur Sullivan', by an old fellow-chorister [Christopher Vickry Bridg[e]man], *Musical Times*, 42, March 1901, p. 167.

8. *See* Appendix I, p. 272.

9 E. Hanslick, 'Musikalisches aus London', *Aus dem Concert-Saal, 1848–68*, Vienna/Leipzig, 1897, p. 578.

10. Sullivan and Flower, *Sir Arthur Sullivan*, 1950 edn., pp. 13–14.

11. Karl Klingemann (1800–62), from 1827 and for some years a member of the staff of the Hanoverian Embassy in London, was a poet and an intimate friend of Mendelssohn and Moscheles. On his death Sullivan wrote to Klingemann's widow, saying that he was 'mourned by his friends as an upright man and true Christian'. See *Mendelssohn and his friends in Kensington* (letters from Fanny and Sophy Horsley), ed. R. B. Gotch, London, 1934, p. 272.

12. See *Musical Times*, 4, March 1854, p. 383: 'It will be recollected that, five years ago, a concert was given, the proceeds of which were to be applied to the foundation of scholarships under the above title [Mendelssohn] . . . It has been stated that, in furtherance of this object the sum of £1,000 has recently been forwarded to Germany: this, however, is not the fact: the English trustees have waited in vain for some steps to be taken in the matter by the promoters of the scheme in Germany, who, to speak mildly, have been extremely dilatory in fulfilling their self-imposed duties.' *See also* April issue, 1854, p. 11.

13. 'When I was about fourteen, I heard that a competitive examination would take place at the Royal Academy of Music for a scholarship founded in memory of Mendelssohn. There was a large number of competitors, and when I saw them I almost gave up all hope of success. However, when it came to the last day of the examination, it was announced that the scholarship lay between the eldest and the youngest of the competitors. Needless to say, I was the youngest. The eldest was Joseph Barnby. During that long summer day Barnby and I went through a most searching final examination. At the close, the judges reserved their decision. I was living at No. 6, Cheyne Walk, with Mr. Helmore.

'I spent the day in a fever of excitement. Every time I heard a knock at the door, my heart was in my mouth. Two o'clock came—three—four, I was beginning to lose hope. At last, rat-tat! The postman's knock. It was unmistakable. I crept into the hall. The maid-servant passed by me, and went to the letter-box.

'"A letter for you, Master Sullivan," she said.

'I took it from her, tore it open, and then—I had won it. I don't think I ever felt such joy in my life. I have that precious letter now, framed and hung on my wall, with other pleasant reminders of happy, bygone days.'

Sullivan's own account, in: R.A.N., 'Sir A. Sullivan and the Scholarship', *Country Gentleman*, December 1900.

14. Appointment ratified on 28th November 1856, to commence on 1st January 1857. (Cheque Book of the Chapel.)

15. *See* note contributed by Edward Peacock to *Musical Times*, 42, March 1901, pp. 165–6.

16. *Musical Times*, 8th August 1858, p. 292. J. B. Turner probably indicates 'J.G.T.', who celebrated Sullivan's setting of *It was a lover and his lass* (R.A.M. Midsummer Concert 1857, see p. 277) with an acrostic. *See* Leslie Baily, *The Gilbert and Sullivan Book*, London, 1952, p. 14.

2
Student in Leipzig

Fortified by the commendation of his London teachers, the affection of his proud parents, and a slender working knowledge of the German language acquired from Mrs Karl Klingemann, Sullivan arrived in the then musical capital of northern Europe in the September of 1858. He took a room near the Königsplatz, at 15 Grosse Windmühle Strasse. As Elgar testified twenty-five years later, even to visit Leipzig for a fortnight was, for a British music student accustomed to the wayward character and financial instability of English musical institutions, an unforgettable and enriching experience. In Leipzig music was a matter for civic pride, and one for which the civic authorities and the public were willing to pay. Sullivan, although initially looking forward to only one year in the city, had the good fortune to spend three there. That he did so was due to his industry and determination to succeed. He went to Leipzig as one of many students who aspired to greatness: he left as one of the few who might conceivably achieve it.

Leipzig possessed many musical organizations, but in one way or another they were interdependent. The most famous, and the oldest, were the choir of the Thomaskirche and the Gewandhaus orchestra. When Sullivan lived in Leipzig the Thomascantor was Moritz Hauptmann (1792–1868), appointed on Mendelssohn's recommendation in 1842, who remained in this office for twenty-six years. From 1848 until 1860 the conductor of the Gewandhaus orchestra was another protégé of Mendelssohn, Julius Rietz (1812–1877), who for some time also conducted the Leipzig opera. After his removal to Dresden in 1860, to conduct the royal opera, his place at the Gewandhaus was taken by Karl Reinecke. During the 1850s the influence of Mendelssohn—strongly marked also in England—was still felt in Leipzig, but rather more on account of his administrative than his purely creative genius. By his efforts on behalf of J. S. Bach he had made the Thomaskirche a place of pilgrimage, and had also made possible the foundation of the Bach

Gesellschaft (1850), with which all the leading musicians of Leipzig (as well as of the rest of Germany) were associated. From this new enthusiasm for Bach had sprung ancillary institutions such as the Riedelscher Verein (1854), whose founder, Karl Riedel (1827–88), gave the first Leipzig performance of the Mass in B minor on 10th April 1859. The *St Matthew Passion* had been re-established in the Good Friday order at St Thomas's in 1854.

As conductor of the Gewandhaus orchestra Mendelssohn had brought that body to a high pitch of excellence, and he had enlarged both the scope of the programmes and the catchment area for visiting virtuosi. He had, on occasion, gone against a strongly held German prejudice and engaged performers from England. By his promotion of Englishmen—in particular Sterndale Bennett, who was also commended by Schumann—he had made it possible even for a composer from England to be taken seriously in Leipzig. Mendelssohn's greatest benefit to the city, however, was the Conservatorium. With the blessing of, and subventions from, the municipality and the State of Saxony, this had rapidly acquired the reputation of the finest school of music in Europe. This reputation is attested by the fact that from its foundation in 1843 until 1868, the number of British students was 109 (73 male, 36 female) and of American 85 (68 male, 17 female).

Among students who entered the Conservatorium in 1858, in addition to Sullivan, were Jessie Reid from Glasgow, Walter Bache (1842–88) from Birmingham, John Francis Barnett (1837–1916) from London, Edvard Hagerup Grieg (1843–1907) from Bergen, and Dudley Buck (1839–1909) from Hartford, Connecticut. In the next year Franklin Taylor (1843–1909) arrived, also from Birmingham, while more Americans came from Albany, New York, Boston and Worcester. The 1860 intake included Madeline Gertrude Schiller of London, Edvard Grieg's brother, John, and Katharina Blanda Fanny Bach of Meiningen. The last-named student belonged to a well-known musical family and was a descendant of Johann Ludwig, J. S. Bach's cousin in Meiningen.

During this time some of the professors appointed in 1843 were still in office. Mendelssohn's intimate, Ferdinand David (1810–73), and Moritz Hauptmann and Karl Ferdinand Becker (1804–77), were the principal teachers of violin and conducting, harmony and counterpoint, and organ, respectively. Hauptmann, a scholar of wide interests and a disciple of Hegel in philosophy, made important contributions to the rapidly developing field of *Musikwissenschaft*; while Becker, organist of the Nikolaikirche, continued to extend the historical boundaries of musical knowledge in the tradition of Nikolaus Forkel. Soon after the Conservatorium had opened its doors, its popularity necessitated additional staff and a number of 'extraordinary teachers' were appointed. Of these the most celebrated was Ignaz Moscheles (1796–1876), a virtuoso pianist who had studied in Vienna with Albrechtsberger and Salieri, and had heard Beethoven play. Prior to his Leipzig appointment, Moscheles, an international figure, had made London his headquarters; he had many friends there, and this fact was of some help to Sullivan. Louis Plaidy (1810–74), although less well known than Moscheles as a performer, also taught the piano and was esteemed for his thoroughness. He was, however, conservative, and one of the principal detractors of Schumann, Wagner and Liszt. Ernst Friedrich Richter (1808–79), University Music Director and conductor of the Singakademie, was a tower of strength on the theoretical side; while Karl Franz Brendel (1811–68), proprietor of the *Neue Zeitschrift für Musik* from 1844, countered Plaidy's influence and wielded a polemical pen in the cause of the 'new music'. The Sunday soirées at Brendel's house were a famous institution, attended by celebrated artists and favoured students, and they exerted a strong influence on Leipzig taste and thought. In 1859 the cult of modernity was decried by, among others, Brahms and Joachim, and Brendel, recognizing the absurdity of rival camps, from then on attempted to reconcile the conflicting interests. In 1849 Robert Papperitz (1826–1903), organist of the Nikolaikirche, joined the staff of the Conservatorium to teach organ, piano, harmony and composition. Two years later Raimond Dreyschock (1824–69), leader of the Gewandhaus orchestra, augmented the violin teaching strength. In 1860 one of the greatest of all the Leipzig teachers came to take the place of Rietz—Karl Reinecke (1824–1910), who supervised choral music and gave lessons in piano and composition. At one period of his life Reinecke taught Sullivan, at another, Delius.

A catalogue of the most famous teachers of the Conservatorium shows a powerful team. But each member of this team was much more than a specialist in one field. None was uncreative—most were composers and/or effective writers and critics—and all, schooled in the most rigorous German tradition, were zealous in the promotion and protection of creativity as it was discovered among their pupils.

Sullivan remarked on the strenuous academic discipline to Mrs Klingemann on 22nd January 1859. While thanking her for her help with the language, he said that in Leipzig his other studies were so pressing that he had little time left over to work at German.

One of the advantages of study at the Leipzig Conservatorium was that the close relationship existing between that institution and the Gewandhaus ensured early opportunity for a promising young artist to test his skills in the open market. There came to be no discrimination on the part of the Gewandhaus committee against those who were not German; nor did the public generally take too much exception to unknown names on the programme. The respect shown to British musicians of promise in Leipzig was greater than most of them were to experience at home.

During Sullivan's first year in Leipzig one Gewandhaus concert stood out above the others, and showed not only that the Leipzigers could on occasion be ungenerous (a fact later noted by George Grove, see pages 57–8), but that in judgment they were not infallible. On 27th January 1859 Johannes Brahms, having already given a programme of the work in Hannover, played his D minor Piano Concerto, the conductor being Rietz. It was received in a silence broken only by the applause of two or three members of the audience, and by those who felt obliged to make public protest against the doctrine of unintelligibility apparently proclaimed by Brahms. The criterion by which new works were assessed in Leipzig was the music of Mendelssohn and—in the judgment of a few only—Schumann. For the latter, regarded by many as the acme of modernism, 1859 was a good season, the Fourth Symphony, *Faust* and *Manfred* all being performed at the Gewandhaus; and Sullivan became a vigorous champion of Schumann.

The year 1859 was otherwise distinguished by the celebrations in honour of the centenary of Schiller's birth. With characteristic devotion to a national hero the Germans prepared solemnities on the grand scale, and 10th November was declared a national holiday. In Leipzig the combined choirs of the Singakademie, the Pauliner Sängverein and the Thomanen-Chor, with the Gewandhaus orchestra, performed Mozart's Requiem. There was also a ceremony in the Market-Place, followed by a lantern-lit procession of the city's choral singers to Schiller's house (now a museum) in the suburb of Gohlis for a celebratory concert. In honour of the centenary, Rietz composed a Festival Overture and Richter a cantata.

Although obliged to live frugally, Sullivan, enjoying independence for the first time, made the most of all these opportunities. As he had been by his London teachers, so also he was more than a little spoiled by his Leipzig professors, whose frequent hospitality he was able to enjoy. Moscheles—whose son Felix was to become a close friend—especially had high hopes of him.[1]

Sullivan was also under the wing of Mendelssohn's sister-in-law, Mrs Schunck, and Walter Bache described how he and Sullivan were on occasion entertained at her house, where they met Mendelssohn's daughters and Konrad Schleinitz, the lawyer, who was a director of the Conservatorium on behalf of the municipality.[2]

The first intention was that Sullivan should become a pianist. At the end of his first year he took a modest part in the *Hauptprüfung* (the graduation concert). It was clear that although his talent was considerable there was no intention to force his development, nor to dissuade him from the principle that it was best to work up from the bottom. Together with Diana Ashton of Durham (whose performance in Beethoven's G major Concerto at the earlier *Prüfung*, in April, had been admired), Helene Jensch of Münster and Bernhard van der Eyken of Haarlem, Sullivan took part in a performance of an unascribed eight-handed fantasy (*Contraste*) for two pianos. Liszt was present at this concert, at which the greatest praise was for Barnett's performance in Weber's C major Piano Concerto.

At the previous concert in April, Barnett's quality as composer had been noted with faint praise.[3] Sullivan was fortunate in that Rietz overruled suggestions that he might also submit a composition, since the impact he was to make a year later would have been blunted by the previous display of a less mature (if charming) example of his talent. The work in question, 'a little romance for four stringed instruments', was, however, played at one of the informal evenings, and Sullivan wrote to his parents that it gave general satisfaction. This work, dedicated to Mrs Sullivan, was composed on 2nd November 1859.

Liszt, although regarded with great suspicion by the more conventional teachers at the Conservatorium, was much in evidence in Leipzig in that summer of 1859. In June he came up again from Weimar for a meeting of the Tonkünstler-Versammlung, and to propagandize for the 'new music'. David gave a party to which everyone who was anyone was invited, and Sullivan was among the guests. Hans von Bülow (1830–94) and Hans von Bronsart (1830–1913)—who conducted the Euterpe concerts in Leipzig for the next two seasons—were also present. After the musical part of the at-home had been concluded Sullivan was delighted to be invited to play cards with David, Bronsart and Liszt, and then to be asked to walk home with Liszt. One of Sullivan's friends of that time later recalled his genius for making profitable social progress:

> It was part of [his] nature to ingratiate himself with everyone that crossed his path. He always wanted to make an impression and, what is more, he always succeeded in doing it. . . . In this way he got into personal touch with most of the celebrities. . . . He was a natural courtier, which did not prevent him, however, from being a very lovable person.

Clara Barnett, who thus remembered Sullivan,[4] was one of the three children (the others being Rosamond and Domenico) of John Barnett (1802–90), in a performance of whose *Mountain Sylph* Thomas Sullivan had once played the clarinet at the Royal Surrey Theatre. The Barnett children inherited musical talent from both sides of the family for their mother was a daughter of Robert Lindley (1776–1855), the famous cellist. Rosamond was a god-daughter of Liszt. Since the children's gifts were apparent early in life their parents took them to Germany (Barnett père was Hungarian-German in origin and a second cousin of Meyerbeer), and one by one they entered the Leipzig Conservatorium.

Mrs Barnett's house in Leipzig (Barnett stayed in Cheltenham to maintain his lucrative teaching practice) became one of a number of homes-from-home for the British colony. In the summer of 1859 Sullivan saw a good deal of the family. Together with Walter Bache, the Barnetts and other friends, Sullivan went over to Halle for the unveiling of the Handel statue on 1st July. He and Bache approved the statue, but considered the performance of *Samson* by the united music societies of the city, conducted by Robert Franz, inferior to those to which they were accustomed in England. Sullivan next visited the Barnetts in their summer retreat at Bad Schandau on the Bohemian border. Clara was captivated by Sullivan, and none too pleased when, towards the end of a deliciously flirtatious fortnight, he examined with some care the charms of a couple of Irish girls who were also holidaying in the neighbourhood. Even at that time, as Clara ruefully remarked, Sullivan was a regular devil as far as girls were concerned. On 3rd December, however, he was busy restoring himself in the graces of at least one member of the Barnett family. On that day he wrote *Ich möchte hinaus es jauchzen*, and dedicated it to Rosamond—a fact which Clara forgot to mention in her memoirs.

The reports on Sullivan that reached London in the summer of 1859 were entirely satisfactory, and the Mendelssohn Committee renewed his scholarship. In September Moscheles wrote to Smart, remarking on Sullivan's growing promise as a composer and also on his often expressed affection for the Smarts. Smart himself began to be slightly doubtful of Sullivan's future intentions. Hearing how he was carried away by a new-found enthusiasm for conducting the old man warned that, since this profession had been devalued by there being in England too many conductors of too little competence, it was better to stay faithful to the piano. Skill on this instrument, he said, could always be turned into funds by way of teaching. But Sullivan's piano technique, according to Walter Bache, was not particularly assured, while his ambition to conduct had been fired by long conversations with David.

His first real opportunity came at the Rietz celebrations on 28th March 1860, when he directed the Conservatorium orchestra in a performance of some of the works of the departing master. 'I come in for all the conducting now,' Sullivan wrote to his father.[5] That his piano studies were secondary was indicated by the exercises proffered at the graduation concerts at the end of the academic year. All the laurels for piano playing were bestowed on Rosamond Barnett, who also distinguished herself as a singer, according to the *Neue Zeitschrift für Musik* (52, 1860). On 23rd April she first sang a recitative and cavatina from Rossini's *Tancredi* 'with great ardour', and then played the first movement of the 'Emperor', 'with the same intensity that marked her singing'.

At the second *Prüfungskonzert* on 25th May, Jessie Reid played the first movement of Moscheles's G minor Concerto; but the main interest on this occasion centred on Sullivan, appearing in the dual role of composer and conductor. During this second year he had made further inroads into the goodwill of the influential. His quartet movement had been approved by Ludwig Spohr (1784–1859), and Wenzel Heinrich Veit (1806–64), an important patron of music and amateur composer; now came an overture of which the merits had already been advertised by Moscheles.

... Arthur Seymour Sullivan, from London [appeared] with an Overture in E major to Thomas Moore's *Rosenfest*. Directed by the young composer himself in the most unassuming manner, this work made a lively impression by reason of its excessively fiery nature. Because in respect of thematic invention and working-out, and harmonic combination, the overture is so completely conceived in Mendelssohnian style it is not possible to give a proper opinion on the future prospects of the composer's independent creative ability.[6]

Another reviewer, in the Leipzig *Signale*, was prepared to go a stage further:

Mr. Sullivan still works preponderantly in Mendelssohnian idiom; but he manipulates this with skill and taste, and his Overture is well-proportioned, organically developed, and most charming in its sonorities. It gives rise to the best expectations for his future as a composer.

Since Sullivan never completely managed to disguise his early affection for Mendelssohn it is hardly surprising that the influence was so evident at this stage of his career. The choice of subject for his Overture—the Persian 'Feast of Roses' as described in Moore's *Lalla Rookh*—suggests, however, that his enthusiasm for Schumann, whose *Paradise and the Peri* was taken from the same work, was increasing. Partly this was due to the frequency with which Schumann's works were performed in Leipzig, partly to the opportunity of hearing Clara Schumann, who, with Joachim, came to the Conservatorium during that year.

After the *Hauptprüfung* of 1860 Sullivan anticipated an early return to England, even though Moscheles and Plaidy were anxious that he should stay in Leipzig for a further six months at least. The Mendelssohn Scholarship was not renewable for another year, and it seemed that there was no chance of raising funds elsewhere. George Smart promised a donation of five pounds towards an extra year, but that left at least thirty-five to be found from other sources. In the end it was Thomas Sullivan who found ways and means of making up the balance. In addition to his Kneller Hall duties he undertook evening-class teaching at Broadwoods, where he attended four nights a week. It was through this paternal effort and act of sacrifice that Sullivan achieved recognition as an outstanding composer. The extra time allowed him in Leipzig gave him incentive and opportunity to write a major work.

With Mendelssohn's *A Midsummer Night's Dream* and Joachim's recent Overture for *Henry IV* (first performance, Gewandhaus, 24th March 1859) in mind, and with knowledge of John Henry Griesbach's *The Tempest* [7] and Potter's *Cymbeline* [8] and *Antony and Cleopatra* [9] Overtures, which had been played at Philharmonic concerts in London, he planned a sequence of pieces illustrative of *The Tempest*. Mendelssohn had once hoped to write an opera based on this theme, but Karl Immermann had failed to produce a suitable libretto. Mendelssohn had also been expected to provide incidental music for the play for the King of Prussia in 1842, but this commission was never accomplished. Sullivan—somewhat inspired, it was said, by the thunderstorm of August 1860 that shook the Leipzigers into declaring it the greatest that had ever struck the city—took up the subject to some extent as Mendelssohn's surrogate. He was the friend of many who had been friends of Mendelssohn; at this juncture the most important of them was Konrad Schleinitz, who arranged for Sullivan to be excused from paying tuition fees during his last year. Sullivan worked intensively at his *Tempest* music during the last months of 1860, and the score was ready by March 1861.

From this period there survive a fragment of a letter from Sullivan to Clara Barnett, now in Berlin, and a complete letter to her sister. Both are of great interest, not only for the light they throw on student life of the time and on the progress of the *Tempest* music, but for their illumination of Sullivan's character. By no means of least interest is the kind of Lewis Carroll fantasy within the fragment to Clara:

> . . . the Town, if the twins have dropped their Leipzig accent and patronised the Berlin, if you ever accidentally put a right article now whilst speaking German, if you have heard from Liszt,—and in fact everything concerning your present life should I like to know, for you know how interested I am in the welfare of you both. If I thought it would interest you, I should tell you how Leipzig itself is the same as it ever was, although its attraction for me is gone now that you have all left, how Bernsdorff and Jadassohn are low spirited in the concerts without you, how people are born and die, and everyone gets older everyday, how I am getting morose and surly, and how I dream every night, that Mrs. Barnett is boiling on the stove, while the teapot plays Chopin's Concerto, and you are pouring

your sister out into the cups for us to drink—how Domenico
[Barnett] is gone to Bubendorff to see Bobby who wrote him a
letter the other day beginning 'My dear Sir' and ending 'yours
truly'—how my 'Tempest' music is progressing and going to
take the world by 'Storm'—How Rudorff and I sat up (last
week) until 4 o'clock one night or rather morning, playing
'Orpheus', 'Armida', and 'Erlkönigstochter', and that it was
the only time I was glad Mrs. Barnett wasn't here, for I should
have caught it—how I have been photographed for [Ferdinand]
David and look so horrible, that I have hid the pictures out of
sight, for I dare not look at them, how [Franklin] Taylor was
ill for two weeks and did not have the measles nevertheless,—
how I must soon leave off and go to the lesson, and how, finally,
wishing you all health and happiness for many, many years to
come I shall always, my dear Miss Clara, continue to be your
sincerely attached friend,

Arthur S. Sullivan

P.S. In remembering me kindly to your Mamma, Aunt, and
the rest of your family, please tell your sister that she ought by
rights to have written to me already, and that if she does not
do so within a fortnight, I shall write to *her*.[10]

Sullivan was as good as his word, and Miss Rosamond received
the following invitation to rekindle the little embers of past flirtation:

Reichel's Garten—Mittelgebäude 8
Leipzig, March 1861

I have treated you badly, *very badly*, my dear Miss Rosamond,
inasmuch as three months have elapsed, and I have not written
to you once, but I know your kind and forgiving disposition
(do you remember our little quarrels in days of yore?) and feel
assured that you will not only rejoice over the repentant sinner,
but will also write to me in return, which is saying a great deal,
for one under the influence of Berlin atmosphere—But you will
write quickly I hope, for I leave here in about a fortnight, and
wish very much to come over and see you, and should like you
to tell me first, that you will be glad to see me, do not forget—
I intend staying about three days in Berlin and going straight
to London from there—If you want anything brought over,
tell me in good time—

It would do your heart good to see how busy we all are now,
how industrious and hardworking, Rudorff has finished his

Overture, and works day and night copying out a fresh score, that the Notenschreiber may write out the parts quickly. My Tempest is done (except one duett) and I suffer 3 hours headaches everyday from correcting the parts which the aforesaid Notenschreiber sends to me in small relays—Taylor is pale from excessive fatigue, he is arranging it for four hands as fast as I write it—Domenico has lost several pounds of flesh, and his appetite from practising the Polonaise of Chopin too much which he played today in the Kleine Prüfung, and [Carl] Rose gets redder and redder everyday (it would be ridiculous to say paler) thinking about the public Prüfung—In fact we are all 'Auf dem Grund' except Payne who is in high spirits, because he is getting an excellent staccato; Miss Schiller has another gathering on her finger, and cannot play in the Prüfung. She is going to write to you in the holidays but she has had such a bad eye for the last two months that she has not been able to write to her *own sister* [sic!] You have heard of course about the nigger affair at the Paynes, and also about Lotto the violin player, they are the only two occurrences of any note that have taken place lately.

[Whial?] was with me today, and desired his kindest remembrances to you all, he says you and your sister promised him something for his Album; send him a few bars 'eigene Composition' for he says the people 'down South' do not believe it possible for a young lady to compose and that you would be considered prodigies of the first order—who is this man, Prince George [grandson of King Friedrich Wilhelm II], that you speak so much of in your letters? Is he any relation to the King [of Prussia], and what dark meaning is hidden under that mysterious hint thrown out by your sister, regarding the Princess Victoria? I am afraid you are getting into bad company with all those Princes and Baronesses, and 'Vous' of various degrees—David says 'Put not your trust in princes' and David is right—You will be so accustomed to titles that you will not be able to tolerate the company of plain 'Misters' and 'Esquires' when you return to England, but 'nous verrons'—

I have still a good deal to say to you, but I prefer doing it verbally, than to writing it—and as we shall most probably see each other very soon, I will put it off till then. If you receive invitations for the evenings that I am in Berlin, you must stipulate with the people, to take me with you. I wish, when you write to your Papa again you would ask to me a great favour—viz: to send me the route he took from Berlin to London, with an account of exactly what it cost him, how long he travelled, when he arrived in London, and other little particulars that may be useful to me—Tell him he would be rendering me a great kindness, if he would be so good—

And now, Good bye, for three o'clock draws near and the Prüfung will begin. Remember me kindly to your Mamma, Aunt and sister, also my much esteemed friends the twins, and believe, my dear Miss Rosamond, in all earnest

your very sincere friend
Arthur S. Sullivan

Write very soon.

The first performance of *The Tempest* took place at the graduation concert on 6th April. Sullivan conducted the work, and a young Leipzig student, Minna Giesinger, sang the solo part. At the same concert Walter Bache played the first movement of Sterndale Bennett's F minor Piano Concerto, and Leonora Schmitz the first movement of John Field's A major Concerto. Thus there was a good deal of emphasis on British music. In respect of Sullivan the *Neue Zeitschrift für Musik* (54, 1861, page 144) commented as follows:

> Mr. Arthur Sullivan, from London, produced music for Shakespeare's *The Tempest* which showed him strongly influenced by Schumann, and, to some extent, by Mendelssohn. The last movement, 'Dance of nymphs and reapers', with its skipping, flirtatious, rhythms, won hearty applause. The composer handles the orchestral medium skilfully, and achieves charming effects. Altogether, although not having considered the deeper meaning of the problem set, his accomplishment is most attractive.

The *Signale* said more or less the same thing, but adding that: '. . . everything has a sense of imaginative mobility, and, above all, appears to be controlled by a very sure and practical hand.' [11]

The Leipzig critics clearly indicated the route Sullivan should take, and their observations show how natural was that part of his talent that was to find its ultimate outlet in the realm of operetta. But it was neither the intention of the committee of the Mendelssohn Scholarship nor of the professors at the Conservatorium that creative skills should be dedicated to this end. Music was a solemn business. At the age of eighteen Sullivan presumed that his seniors knew best, and began earnestly to prepare himself for the severities of the career of a serious composer in a rather cold climate. He stayed in Leipzig long enough to hear the second graduation concert on 13th April (there was a third concert on 20th April), and to applaud the performances of Franklin Taylor, Domenico Barnett, and Madeline Schiller, once his girl friend—who stirred Sullivan's Irish sentiments by playing Moscheles's *Erinnerungen aus Irland*.

Having reached England a first duty was to write to Smart:

3 Ponsonby Street,
Pimlico Square,
London.
22 April, 1861.

My dear Sir George,

Having now returned from Leipzig, after an absence of two and a half years, I feel it a duty incumbent upon me, to offer to the Gentlemen of the 'Mendelssohn Scholarship Committee', my heartfelt thanks, for the means and opportunities they have placed at my disposal, enabling me to obtain the instructions, and gain the friendship of the greatest masters at home and abroad.

The Committee have thus given me the first step in life, that which is most important to a young Artist—a first rate education, and one that does not fall to the lot of everyone; for to have studied under and known such men as Mr. Goss, Dr. Bennett, Mess. Moscheles, David, Hauptmann, Rietz, and Plaidy, are advantages replete with honour, and I trust my future career will prove how entirely I have appreciated and endeavoured to benefit by them.

I therefore beg that you will convey my most grateful thanks to the Committee assuring them how proud I feel to have been a 'Mendelssohn Scholar' (and the first one) and that I shall always strive to do credit to their choice, and show myself worthy of it.

Receive, my dear Sir George, the highest sentiments of my respect, and believe me to remain

Yours most gratefully attached
Arthur S. Sullivan [12]

Next came the necessity of ensuring a livelihood. To this end an advertisement was published in *The Musical World* of 11th May (page 290):

Mr. Arthur Sullivan begs to inform his Friends, that he has RETURNED from Germany.

All communications respecting Pupils, etc., to be addressed to his Residence, 3 Ponsonby Street, Pimlico, S.W.

To subsist on the fees of pupils alone being an impossibility, Sullivan decided to follow English custom and to become a church organist. He almost became organist of a Lutheran church in London, for on 31st May 1861 he wrote to Otto Goldschmidt declining an offer of such appointment 'on religious grounds'. Since Leipzig did not give adequate preparation for an organist's duties within the Church of England, he took lessons with George Cooper (1820–76). Before the course ended, however, Sullivan was launched into the serene waters of English church music on his own account.

St Michael's Church, Chester Square, a large if undistinguished building by the younger Thomas Cundy (1790–1867), served one of the parishes separated from St George's, Hanover Square. It was opened in 1847, the vicar being Joseph Harriman Hamilton who remained in this office until 1870.[13] Hamilton was a mathematician at Trinity College, Cambridge, of which, after his ordination in 1825, he was for a time chaplain. At St Michael's he enjoyed a large stipend—£725 a year. His first organist was John Hopkins (1822–1900), who resigned in 1854 and became organist of Rochester Cathedral in 1856. Hopkins's successor at St Michael's was Walter Hay Sangster, a 'Professor of Music', whose talents, however, were inadequate to support him in his position in a fashionable church. In 1861 Hamilton decided on change [14] (Sangster, living in the parish, continued to worship at St Michael's) and, urged by Captain C. J. Ottley [15]—a friend of Helmore—invited Sullivan, who was living near by in Pimlico, to apply for the post to be vacated by the unfortunate Sangster.

According to custom Sullivan was required to submit himself for trial. The vicar's daughter, who was present, 'was quite enthralled by the performance of the E minor Fugue of Bach, one of the pieces played by the slim, curly-headed, black-eyed youth'.[16] Only lately released from the close supervision of her governess, Miss Hamilton was warned by that lady of the dangers that could arise from a too close contact with a young handsome musician. However, she was a young person of spirit and, ignoring her governess's advice, became Sullivan's pupil. In due course she sometimes acted as his deputy and when, in 1867, Sullivan finished the score of *Cox and Box* at an all-night sitting, she obligingly set to next day to copy out the violin parts. Sullivan's 'Dorabella', in fact.

The congregation of St Michael's was mixed—so mixed in fact that the more exclusive among the pew-renters urged the establishment of a daughter church to superintend the spiritual welfare of the large number of representatives of the working-class who attended at divine service. Since this proved impracticable the congregation continued to include a fair slice of the aristocracy, army and navy officers, surgeons, barristers, Queen's Messengers, servants of the Royal Household and the Houses of Parliament, together with grooms, butlers, bricklayers, engine-drivers, publicans, musicians [17] and policemen. From Sullivan's point of view the most prominent members of the flock were the policemen from the neighbouring Gerald Road station. Constables John Woods, Joseph Holman, John Done, James Sutton, John Haines (whose wife bore triplets at the beginning of 1864), Sergeant George Selby . . . These and many others posted to Gerald Road found that their constabulary duties included compulsory church attendance each Wednesday morning, and, unless totally tone-deaf, membership of the church choir. This had advantages. Sullivan was a companionable young man, with a flashing humour. And, seated up in the west gallery in front of his three-manual organ (built by the firm of Flight and Robson), attention to the sermons could be relaxed. The choir-boys like the policemen were conscripts—from the nearby National School. They, too, took to their organist.

Sullivan was relatively well paid at St Michael's, his stipend being eighty pounds a year. His aspirations, however, envisaged a higher standard of living than this supported. So he augmented it by giving elementary instruction in reading, writing and arithmetic to the Chapel Royal boys on four afternoons a week at Helmore's house. He also hired himself out as an accompanist, an occupation which once prompted him to explode in a letter to Felix Moscheles (5th June 1861), 'I hate concerts!' The prospects for a composer in England were unpromising.

NOTES TO CHAPTER TWO

1. C. Moscheles, *Life of Moscheles*, trans. A. D. Coleridge, 2 vols., London, 1873, II, p. 262.
2. C. Bache, *Brother Musicians, Reminiscences of Edward and Walter Bache*, London, 1901, p. 135.
3. 'The Composition Department was represented by an overture and chorus, *Gross ist der Herr*, by John Francis Barnett, of London. The work provides evidence of a sound musical training. The composer demonstrates a practised hand in respect of thematic and contrapuntal construction; but the exercise that we heard does not rise to the higher level of poetic significance.' *Neue Zeitschrift für Musik*, 50, 1859, p. 194.
4. Clara Rogers, *Memories of a Musical Career*, Boston, 1919, p. 168. Clara Barnett (1844–1931) went to America in 1871 as a member of the Parepa-Rosa Opera Company. She settled in Boston, where she had a fine reputation as singer and teacher. In 1878 she married a Boston lawyer, Henry Munroe Rogers, and their house at 306 Beacon Street became a noted cultural centre.

   Rosamond Barnett married R. E. Francillon, a writer, and a librettist for F. H. Cowen. Their combined recollections of Sullivan give, to say the least of it, an unusual impression: '. . . Among the more intimate of their fellow-students at Leipzig, and the most frequent guests at their mother's hospitable supper-table—a highly popular institution among a cosmopolitan flock of young people mostly with appetites too big for their pockets—was the future Sir Arthur Sullivan, as notable then for easy charm of manner, and adaptability to all sorts and conditions of persons and circumstances, as when he became no less welcome a guest at royal tables. It may interest some who only saw him in after years to learn that he was golden-haired in his student days, and this in spite of the strong strain of African blood that became increasingly perceptible with increasing age. He was, in fact, an Octoroon, and was accordingly subjected to inconveniences and annoyances during his visit [*sic*] to the United States which permanently embittered him against Americans and American ways. . . . In some talks I had with him about my supplying him with a libretto (I quite forget the proposed subject; but that it was essentially un-Gilbertian I need not remember in order to know), I thought I discovered the secret of his charm. It was the tact with which he flattered one's vanity by treating one as if of permanent and exclusive interest to Arthur Sullivan. . . .' Robert Francillon, *Mid-Victorian Memories*, London, [1914], pp. 194–5.
5. Letter quoted in Sullivan and Flower, *Sir Arthur Sullivan*, 1950 edn., p. 27.
6. *N.Z.M.*, 52, 1860, p. 205.

7. First performance, 6th May 1850.

8. Composed, 31st October 1836; first performance, 3rd April 1837.

9. First performance, 12th May 1850.

10. Eduard Bernsdorf (1825–1901), composer and critic who later edited the *Universal Lexikon der Tonkunst*, was a contributor at this time to the *Signale* (*see* Note 11 below). Salomon Jadassohn (1831–1902), composer and teacher, was conductor of the Euterpe concerts. Ernst Rudorff (1840–1916), pianist and composer, became conductor of the Stern Choral Union (*see* p. 146). Izydor Lotto (*b.* 1840), mentioned in the next letter, was a Polish violinist who became leader of the Court orchestra in Weimar. Albert Payne (*see* p. 25) was English, and his father was head of a music publishing business in Leipzig.

11. *Signale für die musikalische Welt*, ed. Bartholf Senff, 9. Jrg., Leipzig, 1861, p. 254.

12. Copy of letter, BM. Add. MS. 41771.

13. Hamilton was succeeded in 1870 by Rowley Hill (1836–87), who as Bishop of Sodor and Man was immortalized in *The Mikado*.

14. cf. '. . . That it shall be lawful for the Minister for the Time being . . . to appoint such Persons as he shall think fit to officiate as Clerk, Organist, Pew Openers, and Beadle or Verger in the said Church, and also from Time to Time to displace and remove such Clerk, Organist, Pew Openers, and Beadle or Verger respectively, and that the Wages or Stipend of such Clerk, Organist, Pew Openers, and Beadle or Verger shall be fixed with the Consent and Approbation of the Bishop of *London* for the Time being.' *St Michael's, Chester Square, District Church Act*, 14th August 1850.

15. Ottley, to whom Sullivan dedicated a song in 1863 (*see* p. 273) was a subscriber to the Philharmonic Society in 1869 and was present at a dinner for Sir John Goss on 24th April 1872.

16. Miss Hamilton later married Rev. Walter Carr (Curate of Ware, 1866), and her reminiscences of Sullivan were published in *Musical Times*, 42, January 1901, p. 101.

17. Among those so described in the Church records during Sullivan's time were the dispossessed Sangster, James Nixon, William Handley, Thomas Ogilvy (singer), Henry Robert Weldhen, and Nicolo de Becker and Charles Philip Mann (both 'Professors of Music'). There were also John Boffin, pianoforte tuner, and William Pilcher, organ-builder.

3

The white hope of English music

Partly out of loyalty, partly out of a natural self-interest, Sullivan
continued to keep his old benefactors aware of his enthusiasms and
intentions. But Helmore, Smart and Potter were back-numbers.
The last-named—his own early hopes of achieving fame as a composer
extinguished by the cares of running the Royal Academy of Music—
was at first displeased by Sullivan's attitude. 'I'm very sorry about
[him],' he is reported to have said; 'going to Germany has ruined
him.' The frontiers of respectability in music, so far as he was concerned, stopped short of the three composers about whom Sullivan
most talked: Schumann, Wagner and Schubert. Of these, the most
problematic was Schumann, Sullivan's favourite. With the innocence
and effrontery of youth Sullivan asked whether Potter had, in fact,
heard any of Schumann's works. Potter was honest: he had not,
and said so. It says much for his patience that he agreed to play
through piano duet arrangements of the symphonies with Sullivan.
Not only did he give up his time to this exercise but he showed a
willingness to change his opinion. Soon he was propounding the
merits of Schumann to his friend George Grove (1820–1900), whom
Sullivan met during the summer of 1861, and with whom he developed a life-long friendship. A civil engineer of distinction, Grove had
worked his way into the field of music, where, by the time he made
Sullivan's acquaintance, he occupied a position of some importance.
He was Secretary to the Crystal Palace, a post which was offered to
him after he had held a similar position with the Society of Arts and
had taken part in the administration of the Great Exhibition of 1851.

The real arbiter of English musical taste in 1861 (outside of church
music and oratorio) was, however, a German. August Friedrich
Manns (1825–1907) was a Prussian military bandmaster who resigned
that appointment in 1854 when a junior officer reprimanded him
for permitting his bandsmen to appear on parade with dirty buttons.
Out of work, Manns was grateful to be offered a job in England.
Heinrich Schallehn, a fellow-German then living in London, and

conductor of the military band recently established at the Crystal Palace, engaged him as E flat clarinettist and sub-conductor. (Schallehn, as it happened, was also a colleague of Thomas Sullivan at Kneller Hall.) After various misadventures with Schallehn, and after Schallehn's subsequent dismissal, Manns was appointed conductor at the Palace in October 1855, where he promptly installed an orchestra in place of the military band. Within a year he had turned musical London upside-down by performing works by Wagner, Schumann and Schubert. On 15th March 1856 he gave the first London performance of Schumann's Symphony in D minor. A month later he introduced the English to Schubert's 'Great C Major'. His missionary zeal was fully supported by Grove. Although dedicated to the cause of German music, Manns (since no one else would do so) accepted the responsibility of promoting the interests of British composers.

On 13th April 1861, a few days before Sullivan left Leipzig, Manns gave a programme of works by Michael Balfe (1808–70), John Hatton (1809–86), William Vincent Wallace (1812–65), George Macfarren (1813–87), Sterndale Bennett, and Henry Leslie (1822–1896).[1] Between the works of these and the contemporary German masters there was a considerable gulf. If the gulf could be lessened no one would be better pleased than Manns. Early in 1862 a private performance of Sullivan's The Tempest took place at the home of Henry Chorley (1808–72), the music critic. Grove, who had already had Schumann's 'Spring' Symphony performed at the Palace at Sullivan's suggestion, sensed a work of major importance in the context of British music and so arranged for it to be put down for performance on 5th April. Sullivan never forgot this signal act of encouragement, to which he often referred in later life.[2] The first London performance of The Tempest was decisive for Sullivan's career. Unknown on the morning of 5th April—except to a small, select circle of acquaintances—by the evening he was being acclaimed as the white hope of English music.

'The concert on Saturday afternoon,' reported The Musical World of 12th April (page 231), 'was one of more than ordinary interest, the programme being almost exclusively devoted to a new work by a young English (or Irish) composer, hitherto unknown to the public.' The report continued:

> The concert-room was crowded to the doors, and a success was obtained by the young musician of which he, and those who

first discerned the germs of talent in him, may well feel proud. So enthusiastic, indeed, were the audience that they insisted on no less than five pieces being repeated. . . . We shall not pay Mr. Sullivan the ill compliment of judging him critically by a single hearing. Enough at present to say that his music to the *Tempest* while betraying a strong partiality for Mendelssohn's fascinating style, exhibits remarkable merits, and amongst the rest a decided vein of melody, a strong feeling of dramatic expression, and a happy fancy in the treatment of the orchestra. . . . The band, good throughout, shone most brilliantly in the 'Dance of Nymphs and Reapers', and in the overture to the fourth act. The Shakespearian text (that is, so much of it as Mr. Sullivan has included in his plan) was read, as clearly and effectively as possible under the circumstances, by Mr. A. Matthison. At the conclusion there was a loud call for 'the composer', who, being led forward by Herr Manns, was greeted with the heartiest applause from all sides.

A week later *The Tempest* was repeated, and heartily applauded by, among others, Charles Dickens. 'This,' Sullivan subsequently wrote, 'was the great day of my life!' [3]

Between the two performances a letter from Helmore appeared in *The Times* of 8th April:

The young English composer, Arthur Seymour Sullivan, whose music for Shakespeare's Tempest was so favourably noticed in *The Times* of Monday, was a chorister in the Chapel Royal, St. James's, at the time he was chosen Mendelssohn scholar; he then studied for two years at the Royal Academy of Music and was afterwards sent to the Conservatorium, Leipzig. He entered the Chapel Royal in April, 1854,[4] and left in June, 1857, and it seems just to the oldest school of English composers that this fact should not be wholly ignored in any notice of his educational career.

Sullivan responded promptly and sent a heartfelt thank-you letter to Helmore the next day. His warmth of gratitude and affection—generously bestowed on his friends and benefactors throughout his life—must have moved his old teacher, as he read:

. . . If any little success attends me in my professional career, surely you ought not to be overlooked amongst those to whom

the chief credit is due, for to you I owe more than to any one else
perhaps. . . . (Letter sold at Sotheby's on 11th May 1959.)

Sullivan's affection for Helmore was very real and later that year,
on 24th September, he invited him to dine at Sydenham, where
Sullivan had rooms for a short time.

As an ex-chorister of the Chapel Royal Sullivan truly belonged
to a great tradition. But he was the last great composer in England
to have been educated within that tradition, and his initial success
was registered in an unaccustomed field. The Chapel Royal tradition
in itself, indeed, was virtually dead, for English church music was
at its lowest ebb. After his conquest of the London public at the
Crystal Palace, Sullivan next had the opportunity to present his
credentials to the no less discriminating music-lovers of Manchester,
where Charles Hallé (1819–95) conducted *The Tempest* on 2nd April
1863. The programme also included Mendelssohn's *Midsummer
Night's Dream* music and the march from *Athalia*, Beethoven's
overture to *Fidelio* and Auber's to *Masaniello*, and some other items.[5]
Concerning this performance a perceptive notice appeared in *The
Manchester Guardian* the next day which concluded:

> There are many scattered beauties throughout the work
> which we cannot pause to notice. We do not content ourselves
> with saying that it is a work of promise merely. It is evident,
> even upon the first hearing, that it is an achieved composition
> which may boldly challenge criticism. The instrumentation is
> masterly throughout, and is always in keeping with the dramatic
> elements, while every movement is constructed with a severe
> care for unity of purpose and idea, without ever becoming
> monotonous. . . .[6]

It is already evident that Sullivan was indebted to German
musicians both in Germany and in England, in this, as in other
aspects, anticipating somewhat the career of Elgar. The expatriate
element in Manchester (the mainstay of the city's music) impressed
itself on Sullivan's notice, and in writing to Mrs Lehmann of the
Hallé concert he seems to have implied a certain, possibly perverse,
tendency towards anti-Semitism in his make-up (cf. pages 2 and 240):

> I bow six times, twice to the orchestra (who throughout have
> been so kind and friendly) and shake hands with Hallé; then
> down again and all is over. I stay behind during the 15 minutes

interval and am overwhelmed with—not reproaches—from
critics, artists, rich merchants with hooked noses etc. . . .

Sullivan, of course, was flattered by the attentions of the *cognoscenti*,
and his talent for ingratiating himself with the influential—noted
by Clara Barnett in Leipzig—was marked. Honoured by Manns,
fêted by Hallé (whose hospitality also offered opportunity for Sullivan
to meet Mrs Gaskell), praised by Dickens, promoted by Grove, and
protected by the incumbent and officers of a fashionable church,
Sullivan, at the age of twenty-one, had the world at his feet.

At this time he was much indebted to the Lehmann family, both
for their kindness and interest, and also for their mediation on his
behalf in the social and intellectual milieu of London. Rudolf
Lehmann, Hamburg-born, was a painter; his wife, Amelia, was the
eldest daughter of the Edinburgh author and publisher Robert
Chambers. A frequent visitor to the Lehmanns (as also was Grove),
Sullivan spent his twenty-first birthday with them, the most memorable event of the day being a visit to Madame Tussaud's. 'With
every gaiety of London open to us,' wrote Sullivan thirty-one years
later, 'we chose the delirious dullness of Madame Tussaud's.' [7]

Other friends who belonged to the Anglo-German intelligentsia
at that time conspicuous in London were the Goldschmidts. Otto
Goldschmidt (1829–1907), a native of Hamburg and a Mendelssohn
pupil in Leipzig, a pianist and conductor with an international
reputation, married the Swedish singer Jenny Lind (1820–87) in
1852. From 1858 they made London their headquarters and in 1863
Goldschmidt became Vice-Principal of the Royal Academy of Music.
By this time the Goldschmidts had taken Sullivan under their wing,
and their belief in his genius was an invaluable aid to further pro-
gress. For his later interest in authentic performances of Bach's
music (see pages 211 and 215) Sullivan was greatly indebted to the
Goldschmidts. In *Pages from an Unwritten Diary* (page 54) C. V.
Stanford relates how he heard Mrs Goldschmidt sing *Ich hatte viel
Bekümmerniss* at an amateur performance conducted by Sullivan at
Arthur Coleridge's house in 1873.

Down at Sydenham, where Grove lived, there was another cosmopolitan family whose interest in Sullivan was helpful in his early
years. Robert von Glehn (1800–85), Estonian by birth, had married
a Scotswoman, settled permanently in England and taken British
nationality. Like many other immigrants who had prospered in

commerce, von Glehn became more British than the British, and was prominent among those who cared for the protection of native cultural standards. On 22nd July 1864 Sullivan stood as god-father to Arthur, Grove's youngest son. The other god-parents were Olga von Glehn—one of Robert's numerous daughters—and Arthur Stanley, soon to become Dean of Westminster Abbey.

At this time Sullivan appeared to be well established on the road to eminence. Everybody's blue-eyed boy, he was surrounded by adulation and opportunity. In addition to his organ appointment and his part-time teaching at Helmore's, he was 'Professor of Pianoforte and Ballad Singing' at the Crystal Palace Company's School of Art, Science and Literature, which had been established in 1860. This institution, mainly concerned with providing lessons for indifferent lady amateurs, was set up with the best of intentions in order to supplement the inadequate facilities of the Royal Academy of Music. But being without any kind of official backing, it was never able to fulfil the aim of becoming a national school of music.

Early in 1865 Sullivan joined the staff of the short-lived National College of Music, 'Founded to promote the Musical Education of persons who desire to enter the Profession . . .' This institution, of which the Principal was Henry Leslie, had an impressive list of professors. George Macfarren gave a special course in harmony; Thomas Harper, the prince of trumpeters, taught the trumpet; Henry Lazarus, the leading clarinettist of the day, taught the clarinet; Julius Benedict was one of the composition tutors, and Sullivan another; Franklin Taylor gave instruction in pianoforte and harmony; while declamation was supervised by Rev. W. W. Cazalett.[8]

Neither then nor at any other time, however, did Sullivan find teaching at all congenial, and he treated it merely as a subsidiary means of subsistence. According to Sullivan himself he was offered a teaching post at the Royal Academy of Music, but there seems some doubt as to whether any such firm offer was really made.[9]

In the meanwhile he had acquired another, albeit modest, source of income. Through Costa he became organist at Covent Garden, a job that alerted him to the virtues of quick thought and decisive action in emergency, and opened up to him vistas that lay beyond the range of The Tempest. Under Frederick Gye's management and the incentive of lively competition from J. H. Mapleson's Italian Opera at Her Majesty's Theatre, Covent Garden was enjoying a brief period of brilliance. The stars were Pauline Lucca, Adelina

Patti, Jean Baptiste Faure and Giuseppe Mario. While Sullivan was organist at Covent Garden he had opportunity to learn *Faust*, *Don Giovanni*, *William Tell*, *L'Africaine*, and popular repertory works by Bellini, Donizetti and Verdi. It is clear from his own observations that he sometimes went to the rival house where, in 1864, he could see *Fidelio* and—a work which appealed greatly to him—Nicolai's *Falstaff* (under which title *The Merry Wives of Windsor* was then played).

At this time Sullivan was at work on a libretto by Chorley, *The Sapphire Necklace*, for the Pyne-Harrison Opera Company. Ultimately the task of making an opera out of Chorley's words proved too great. But Sullivan did not jettison the work quite light-heartedly as has hitherto been supposed. He assigned the rights in it (now entitled *The False Heiress*) to Cramer in 1868 for an advance of £251 10s. Nothing, however, came of this, and although the overture went into the repertoire for a time, and one or two other movements found new homes, the main part of the score was still-born. In the meantime Costa, having got over his irritability at Sullivan's occasional lateness at rehearsal,[10] offered him the chance of writing a ballet. This, *L'île enchantée*, was performed at Covent Garden on 16th May 1864, bu without conspicuous success.[11] By now, however, Costa had put his money on Sullivan as the man of the future. He saw in him 'the only man in England capable of succeeding himself as conductor of the Handel Festival',[12] and as one competent to replenish the repertoire of the other great choral festivals.

Writing from 47 Claverton Terrace [13] on 26th February 1864, Sullivan thanked Costa for having recommended him as a prospective composer to the Birmingham Festival, of which Costa was the chief conductor. On 2nd March J. O. Mason, chairman of the orchestral committee at Birmingham, visited Sullivan, who was able to write to Costa again on the following day to say that everything was now in order; that the work, to a libretto by Chorley, would be entitled *Kenilworth*, and that it would be published by Chappells. In his programme note Sullivan wrote:

> My fancy was directed to this Kenilworth pageant [of 1575], not merely from its local interest to those interesting themselves in our great Midland Festival, but because I have long known, almost by heart, Scott's wondrously musical, but as wondrously simple description of the arrival of England's maiden Queen at her subject's palace, on 'a summer night'.

It is possible that Sullivan's attention was also drawn to the subject by Auber's *Leicester, ou le château de Kenilworth* (1823), a work in which sources of some part of Sullivan's general musical inspiration may easily be found.

If anyone was capable of reducing the most promising of subjects to a mess of platitude it was Chorley. A man of set opinions, he had at this time two fixed ideas: first, that he was a literary genius; the second, that Arthur Sullivan had no peer among contemporary composers. *Kenilworth*, the only redeeming feature of the libretto being the inclusion of the Shakespearian lines 'How sweet the moonlight sleeps', etc., gave Sullivan little chance to show that Chorley's evaluation was correct.

In the Birmingham Festival of 1864 the principal 'novelty' was Costa's oratorio *Naaman*. Sullivan's masque (as it was called) and Henry Smart's (1813–79) *The Bride of Dunkerron*, a secular cantata, were in the second line.

Kenilworth was performed on the evening of Thursday, 8th September. The principal singers were Helen Lemmens-Sherrington, Bessie Palmer, W. H. Cummings and Charles Santley—Cummings deputizing for Mario, whose indisposition came as a great disappointment to the patrons of the Festival. The Town Hall was filled with an audience of 2,188, and among those present was Jenny Lind Goldschmidt, anxious to see her young friend register an expected triumph. But the people of Birmingham had minds of their own and were not prepared to be influenced by the Sullivan publicity that was propagated in London. When they disapproved of anything they said so. They disapproved of *Kenilworth*. Sullivan suffered the first setback of his career. A famous old Birmingham chorister, William Pountney, who had sung in the first performance of *Elijah* and was also to sing in that of Elgar's *Gerontius*, later recollected the débacle. He also gave the impression of a Sullivan unusually ill at ease:

> Sullivan's *Kenilworth* was a disappointment. The young and gifted composer, it was thought, was about to clinch the success he had made by his *Tempest* music, and the musical world looked forward with exceptional interest to the new work. But in spite of a good performance, conducted by the composer, the work, I remember, fell flat.
>
> I think Sullivan himself was a little doubtful as to its success. I remember meeting him on the day of the performance

strolling round the picture galleries of the Society of Artists all
alone. I asked him how he was, and, with a look of anxiety, he
replied that he was 'very squeamish'. *Kenilworth* has scarcely
been heard since its initial performance.[14]

H. C. Lunn, in the October issue of the *Musical Times*, exposed an
undercurrent of resentment that a young man should be pushed so
quickly to the front. Nevertheless, a month after the Birmingham
performance the 'Brisk Dance' from *Kenilworth* was played at the
Crystal Palace, where the complete cantata—Miss Banks, Miss E.
Haywood, Cummings and Santley being the soloists—was given on
12th November.

But by now Sullivan was deep in other projects. That he was Irish
was brought home to him by Robert Browning, who tried to put
Sullivan in touch with William Allingham (1824–89), an admirable
and sensitive miniaturist who had just published *Laurence Bloomfield
in Ireland*. Allingham, a native of Ballyshannon, would have made a
good partner for Sullivan, which Browning was perceptive in noting:

> . . . He knows and admires your music; if you know his
> poetry the business of 'introduction' will not be a long one.
> What concerns you particularly is, that I don't believe anyone
> could write a better, nor so good a lyric opera with a view to the
> requirements of music as well as of poetry—and one day you
> may want such a poet, as, I hope, now he wants a musician.[15]

Having finished the score of *Kenilworth*, Sullivan betook himself
to the land of his fathers. He was a guest of the Dunvilles (who lived
at Richmond Lodge, Holywood Road, Belfast) at a particular point
of creative inspiration, for during the summer he wrote to his mother
from Belfast expressing contentment and a renewal of energy:

> . . . already I feel my ideas assuming a newer and fresher colour.
> I shall be able to work like a horse on my return. Why, the other
> night as I was jolting home from Hollywood (a suburb of Belfast,
> on the north bank of the Lough) through the wind and rain on
> an open jaunting car, the whole first movement of a symphony
> came into my head with a real fresh flavour about it—besides
> scraps of other movements.[16]

The 'Irish' Symphony,[17] kept in cold storage awhile because the
production of a British symphony was a risk most managements
were reluctant to take, was eventually put into the Crystal Palace

programme for 10th March 1866. That it was accepted by Manns was due to the passionate championship of its, and its composer's, virtues by Jenny Lind, whose appearance on the platform was taken by the 3,000 people present as if it were a regal gesture of approbation. Apart from the new symphony the programme included *Leonora No. 3*, Weber's *Jubilee Overture*, some violin pieces played by Sullivan's one-time fellow-student in Leipzig, Carl Rose, and songs sung by a Miss Edmonds and by Santley. *The Times* duly recorded the enthusiasm with which Sullivan's symphony was received, and proceeded to its evaluation in a critique that is also interesting for the light thrown on the contemporary rating of certain other composers:

> The symphony . . . is not only by far the most noticeable composition that has proceeded from Mr. Sullivan's pen, but the best musical work, if judged only by the largeness of its form and the number of beautiful thoughts it contains, for a long time produced by any English composer. . . . Mr. Sullivan should abjure Mendelssohn, even Beethoven, and above all, Schumann, for a year and a day—like the vanquished knight errant, who, when conquered, foreswore arms for a like period. Not that Mr. Sullivan has been conquered, but that he must conquer; and the best way to do this is to study the most legitimate and natural models, in the works of Haydn and Mozart, trusting to himself for the rest. . . .
>
> The works of Haydn and Mozart in one sense, Bach and Handel in another, should be the text books of every young composer, who, ungifted with the genius of a Beethoven, is incapable of declaring himself, like Beethoven, independent of all precedents. Meanwhile, Mr. Sullivan, who, though young, is already shrewd enough to have steered clear of that dangerous quicksand, Spohr, the most mannered of all mannerists, has composed a first symphony, which, or we are greatly mistaken, will, for some time hence, engage the attention of the musical world, and lead to a second that may possibly fix it for at least a generation.

After the performance John Goss wrote his congratulations, hoping that his former pupil would 'prove a worthy peer of the greatest symphonists'. A month later the symphony was played again, at the second concert of the year of the Musical Society of London. Each movement was rapturously applauded, and when he appeared on the

platform Sullivan was acclaimed not only by the audience but also—
and this was worth more than any other signs of favour—by the
orchestra.

Piatti played the Schumann Cello Concerto ('a hopelessly dreamy
work' according to *The Times*) at the same concert, a circumstance
which led to Sullivan's also composing a cello concerto.[18] This was
played at the end of the year and was moderately well received, at
any rate by *The Musical Standard* [19]:

> . . . It consists of three movements—*Allegro moderato, Andan-
> tina expressivo* [*sic*], and *Molto vivace*. The chief attraction of the
> work is found in the *Andantino*, which is a gem of loveliness, and
> gave the great cello player a fine opportunity for the display of
> his unequalled cantabile We hope soon to see this charming
> movement in the form of an organ voluntary, for which it is
> eminently fitted. The *Molto vivace* is marked by Mr. Sullivan's
> invariable elegance, and is more interesting than usual with
> music written with the primary object of bringing out the
> 'points' of a brilliant performer. We may soon have an oppor-
> tunity of enlarging upon this theme; and shall for the present
> dismiss it, with the remark that Mr. Sullivan has now added
> another leaf to his fast gathering laurels. . . .

This concerto, however, was not destined to survive beyond its first
performance, being quite overshadowed by a work which the public
took to its heart for the worst of reasons, and which considerably
helped to turn the composer's pen in the wrong direction.

Like the other major English festivals, that at Norwich took pride
in the production of 'novelties'. In a lean period the meteoric rise
to fame of Sullivan was a godsend. There is nothing like youth, unless
it be extreme old age, for stimulating the box-office. While contem-
plating the success of his symphony Sullivan received a commission
to furnish a work for the Norwich Festival of 1866. As always hereto-
fore he reported on this to his father, whose opinion he respected and
by whose devotion he was always moved.

> 'I have a mind to give up the whole affair,' he remarked to his
> father; 'I don't know what to choose for a subject.' 'Don't do
> that, my boy,' said his father; 'don't give it up, something will
> happen that may furnish you with an opportunity.' And three
> days afterwards something did happen: his father died.[20] Half
> mad with grief, his son followed the coffin to the grave, and

when he came home and sat with his mother brooding over his loss, he suddenly jumped up and said: 'Mother, I can't bear it. I must cry out my grief in music.' And he sat down then and there and wrote the *In Memoriam* overture.[21]

Meanwhile Sullivan had been strengthening his many other bastions. On 7th March 1863 Princess Alexandra arrived from Denmark to marry the Prince of Wales at Windsor three days later. As was the Consort of James I (also Danish) some two and a half centuries before, she was greeted with 'her own country music'. On this occasion Danish airs were arranged into a *Princess of Wales' March* by Arthur Sullivan. This work, dedicated to the Prince of Wales, was first performed at a 'Wedding Festival Concert' at the Crystal Palace on 14th March 1863. Sullivan's *Bride from the north* was also performed for the first time at this concert. Other works included Niels Gade's Fifth Symphony in B flat and a new Festival Overture by Manns. Sullivan was presented to the Prince of Wales after the concert, and also to the Duke of Edinburgh, who was to become a very close friend of the composer.

Two years later Sullivan paid his first visit to Paris, accompanied by the Lehmanns and Chorley. Charles Dickens was also in Paris—a rather melancholy Dickens, saddened by the deaths of Eugène Scribe and Victor Hugo. Dickens made no mention of meeting Sullivan at that time. Sullivan, on the other hand, did say a good deal about his meeting Dickens. The primary purpose of the visit, according to Sullivan, was to hear Pauline Viardot (1821–1910) sing the title role (restored from tenor to alto by Berlioz) in Gluck's *Orfeo*. This was reckoned as one of the most sensational interpretations in opera in the nineteenth century, and Sullivan endorsed the general opinion. 'She was,' he wrote, 'intensely emotional, and her performance was certainly one of the greatest things I have ever seen on the stage.' Chorley, Dickens, Sullivan and (presumably) the Lehmanns were so affected that they all wept copiously.

The company also went to the Opéra Comique where *Lalla-Roukh*,[22] a new opera by Félicien David (1810–76), was playing. Since Sullivan's own career had effectively started from the same subject he was interested in the Frenchman's treatment of it, but disappointed by its monotony.

Having previously met Viardot in London, Sullivan renewed his acquaintance with her, and was delighted that through her he was invited to some of Rossini's levées. At one of them he met Carl Rose, and was amused when someone tried to introduce them to each other as if for the first time. At others he persuaded the aged master to play the piano duet version of *The Tempest* with him. Rossini, Sullivan reported, took a great fancy to the music, and when he left he was asked by Rossini to send copies of all his works to him.

At home Sullivan was assiduous in cultivating new friends and keeping in close touch with those who were in a position to further his interests. The way of a composer was not easy. Large works brought prestige but little financial return. Popularity was ensured by invasion of the drawing-room song and ballad market. Since this, for the time being, also brought minimal material rewards (*Orpheus with his lute*, for instance, was sold outright to Metzler for five pounds), the only hope was that success in this field would guarantee a continuation of commissions in others. Through the Lehmanns Sullivan met Adelaide Procter (1825–64), the wife of Barry Cornwall. 'I have a note from Mr Sullivan,' Mrs Lehmann wrote on 15th August 1866, 'who has set Adelaide's words "Hush" to music for Madame [Charlotte Sainton-] Dolby.' [23] The settings of Shakespeare that engaged Sullivan's interest at this time were also discreetly dedicated—one to Mme Dolby, the others to Louisa Crampton, Santley, Sims Reeves and Cummings. Two friends who had been fellow-choristers at the Chapel Royal were also in the forefront of Sullivan's thoughts at this time, Fred Clay (1838–89) and Alfred Cellier (1844–91). Very much a dilettante, Clay was for a time a clerk in the Treasury. But, a gifted melodist, he escaped from this occupation and devoted himself to the composition of popular songs, small dramatic works and cantatas. To Clay Sullivan dedicated his *Arabian love song*,[24] which soon became a standard number in Arthur Chappell's 'Monday Pops', established in 1858. This was a fitting dedication in that Clay's own musical fame ultimately depended on his 'I'll sing thee songs of Araby' (*Lalla Rookh*, 1877).

In the summer of 1866 Sullivan did Clay a service by giving a first performance of a new cantata by him:

THE CIVIL SERVICE MUSICAL SOCIETY gave a concert on 20 [July], at St. James's Hall (in aid of the funds of King's College Hospital), which we are glad to say was extremely well attended. A Cantata by Mr. Fred Clay, called 'The Knights of the Cross' (words by R. Reece, Esq.) was produced for the first time, and sufficiently proved that, as an amateur, Mr. Clay has many claims to attention. . . . Mr. A. S. Sullivan made a most efficient conductor.[25]

Cellier went to Belfast in 1865 as conductor of the Philharmonic Society, and a visit by Alfred J. Hipkins (1826–1903) to Northern Ireland in 1866 afforded opportunity for Sullivan to send messages to those of the establishment there who had befriended him two years previously. On 5th October he wrote to Hipkins as follows:

My dear Hipkins,
Put the enclosed [letter to Cellier] in an envelope, and tell Cellier that I couldn't write more on account of my present trouble [the death of his father]. I enclose two or three cards in case you would like to present them to Dunville or the Tennants, or any friends of mine over there.
Many thanks for your kind and sympathetic letter. It is pleasant to find one's friends don't forget one in trouble.
Yours sincerely,
Arthur Sullivan.[26]

The summer and autumn of 1866 were decisive in many ways. Sullivan was prominent as a composer, establishing himself as a conductor, and beginning to reap the first substantial dividends on his invested charms. On 11th July George Grove noted in his 'Diary' his attendance at 'Arthur's concert'.

MR. ARTHUR S. SULLIVAN'S Concert at St. James's Hall . . . was in every way a highly successful one. Appealing to the public as a composer, Mr. Sullivan was perfectly right to print his own name as often as he pleased in the programme, and to stand or fall by the result. We have already given opinion on his Symphony [27] . . . which of course occupied a conspicuous place in the Concert—and of his Overture to the *Sapphire necklace*, we may say that there is very much to admire, and that, without contrasting it with mature works, it contains sufficient to show that Mr. Sullivan has power to advance to a high place provided that power is rightly directed in time. A great feature of the Concert was Madame Goldschmidt's singing of two songs by the Concert-giver, and her brilliant execution of Handel's 'Sweet bird' . . . which made us feel how little the lapse of time can weaken the charm of a real artist. Mr. Santley's song (also by Mr. Sullivan), 'O mistress mine', is a clever composition, and was enthusiastically encored. Bach's Concerto in C minor, for two pianofortes, was played to perfection by Madlle. Mehlig [28] and Mr. Franklin Taylor, and later in the evening Madlle. Mehlig performed Moscheles' 'Recollections of Ireland', at the end of which the composer, who was present, received quite an ovation. The programme also included the duet, 'In such a night as this' . . . and the 'Brisk Dance', two of the best pieces in . . . *Kenilworth*. The concert was extremely well attended.[29]

It is clear that at this time Sullivan was hardly under-employed (the time he was able to give to his church duties would appear to have been limited). Nonetheless in the autumn, while still busy with *In Memoriam*, he was able to find time to go down to the Isle of Wight with Grove, to visit Tennyson at Freshwater.[30] Writing to Olga von Glehn,[31] Grove said:

I had proposed to [Tennyson] to write a *Liederkreis* for Sullivan to set and Millais to illustrate . . . Sullivan went down with me, and pleased Mr. and Mrs. Tennyson extremely. In the evening we had as much music as we could on a very tinkling piano, very much out of tune, and then retired to his room at the top of the house where he read us the three songs,[32] a long ballad, and several other things; and talked till two o'clock in a very fine way about the things which I always get round to sooner or later—death and the next world, and God and man etc.[33]

It is independently recorded that Tennyson was pleased at the idea of a 'song-cycle in the German manner', and also with Sullivan's visit. As he went on with the composition of the poems, however, he was less than pleased with what he wrote and at the end of the month observed to William Allingham of the cycle: 'It is quite silly.' Three years later he did all he could to prevent Sullivan from publishing the songs, even offering to pay him £500 in compensation for estimated lost earnings. Sullivan refusing to withdraw, Tennyson honoured his agreement; the two men remained on good terms.[34]

After Norwich, and the acclaim which *In Memoriam* received, Sullivan prepared for another popular success. On 5th November his setting of Scott's *A weary lot*, sung by Santley and accompanied by Benedict, was greeted as 'an extremely pretty new ballad' and was 'loudly encored, [and] repeated as a matter of course'.[35]

At the beginning of the next month Sullivan—travelling with Sym Egerton (later Lord Wilton) to Manchester—heard the symphony played at the Hallé Concert of 6th December. *The Guardian* was not altogether complimentary, observing next day that the work appeared

> ... fragmentary and disjointed ... it is impossible to ignore the fact, which is only too apparent, that the symphony wants that inventive genius and coordinating power without which such works are mere sound ...

Hallé, however, maintained his faith in Sullivan. On 31st January 1867, Santley sang *If doughty deeds,* and on 27th February *In Memoriam* had its first performance at a Hallé Concert. One of the agreeable features of Sullivan's character was his firm loyalty to those who first helped him towards success. In a few years' time he was able to assert his loyalty and gratitude to Hallé in a wholly admirable manner (see page 95). At this juncture the fact may be noted that Sullivan's reputation was not made in London alone, but that a good deal of credit for it belonged to the greater provincial centres.

NOTES TO CHAPTER THREE

1. British composers were also encouraged at the concerts of the Musical Society of London, which were conducted by Alfred Mellon. But to the foreign critic such composers were a joke. 'They swear by what Sterndale Bennett once stated as an article of belief in a public lecture: that English music is of equal rank to that of Germany, France and Italy. How many English music-lovers go so far as really to believe this is not known.' Hanslick, *Aus dem Concert-Saal,* p. 579.
2. *See* letter from Sullivan to Manns of 12th April 1895, published in H. Saxe Wyndham, *August Manns and the Saturday Concerts,* London, 1909, p. 41.
3. *Birmingham Mail,* 23rd November 1900.
4. Helmore's memory played him false, *see* p. 50.
5. In a letter of 23rd January to Mrs R. Lehmann, Sullivan oddly failed to mention the Mendelssohn works and wrongly stated that it was Beethoven's *Egmont* overture that was played. R. C. Lehmann, *Memories of Half a Century,* London, 1908.

6. Possibly written by George Freemantle (1833–94), organist at Cross Street Chapel (of which Mrs Gaskell's husband was minister), a music critic and business man who exercised a considerable influence on the musical life of Manchester.

7. Letter of 29th May 1894 to Mrs Lehmann: see Lehmann, *Memories*, pp. 253–4.

8. *See* advertisement in *Musical Times*, 12, March 1865, p. 1.

9. A. G. Mackenzie, 'The Life and Work of Arthur Sullivan', in *Sammelbände der Internationalen Musik-Gesellschaft*, Jrg. III (1901–2), Leipzig, 1902, pp. 539–64.

10. C. V. Stanford, *Interludes*, London, 1922, p. 34.

11. Two themes from *L'île enchantée* were used in *The Merry Wives of Windsor* in 1874 (see p. 103).

12. Mrs W. Carr, *Musical Times*, 42, 1901, p. 101.

13. Prior to this and after leaving Ponsonby Street, Sullivan lived at 139 Westbourne Terrace.

14. 'Recollections of Past Birmingham Musical Festivals', in *Midland Counties Herald*, 9th July 1885.

15. Quoted, without date, in Sullivan and Flower, *Sir Arthur Sullivan*, 1950 edn., p. 45.

16. Also undated: *ibid.* p. 46.

17. Referring to a programme in 1893, Sullivan wrote to Bennett on 8th March of that year: 'You will see I have called my Symphony "In Ireland". I sketched it when I was in Ireland in 1864, and always meant to call it the "Irish Symphony", but I modestly refrained, as it was courting comparison with the "Scotch Symphony". But Stanford called his symphony the "Irish", so I didn't see why I should be done out of my title abroad!' Joseph Bennett, *Forty Years of Music, 1865–1905*, London, 1908, p. 71.

18. H. Sullivan to F. G. Edwards, 28th June 1905: 'The *Concerto in D major* was written for and dedicated to Piatti who played it Nov. 26, 1866 at the Crystal Palace. I have written out the first page.' BM. Eg. MS. 3096.

19. Vol. v, no. 122, December 1866, p. 335.

20. On 22nd September: see Sullivan's letter of 18th October to Mrs Lehmann, quoted in H. Saxe Wyndham, *Arthur Seymour Sullivan*, London, 1926, pp. 87–8.

21. Obituary in *The Birmingham Post*.

22. First performance, Opéra Comique, 12th May 1862.

23. Lehmann, *Memories*, p. 163. Charlotte Sainton-Dolby (1821–85) was a contralto of whom Mendelssohn thought highly. He invited her, together with Jenny Lind, to sing at the Gewandhaus concerts in 1845. She was also a composer. This song was not published.

24. cf. G. Macfarren's *Songs from the Arabian Nights*, well known from the 'Monday Pops'.

25. *Musical Times*, 12, August 1866, p. 350. W. E. Gladstone, the future Prime Minister, was a member of the choir at this time.

26. This, and the letter to Cellier, are designated BM. Add. MS. 41636, ff. 32, 33. cf. the dedication of *Thoughts* No. 2 to Miss Dunville (*see also* p. 272). The Tennants were (presumably) the family of Charles Tennant, a Glasgow manufacturing chemist with a branch factory at 4 York Street, Belfast.

27. *Musical Times*, 12, April 1866, p. 263: 'Mr. Sullivan's new Symphony has been an interesting feature . . . and seems to have achieved a success which we trust may have a healthy effect upon the young composer. At our concerts in the metropolis we hope to have an opportunity of shortly hearing this work, for there can be no doubt that the puerilities of *Kenilworth* have (in spite of ill-advised laudation) disappointed many who believe in the composer of the *Tempest* music.'

28. Anna Mehlig (1846–1928), a native of Stuttgart, was a pupil of Liszt at Weimar. Her first appearance in England was at a Philharmonic Concert on 30th April 1866.

29. *Musical Times*, 13, December 1867, p. 220.

30. On 17th October: *see* C. L. Graves, *The Life and Letters of Sir George Grove, C.B.*, London, 1903, p. 133.

31. Letter dated 28th October: *ibid.* p. 133.

32. Out of seven then projected, but *see* p. 275.

33. cf. the contents of Tennyson's last poem, *God and the Universe*.

34. Charles Tennyson, *Alfred Tennyson*, London, 1949, pp. 365, 392.

35. *The Times*, 6th November 1866. cf. *Daily Telegraph*, which referred to the song as 'a quaint and original setting'.

4

Straws in the wind

At the age of twenty-five Sullivan had various options open to him. He could stabilize his position in the field of 'serious' music and—with the good fortune that had so far attended him—perhaps go on to become the first great British symphonist. He could exploit his talent for the commonplace, and with the backing he already enjoyed, and a quickening business acumen, make a lot of money. He could invest his critical faculty in musical scholarship, and complement Grove's enthusiasm and historical interest with the special knowledge possessed by a trained musician. Or, emboldened by his friendships and his adventures in the drawing-rooms of the polite, he could aim at the higher ranges of social success. He tried in fact to keep all these options open, but in the end, as will be seen, incompatibility between the possible aims defeated him.

The year 1867 was a fateful one, for it saw Sullivan attempting to pursue all his objectives more or less at the same time. In February we find him delicately poised, as guest but also as entertainer, in Chorley's home. There was something of indignity in the scene as described by Mrs Lehmann on 24th February, but Sullivan was prepared to put up with a good deal in his progress towards the flesh-pots.

> I went on Valentine's Day to Mr. Chorley's. Only Peeresses dined, with a few men to do the agreeable. I found only the Women and Chorley. Lady Molesworth in a *red jacket*. Each of the Ladies, six in number, found a Valentine upon her plate—a poem written by Chorley. He never treated me in that way. Sullivan played, and there was a whist table.[1]

It was at this time that Bennett began to entertain doubts about Sullivan's future.

> [In 1867] the Power which shapes our ends had drawn him very near the line dividing Society (with the large S) from

Arthur Sullivan, aged 10, portrait by an unknown artist

Exercise in fugue, after Mozart, 1858 (autograph)

Julius Rietz

Below: Moritz Hauptmann
and his family, from an
original photograph
Below right: Ferdinand David,
from an original photograph

Unveiling the
Handel Monument
in Halle, 1st July
1859

Reichel's Garten. Mittelgebäude 8.

Leipzig. March 1861.

I have treated you badly. very badly, my
dear Miss Rosamond, inasmuch as three
months have elapsed, & I have not
written to you once, but I know your
kind & forgiving disposition (do you remember
our little quarrels in days of yore?) & feel assured
that you will not only rejoice over the
repentant sinner, but will also write
to me in return, which is saying a great
deal, ~~which~~ for one under the influence of
Berlin atmosphere — But you will
write quickly I hope, for I leave here
in about a fortnight, & wish very

Letter from Sullivan to Rosamund Barnett, March 1861

Einladung und Programm

zur

HAUPT-PRÜFUNG

im Conservatorium der Musik zu Leipzig

Sonnabend den 6. April 1861

im Saale des Gewandhauses.

(I. Prüfung.)

(Orchester-Composition. Solo-Spiel und Solo-Gesang.)

Concert für das Pianoforte von W. Sterndale Bennett (F moll, erster Satz), gespielt von Herrn *Walter Bache* aus Birmingham.

Concert für die Violine von L. van Beethoven (erster Satz), gespielt von Herrn *Ernst Friedrich Fabritius* aus Wiborg in Finnland.

Concert-Arie von F. Mendelssohn-Bartholdy, gesungen von Fräulein *Sara Oppenheimer* aus Esens in Ostfriesland.

Concert für das Pianoforte von Field (As dur, erster Satz), gespielt von Fräul. *Leonora Schmitz* aus Edinburg.

Musik zu Shakspear's „Sturm", componirt von Herrn Arthur S. Sullivan aus London (unter Leitung des Componisten).

Hieraus:

    a) **Einleitung.**
    b) **Lied des Ariel,** gesungen von Fräul. *Minna Giesinger* aus Leipzig.
    c) **Entreact.**
    d) **Grotesker Tanz.**
    e) **Entreact und Epilog.**
    f) **Tanz der Nymphen und Schnitter.**

Concert in Form einer Gesangsscene für die Violine von L. Spohr, gespielt von Herrn *Carl Rose* aus Hamburg.

Concert pathétique für Pianoforte von J. Moscheles (erster Satz), gespielt von Herrn *C. Aug. Heinrich Werner* aus Genf.

Scene und **Arie** aus dem „Freischütz" von C. M. v. Weber, gesungen von Fräul. *Minna Giesinger* aus Leipzig.

Concert für die Violine von F. Mendelssohn-Bartholdy (zweiter und dritter Satz), gespielt von Herrn *Henri Schradiek* aus Hamburg.

Einlass halb 6 Uhr.   Anfang 6 Uhr.

Das Directorium des Conservatoriums der Musik.

Druck von Breitkopf und Härtel in Leipzig.

Programme of the Leipzig Conservatorium Graduation Concert of 6th April 1861

St Michael's Church,
Chester Square,
c. 1861

Sir Francis Cowley
Burnand, pen-and-
ink portrait for
Punch by
H. Furniss

Music and oysters
with Arthur J.
Lewis, 1865

society (with the small s). It would have been better for music, perhaps, if he had never overstepped that line, but the crossing was almost inevitable. 'Society' leading, for the most part, an empty and vapid life, wants to be entertained, and cannot afford to be particular about the entertainers; so it happens that Sullivan, who was already on the side of the angels as far as that position is assured to a church organist, drifted across to the butterflies, became a friend of Royalty, and a darling of the drawing-rooms. He could hardly help himself, poor boy! Was he not under the control of his own fascinating gifts and sunny temperament.[2]

Sullivan may have been showing signs of forsaking the high ideals which his older friends and former teachers supposed he should pursue. But his gratitude to those who had formerly assisted and encouraged him was genuine, and he never failed to express it. This is one of the engaging features of his personality. On 23rd February Sir George Smart, to whom perhaps he owed most, died. Sullivan wrote to his widow.

> 47 Claverton Terrace,
> St. George's Road, S.W.
> [no date]

My dear Lady Smart,

You I am sure will not think I am intruding upon your grief, if I venture at this early period to write and assure you how deeply and earnestly I feel with you, and how sincerely I mourn for the loss of my kind and revered old friend. Upon no one has his memory greater claims for love and honour than myself. Since I owed him so much, and although in his last days I was not permitted to see much of him, I never failed in my warm affection or gratitude to him. After all the first bitterness of sorrow is over we shall be able to look back calmly upon the noble example which his blameless unsullied life has left us— an example to follow which will (please God) be my great aim and the greatest respect I can pay to his memory—I dare not of course ask to see you yet, but when you are quite strong enough I should like to come and talk over his many great and endearing qualities. One privilege I hope you will not refuse me. Viz: that of following him to his last home on earth. I should be grieved if I could not pay him that last tribute of respect. With *Him*, in whom I sought comfort, lately in my own great trouble, You will I know find peace and happiness.

> God bless you, dear lady Smart,
> Ever affect. Yours
> Arthur S. Sullivan.

If there is anything in the world in which I can be of service to you, pray rely upon me.[3]

In the summer Sullivan advanced on two fronts—the social and the ecclesiastical—simultaneously. Sir Charles Freake had just built the Church of St Peter's, Cranley Gardens, and the Perpetual Curate, Hon. Francis Byng (later Lord Strafford) needed an organist. Advised by Sym Egerton, as has already been seen, who had become acquainted with Sullivan and had spoken of him to Byng previously,[4] he approached Sullivan. Byng's offer was acceptable and Sullivan relinquished St Michael's to Franklin Taylor,[5] for the time being, however, retaining his post at Covent Garden. He took up his appointment at Cranley Gardens on St Peter's Day (29th June) 1867, the day of the consecration of the church. The service of consecration, in which Helmore took part, was not without its comic side, as Byng himself was to indicate:

> . . . the Bishop of London had appointed 11.15 as the Hour—but in the morning—sent a message to say—he could not come—until 11.45—so Sullivan very kindly kept the congregation interested by playing—I went up to thank him—and he jokingly remarked he had almost come to the end of his repertoire and he asked what shall I play? and *I* suggested (I think it was!) [Sullivan's] 'Will he come'—then very popular. . . . Helmore was in my Church with some of the Boys and began in his loud and powerful musical voice (the Athanasian Creed, which is not proper for St. Peter's Day)—but I had begun reading the Apostle's Creed—so that for a second or two we were both reciting different creeds . . .[6]

Sir John Goss was also present to hear his own setting of 'Praise, my soul, the King of heaven'. After that, whenever Goss was present at Evensong Sullivan would put this hymn into the service. Another old hero who occasionally came to St Peter's was Ouseley, and it is recorded that once he played an extempore fugue on the hymn-tune 'Hanover'.[7] This provided a change for the congregation, since Sullivan (whose strong point was his accompanying of the choir) largely eschewed counterpoint in church, preferring to play as voluntaries his own arrangements of concert pieces and oratorio arias.

Only seven years older than his organist, the vicar of St Peter's not only had a high regard for Sullivan but was on terms of friendship with him. The distance Sullivan had travelled in the social rat-race is indicated by the fact that he felt able to ask his vicar to dine with him, and that Byng, in accepting, was conscious of an honour done to him:

> I was present, by his Invitation, at a Dinner when he—Tennyson, and Millais [8] dined together at his house. Tennyson read The Window—Song of the Wren—Millais gave his notions of the Illustrations suitable—Sullivan suggesting the Music—An unique pleasure and privilege—
> I suggested to A.S. that I represented 'Ignorance' of all three Poetry—Music and Art. [9]

Byng was also grateful to Sullivan that the song *O sweet and fair* was dedicated by the composer to Mrs Byng. Sullivan remained organist at St Peter's until the beginning of 1872. [10]

Although not appreciated at the time, the real turning-point in Sullivan's career was the production of the operetta *Cox and Box*. Its coming into existence, however, was purely fortuitous, the consequence of Sullivan's gregariousness on the one hand and his easy good nature on the other. The account of its parturition is uncommonly complicated.

Arthur Lewis, the managing director of a Regent Street store and husband of Ellen Terry's sister, Kate (also an actress), lived in west London at Moray Lodge, Campden Hill. He was in the habit of giving parties to which the artistic and the fashionable were invited in more or less equal proportions, and at which large quantities of oysters, champagne and cigars were consumed. At Moray Lodge could be met the Duke of Sutherland, the Marquis of Lorne, Lords Dufferin and Houghton, Frederick Leighton, Wilkie Collins, Rossetti, Landseer, Daubigny, Doré, Leech, Keene, Tenniel and Francis Burnand (1836–1917).

Burnand was one of a number of *Punch* contributors who attended these parties, and he was also author of several burlesques, some of which he had adapted from French originals. Sullivan was present at the Lewises' sometime towards the end of 1865, and during the next

year the idea of adapting John Maddison Morton's (1811–91) farce
Box and Cox (1847) for an operetta was mooted.

Various legends developed concerning the origins of *Cox and Box*,
some of which are disposed of by Burnand in a letter which is also
interesting in other respects. Burnand wrote to F. G. Edwards on
14th January 1901 as follows:

> My dear Sir:
>
> Sir G. Grove's account of performance of 'C. & B.' at Moray
> Lodge [11] may be accurate as to *date* but is *inaccurate* as to its
> being the *first* performance, which, as Harold Power (who played
> in it) remembers, and as my wife (who saw it) remembers,
> also Mr Arthur à Beckett [12] (who saw it & who I believe has
> the date in his diary) reasons and as I, for various reasons which
> I retain in my 'Reminiscences', distinctly and unhesitatingly
> remember took place in my home. The *exact* date I shall
> endeavour to find out: if the *raison d'être* of the party I gave was
> my birthday (not at all unlikely) then it was certainly in 1866
> November. But of this I can't be as yet at all sure. However I
> will be if any of my copies has a date.
>
> You astonish me as to the musical world saying there being
> no overture to 'Cox & Box' at the Adelphi. It certainly had a
> *prelude* to Cox & Box—I believe 'overture'—as I saw him
> [Sullivan] at work at it (and he called it 'overture') which
> commenced with the *Handelian Bouncer's* Song.
>
> The story as to Cox & Box being started by A.S.S. & self on
> returning from Church one Sunday [13] is utterly without a
> semblance of foundation: as I should never have been going
> on a Sunday to a Protestant Church with him [14] nor would he
> have been going with *me* to a Catholic Church. He did, I
> believe, occasionally accompany his mother to the little Catholic
> Church [of St Peter and St Edward] in Palace Street where in
> those days I never went and moreover my early hours for going
> to Mass would never have suited Arthur S. who if he ever
> visited a Catholic Church would have visited it on account of the
> music that is at High Mass at 11. . . . [15]

Partial support, at least, for the statement that *Cox and Box* was
tried out at Burnand's in November 1866 comes from the fact that
on 17th December an amateur performance of the operetta was
given at the Prince's Theatre, Manchester, 'in aid of the Widow of
[the] late John Hudspeth, comedian'. This—which has hitherto

escaped notice—was in fact the first public performance of *Cox and Box*. A classic case, perhaps, of what Manchester thinks today, London thinks tomorrow. Box was played by a Mr Sampson, Cox by Mr Hudspeth (presumably not the deceased), while the third part—for *Mrs* Bouncer—was assigned to a Mrs Chas. Jones.

The celebrated performance in London, previously regarded as the first, took place at Lewis's house on 27th April 1867, with Sullivan at the piano. The part of Cox was taken by Harold Power, an Irishman; that of Box by George du Maurier, who like Burnand was on the staff of *Punch*; and that of Bouncer by John Foster. On 11th May the production was taken to the Adelphi Theatre for a charity performance in aid of the family of C. H. Bennett, also of *Punch*, who had lately died. On this occasion Quintin Twist played the part of Cox, and Arthur Cecil that of Bouncer. Two years later the piece was revived with startling success, as will be discovered.

In the meanwhile Sullivan's friendship with Grove had reactivated his missionary zeal. It also led him back to the point at which he had started—in Leipzig—where, however, he was to discover that time had not stood still. Sullivan, it will be remembered, had returned from his student days in Leipzig full of enthusiasm for the music of Schubert. Although Grove had doubted that the work would be well received, and counselled against its performance, Manns insisted on playing the 'Great C major' at the Crystal Palace in 1856. Having heard it, Grove was fired with ardour for Schubert, but until he met Arthur Sullivan, found it difficult to raise general sympathy. Schubert remained an 'unknown' composer to the English public, but on 8th March 1863, Charles Hallé struck a blow on his behalf by giving the first English performance of the B flat Piano Sonata at a Monday Pop. Two years later Heinrich Kreissle von Hellborn's then authoritative biography appeared, which was issued in A. D. Coleridge's translation in England in 1869. (This contained an appendix by Grove.)

Grove was intrigued by the catalogue of works given by von Hellborn, particularly by the description of the *Rosamunde* music. Having previously had correspondence with Karl Anton Spina (1827–1906)—who succeeded to Diabelli's former publishing business—concerning music for the Crystal Palace, Grove wrote to him anew asking what works of Schubert might be available. In October 1866 he received from Vienna the entractes in B minor and B flat, which were played at the Crystal Palace on 10th November. Soon afterwards nos. 2 ('Ballo' in B minor) and 9 ('Ballet Air'), from the same work, were sent to Grove, and they were performed on 16th March. Other music by Schubert performed at the Crystal Palace at this time included the overtures to *Alfonso and Estrella* and *Fierrebras* (3rd November 1866 and 2nd February 1867), the *Overture in Italian Style* (1st December 1866), and the 'Unfinished' Symphony (6th April 1867).[16]

At this juncture Grove decided to go to Vienna to see for himself what Schubertian treasures might be still hidden away. He went

> . . . in company with a gentleman who is at once one of my best friends, and—in the absence of Mr. Manns, then unable to leave his duties—better able, perhaps, than anyone else to advise and assist me in my search, namely, Mr. Arthur Sullivan.[17]

The pilgrims reached Vienna on 5th October, and when they had booked in at the Zur Kaiserin Elisabeth, made straight for Spina's shop at 6 Kohlmarkt. Having withstood the first shock of Viennese hospitality, and Spina having passed favourable opinion on Sullivan's *Day Dreams* (which Sullivan played to him), they got down to work. They were shown all sorts of items relating to the great Viennese composers, about whom they heard innumerable anecdotes from Spina's manager, Josef Döppler, a friend of the Schubert family from boyhood. From Dr Eduard Schneider, a lawyer who was the son of Schubert's sister Therese, they obtained MSS. of the 'Simfonie in "C" Major', the 'Simfonie in "C" Minor (Sogenannte "Tragisit")', and the 'Overture in "D", "Die Freunde von Salamanca"'.[18] But their main aim was the discovery of the complete *Rosamunde* music. Of this there was no trace, and, disappointed, Sullivan and Grove went off to visit Clara Schumann in Baden, the picture gallery and Dr Döllinger in München, and the Mozarteum in Salzburg. From here they came back to Vienna for a day or two before making their final departure. One last effort was made to find the *Rosamunde* music. This was successful. The part-books of the whole work were finally unearthed in a cupboard in Schneider's house. With the assistance of Karl Ferdinand Pohl [19] the parts were transcribed and, after the travellers' return to England, were immediately passed to Manns. The first complete performance of the *Rosamunde* music took place at the Crystal Palace on 10th November.

Sullivan went to Prague and then on to Leipzig, where he was rejoined by Grove. Before leaving for Leipzig he wrote to Ignaz

Moscheles indicating his intention to visit the city, and asking if any of his works could be included in the Gewandhaus concerts. He mentioned particularly the Symphony and *In Memoriam*. The latter was included in the second concert of the season on 17th October. The programme included three 'novelties', Sullivan's work, Karl Reinecke's *Ave Maria* (soprano and orchestra), and Anton Rubinstein's D minor Piano Concerto (No. 4) in which Rubinstein was the soloist. Sullivan's overture, which he conducted himself, followed Rubinstein's work, and

> . . . was rather less pleasing. Sullivan was a student at the Leipzig Conservatorium, since when he has learned how to gain the particular goodwill of his fellow-countrymen, the English. His Overture, with its special title, offered too little that is original for us Germans. Against this, the composer blends the tone-colours into very beautiful sonorities, while the bass part, the harmonies, etc., are clear throughout and his style is noble. This caused the Overture to be given more applause than it deserves.[20]

The *Neue Zeitschrift für Musik* was a little more encouraging:

> This work was acclaimed on its performance at the Birmingham [in error for Norwich] Festival. Although not of marked individuality the whole work still gives an impression of music of true feeling. It commends itself because, while maintaining the customary shape of an overture, it is fresh in its avoidance of dull formality and displays a psychological consistency in conception and disposition. We would only have wished to have been without the concluding display of effects which are overwhelming and out of proportion in the concert hall. The way in which the work was received was creditable to the composer, who was recalled.[21]

On the Sunday following, the Gewandhaus orchestra played through the 'Irish' Symphony, but it was neither then nor at any other time publicly performed in Leipzig. A lot of water had flowed along the Pleisse since Sullivan was a student, and there were other names which commanded more attention than his. Grove, writing to the von Glehns, was disappointed at the lukewarm attitude of the Leipzigers to Sullivan's music, and ascribed it to their bad taste: 'To please them, everything must be dreadfully grim and earnest,

and as soon as a bit of tune comes, they think it all "*ganz trivial*"—
a state of mind which I hope we shan't get into. . . .' [22]

What, perhaps, Grove did not recognize (Sullivan certainly did
not, for in political matters he was naïve) was that since the coming
to power of Bismarck in 1862 the Germans—especially the Prussians
—had become considerably more 'earnest'. The political aims—
the natural conclusion of the nationalism that had long been bur-
geoning in all classes of society—were the unification of Germany
and the reduction of the power, and potential threat, of France. A
state of tension existed between the two countries, and each played
its cards in the game of diplomacy whenever it seemed a trick might
be taken. Culture had its place in this game. So the Universal
Exhibition, held in Paris at the beginning of July 1867, was a
glittering public relations exercise on the grand scale: there were
17,000 people present at the Prize Distribution in the Palais de
l'Industrie. The most spectacular aspect of the Exhibition was
Eiffel's exciting and futuristic Galérie des Machines, but there was
a good deal of music.[23] Behind the façade the princes and statesmen,
among whom were the Crown Prince of Prussia, the Prince of Wales
and the Duke of Cambridge, met and bargained. On behalf of the
British delegation Lord Granville, an experienced diplomat and
former Foreign Secretary, gave a banquet at which Sullivan directed
a group of glee-singers in a performance of the traditional grace,
'Non nobis, Domine'. He was present in an official position, as a
special 'commissioner'. Parisian life was much to his taste, and as the
years went by he visited France with ever increasing frequency.

Altogether it was a full life. Disinclined to renounce the pleasures
of the world the more purposefully to pursue his vocations, Sullivan
lived well and delighted in company, particularly distinguished
company. At Sydenham, as Grove's constant guest, he dined on
various occasions with Adelina Patti, August Manns and Ferdinand
David. His already wide circle of acquaintance was there extended
to include J. R. Green, the historian, Canon Alfred Ainger, Reader
at the Temple Church and teacher of English language and literature
at the Crystal Palace, Lionel Lewin, a wit who wrote verses for
Sullivan from time to time, and Emanuel Deutsch, the orientalist.
In the autumn of 1868 Sullivan was back in Germany, as the guest
of Clara Schumann in München. A chronic victim of *Wanderlust*, a
restlessness of temperament began to show itself more strongly in
him. He travelled to Brussels in the following summer, and thence

to Aix-la-Chapelle where he sought and found Burnand on holiday. During these two years, songs—with some instrumental music, some anthems and a few hymn-tunes—came more abundantly. The dedications of his works, particularly those of lesser importance, serve as annotations on Sullivan's social life. On 29th April 1868 (according to a marginal note in the copy in the British Museum), Chappell published *Twilight*, a piano piece inscribed to 'Miss Rachel Scott Russell'. In the same year Sullivan also dedicated to the same lady an appealing song, *O fair dove, O fond dove*.

John Scott Russell, F.R.S. (1808–82), a naval architect and as such responsible for the construction of the ill-fated cable-ship *Great Eastern*, was a friend of Grove and a constant visitor at his home. A member of the governing body of the Crystal Palace, Russell was much interested in Sullivan, whom he frequently entertained (it was at Russell's house that Stanford first met Sullivan). He had three daughters, and in one of these, Rachel, Sullivan was also much interested. Sullivan's interest was reciprocated and the two 'came to an understanding'. It would seem (and it would be likely) that Rachel was the more passionate of the two. She it was who, when forbidden to see Sullivan by her parents, arranged clandestine meetings in the potting-shed or, in colder weather, in Grove's office at the Crystal Palace. And she could throw fits of jealousy. Not, perhaps, that one should criticize her for taking umbrage at the sight of Sullivan squiring Lady Katherine Coke, dedicatee of *Will he come?*, in Bond Street. Rachel urged Sullivan to aim high, recommending him at various times to write a Symphony in D, an octet, and an opera with the title *Guinevere*.

A hundred years ago, marriage between a young lady of gentle upbringing and a professional musician was thought by the majority of the well-to-do to be both impolitic and improper. Scott Russell in this matter went with the majority. Rachel made a grand gesture of renunciation in 1869, but instead of following Guinevere into a nunnery married an Indian Civil Servant in 1872. Ten years later, aged thirty-seven, she died. Her poor memorials are Sullivan's crepuscular trifle for piano, and a song. She had signed her letters to him, 'Fond dove'. After this chapter closed, Sullivan referred to Northern Ireland for female inspiration—or so it was coyly stated by his nephew.[24]

Throughout this period Sullivan's name was kept prominently before the public—all of it. His songs and part-songs were deemed

to be admirable on account of their 'graceful melodic phrases' and
their 'chaste and flowing harmonies'. Sullivan possessed the rarest
gift, according to a somewhat ambivalent notice in the *Musical
Times*, of being able to 'produce trifles impressed with special value
and marked character'.[25] The trifles were excellent properties. After
the initial outright sale of the Shakespeare songs, Sullivan, assisted
by his formidable and rising popularity, was able to bargain with his
publishers from a position of strength. In this he was, for that time,
in an almost unique situation—a fact that is made the more striking
by reason of the agreement reached with Boosey's on 9th April 1868.
By this, the firm was obliged to pay him £400 a year for 1868, 1869
and 1870, in return for the publishing rights in his works. This was
without prejudice to his royalties.[26] His minor pieces were published
on a royalty basis (singers who plugged the songs got their cut!),
while mutually profitable contracts were drawn up in respect of
larger works. So far as these were concerned, in order to receive any
kind of adequate return on the time and labour invested it was
desirable to make available piano, or piano duet, scores. Herein lies
one reason, and one of particular cogency, for Sullivan's abdication
from the symphonic field; and, at a later date, for Elgar's slow entry
into it. Sullivan's symphony was not published until 1915. His
cello concerto remained unpublished. The overture, *Marmion*,
which he wrote for, and which was played at, a Philharmonic
Society Concert on 3rd June 1867, suffered the same fate. For
the ambitious young composer in England a century ago, the options
were limited. Survival depended on collusion with those who wielded
economic authority. It also depended on acquiescence in accepted
attitudes, and the understanding, and even acceptance, of prevailing
canons of taste.

In 1868 Sullivan appeared at the Three Choirs Festival at
Gloucester. His success on that occasion reminded the Festival
Committee of its obligation to native composers, and Sullivan was
therefore invited to provide a new work for the following year. The
result was *The Prodigal Son* (the subject of an oratorio by Samuel
Arnold in 1773), which was considered to be an advance on anything
the composer had previously done. Sullivan conducted, and his
soloists were Therese Tietjens (1831–77), a German-born soprano
famous as a London opera singer at that time, Zelia Trebelli (1838–
1892), a French mezzo-soprano also popular in the London theatre,
Sims Reeves, and Santley. The work was repeated at Hereford in the

following year. Sullivan was a quick worker and *The Prodigal Son* was composed at breakneck speed in a matter of weeks. Not unexpectedly, his prolificacy tended sometimes to be condemned absolutely. Sir John Goss was not among those who did this, but he did have his doubts and, after praising the virtues of the oratorio, observed:

> Some day you will I hope try at another oratorio, putting out all your strength—not the strength of a few weeks or months. Show yourself *the best man in Europe!* Don't do anything so pretentious as an oratorio or even a Symphony without *all your power*, which seldom comes in one fit. Handel's two or three weeks for the 'Messiah' may be a fact, but *he* was not always successful, and was not so young a chap as you.[27]

As it happened, Sullivan at this time was following the example of Mozart, Robert Franz, Costa and George Macfarren, and putting into Handel's scores what it was thought Handel would have approved. His commission to provide 'additional accompaniments' for *Jephtha* came from Joseph Barnby, whose choir had been founded in 1867.[28] For Barnby to essay *Jephtha* was a bold undertaking, and

> To render the Oratorio attractive to a modern audience . . . it was necessary to make the most unsparing excisions. . . . Respecting Mr. Sullivan's share in the work as it was presented at this concert, we have nothing but praise. The bald manner in which Handel has left his scores must be a matter of surprise to those who do not believe, as we do, that additional parts were continually written by the composer for various performances of his works which were afterwards lost; and that the scores as they now appear are but skeletons of what was really heard by an audience during Handel's lifetime. There can be little question that the true office of an artist who undertakes to supply accompaniments to these oratorios is not so much to write from himself as from Handel: to allow the score of the composer, in fact, to suggest what he would probably have added, and it is because Mr. Sullivan has reverently followed this plan throughout his arduous task that he is entitled to our thanks. In many of the choruses the richness of the wind instrument parts added materially to the vocal effect, and if in some instances the brass was somewhat too prominent, it was rather the fault of the executant than the author . . .[29]

The performance, at St James's Hall, took place on 5th February

1869, and was so successful that it was repeated 'for the Director's
Benefit' on 15th June, and again on 23rd February 1870. In that
year excerpts from *Jephtha* were given at the Hereford Festival,
while at the 1873 Festival the 'whole' work was performed, still
with Sullivan's additions—and some excisions.

The supplementing of Handel's scores has not generally been
approved on musicological grounds. The practice, however, was
beneficial to players who by this means were able to gain additional
employment. Handel certainly would have supported that. And in
February 1870 the matter of opportunities of employment for orchestral players was very much on Sullivan's mind. He wrote to the
Prince of Wales's Private Secretary asking whether, in the event of a
series of orchestral concerts being instituted by Sullivan in order to
further the interests of the profession, the Prince would lend his
patronage. The intention was good, but was never fulfilled.

Meanwhile commissions continued to flow in. In the summer of
1870, Sullivan, now an Associate of the Philharmonic Society, was
back in Birmingham for the première of his new overture, *Di Ballo*.
Performed in the same programme (on the evening of Wednesday,
31st August) as R. P. Stewart's *Ode to Shakespeare*, it was bound, in
comparison with that, to sound like a masterpiece.[30] It was indeed
the only work in the whole Festival to have any power of survival.
The other novelties were Hiller's *Nada and Damajanti*, Benedict's *St
Peter* and Barnett's *Paradise and the Peri* (of which three movements
were encored).

For the Annual International Exhibition, which opened in the
Albert Hall on 1st May 1871,[31] Sullivan wrote a work of the 'higher
class'. Others who contributed new works for the occasion were
Charles Gounod (1818–93), Ferdinand Hiller (1811–85) and Ciro
Pinsuti (1829–88). Sullivan's *On Shore and Sea*, the words by Tom
Taylor (1818–80), was dedicated to Grove. It served its immediate
purpose, was performed in Manchester a year later, and was then
forgotten. In September Sullivan conducted promenade concerts at
Covent Garden. At one concert he had to cope with Julia Wolff's
lapse of memory during Weber's *Concertstück*; at another he presented
a Mendelssohn programme which included the *Hebrides* Overture
and the 'Scottish' Symphony. On 19th September Sullivan's incidental music for *The Merchant of Venice* was played for the first time
for a production of the play at the Prince's Theatre, Manchester.
But by now it was beginning to become quite apparent what Sullivan

should be doing. *Di Ballo* was the best evidence of his true genius so far, for this overture is not only a work of charm but also of wit. It is, especially when considered in context, a work of vitality and power.

Meanwhile Sullivan's reputation had increased in another direction through the unexpected persistence of *Cox and Box*, and the *succès d'estime* enjoyed by its successor in the same genre, *The Contrabandista*. That Sullivan became fully aware of his capacity to write comedy pieces was due to a remarkable husband-wife team, the German Reeds.

The son of a theatrical musician, Thomas German Reed (1817–1888) was composer, adapter, church organist and theatre music-director. For some time, when Thomas Sullivan was clarinettist there, he was in charge of occasional productions of English opera at the Surrey Theatre. From 1838 until 1851 he was musical director of the Haymarket, after which he free-lanced until 1855, when he and his wife inaugurated their own enterprise. Priscilla German Reed (1818–95), who was talented both as singer and actress, had a rare range of gifts, and she and her husband made an ideal combination. From the 'Entertainments' which they started in 1855 at St Martin's Hall and removed to the Gallery of Illustration in Regent Street a year later, grew the outline, at least, of the idea of English chamber opera.[32] The German Reeds successfully devised small-scale pieces to which German Reed himself devised the music. On 11th May 1867 they saw *Cox and Box* at the Adelphi and, liking what they saw, bought the rights in its future productions. A week later they put it on at the Gallery of Illustration. This performance was reported by a contributor to the journal *Fun*. His name was W. S. Gilbert, and under the heading 'From our stall', he wrote on 1st June:

> Mr. Sullivan's music is, in many places, of too high a class for the grotesquely absurd plot to which it is wedded. It is funny here and there, and grand or graceful where it is not funny; but the grand and graceful have, we think, too large a share of the honours to themselves.[33]

After one performance of *Cox and Box* the German Reeds put it into cold storage, but commissioned another piece from Burnand and Sullivan. This was *The Contrabandista*, half pantomime, half operetta, which was given its first performance at St George's Hall, Langham Place, on 18th December 1867. Emboldened by previous success

German Reed had taken a lease of this hall (while still maintaining the Gallery of Illustration), and for Sullivan's work engaged an orchestra of forty players and a professional chorus. In addition to *The Contrabandista* he performed Auber's *L'Ambassadrice* [34] and *The Beggar's Opera*. Sullivan's work, of which the songs were immediately published by Boosey, was well received.

> The music . . . is conceived in a spirit of true humour, and is as happily scored as it is admirably written; it possesses true melody, clear and able part-writing, goodorc hestral colouring, and originality in construction. . . . We counsel those of our readers who have not as yet heard this operetta at once to seek an opportunity of doing so; and think that they will agree in our having at least one native composer who can write something worth hearing for the English stage.[35]

The Contrabandista, however, was withdrawn. But on 29th March 1869 *Cox and Box* was brought back—with German Reed himself playing Cox, Arthur Cecil, now a regular member of Reed's company, Box, and J. Seymour the part of Bouncer. The accompaniment was reduced to piano and off-stage harmonium. Nonetheless *Cox and Box* was enormously successful and ran for 300 performances. It was on the same bill as a piece by Gilbert, *No Cards*, for which German Reed provided the music. Both pieces were welcomed by the critics. Referring to Burnand's alteration of the original farce, *The Musical World* of 3rd April (page 234) observed:

> . . . The only way to make Box and Cox still funnier was to make certain portions of it lyrical. Nothing can be better than Box's sentimental apostrophe to the rasher of bacon; or than the serenade, accompanied by Box on the gridiron, and by Cox on his hat . . . [it was] a good notion to substitute for the original female housekeeper, a landlord, Mr. Bouncer, who, being a retired Volunteer, incessantly, and . . . at all sorts of irrelevant moments, breaks out into a spontaneous 'Rataplan! Rataplan!'. . . . The music . . . has the genuine comic ring, is full of sparkling melody, and . . . essentially dramatic.[36]

The *Musical Times* (May issue, page 315) was quite overcome by 'the really comic music' and went on to prophesy that *Cox and Box* was 'likely to become a decided favourite in this establishment'. Then, more significantly, began to lay an obligation on the composer:

The excellent vein of humour so apparent in this little piece
of extravagance, as well as in the more important *Contrabandista*,
justifies us in the hope that Mr. Sullivan may give us, at no
distant date, a real comic opera of native manufacture.

It was, however, Gilbert who made the next move. On 22nd
November 1869 his *Ages Ago* went into the repertoire of the Gallery
of Illustration, followed on 20th June 1870 by *Our Island Home*. In
the former—in which the animation of a series of portraits in a
Scottish castle anticipates a similar operation in *Ruddigore*—Gilbert's
collaborator was Fred Clay, who dedicated the music to Sullivan.
Such was Clay's appeal to the public that it looked not impossible
that a more permanent arrangement might be contrived. In which
case there could have been a series of Gilbert and Clay operettas—
with Sullivan left free to concentrate on more 'serious' undertakings.
Sullivan and Gilbert did indeed meet for the first time during a
rehearsal of *Ages Ago*, and German Reed did tentatively propose
that Sullivan should write music for another of Gilbert's pieces;
but nothing positive was then arranged. Gilbert went in one direction, and, it seemed, Sullivan in another.

NOTES TO CHAPTER FOUR

1. Lehmann, *Memories*, p. 165.
2. Bennett, *Forty Years of Music*, p. 65.
3. BM. Add. MS. 41771, f. 177.
4. When Byng was vicar of Holy Trinity, Twickenham, and chaplain
   at Hampton Court Palace. Letter from Byng to F. G. Edwards,
   28th November 1900. BM. Eg. MS. 3095.
5. While working on *The Sapphire Necklace* Sullivan took rooms in
   Sydenham to be near Grove. Franklin Taylor lived with him for a
   time. Graves, *Life of Grove*, p. 92.
6. Letter of 29th November 1900, quoted in Graves, *Life of Grove*.
   Will he come? had been launched by Sainton-Dolby at a Boosey
   Ballad Concert in March.
7. Letter from Edward Mills, sometime deputy to Sullivan, in *Musical
   Times*, 42, January 1901, pp. 22–3.
8. Sir John Everett Millais (1829–96), one of the founders of the Pre-
   Raphaelite school of painters. It was intended that Millais should
   illustrate the Tennyson-Sullivan songs.
9. Letter of 29th November 1900.

10. His successor was James Hamilton Clarke (1840–1912), who subsequently conducted for Sir Henry Irving's company and at various London theatres. A prolific composer, he was best known for his incidental music for Shakespeare's plays.

11. Graves, *Life of Grove*, p. 133, where *Cox and Box* is ascribed to 13th May 1866.

12. Arthur William à Beckett (1844–1909), who left the Civil Service in 1865 to become a journalist. Subsequently he edited the *Sunday Times* and contributed to *Punch*.

13. The facts concerning the true origins of *Cox and Box* are not to be established since the reports of those who were involved are confused. In one place (*see* H. Saxe Wyndham, *Sullivan*, pp. 91–2) Burnand claimed to have met Sullivan in Bond Street and there and then to have floated the idea. Felix Moscheles, on the other hand, reported that after musical duologues performed by Du Maurier and Power (including Offenbach's *Les deux aveugles*), Lewis asked Sullivan to provide such a piece. Signifying his readiness to do so, he inquired about libretto, whereupon Lewis immediately nominated Burnand. According to Moscheles, *Cox and Box* was rehearsed a fortnight later at Burnand's home and performed on the Saturday following at Moray Lodge. *See* F. Moscheles, *In Bohemia with Du Maurier*, London, 1896, pp. 132–4.

14. Burnand was converted to Roman Catholicism in 1858.

15. BM. Eg. MS. 3095.

16. *See* K. von Hellborn, *The Life of Franz Schubert*, trans. A. D. Coleridge, London, 1869; 'Appendix by George Grove Esq.', pp. 297–332.

17. *Ibid.* p. 300.

18. Sullivan's Vienna diary, quoted in Sullivan and Flower, *Sir Arthur Sullivan*, 1950 edn., p. 54, fn. 1. *See also* O. E. Deutsch, *Schubert: Memories by His Friends*, London, 1958, pp. 447–8.

19. Karl Ferdinand Pohl (1819–87), German musician and music historian, lived in London from 1863 to 1866 while researching on Haydn and Mozart in the British Museum. From 1866 he was librarian to the Gesellschaft für Musikfreunde in Vienna.

20. *Leipziger Allgemeine Musikalische Zeitung*, 2. Jrg., p. 346.

21. *N.Z.M.*, 63, 1867, p. 386. The author of the notice was J. Stade.

22. Graves, *Life of Grove*, p. 149.

23. See *Musical Times*, 13, June 1867, p. 73, for a letter from Laurent de Rille (Secretary) to Sterndale Bennett asking him to advertise the choral competition at the Exhibition, to be held on 8th July.

24. *See* Sullivan and Flower, *Sir Arthur Sullivan*, 1950 edn., pp. 71–2.

25. Review of *Day Dreams* in *Musical Times*, 13, January 1868, p. 261.

26. On 17th June 1872 he sold all his rights in *Cox and Box*, *The Prodigal Son*, *Birds in the night* and other songs, to Boosey for £500. This agreement was terminated on 23rd May 1871. *On Shore and Sea* was assigned to Boosey for £150, *Six Part-songs* for £60, while

Sullivan was also credited by the firm with £140 for editing the operas for the Royal Edition.

27. Sullivan and Flower, *Sir Arthur Sullivan*, 1950 edn., p. 62.

28. The first concert took place on 23rd May 1867. A pioneer of the English Bach movement, Barnby then performed the motet *I wrestle and pray*. He also included Sullivan's *O hush thee my babie* in the programme, a piece which enabled the choir to show its superlative control of *piano* effects.

29. *Musical Times*, 14, March 1869, pp. 11–12.

30. *Musical Times*, 14, October 1870, p. 617. Sullivan's *The snow lies white* was sung by Sims Reeves at the concert on the evening of 30th August.

31. The Albert Hall itself was opened on 29th March of the same year, the Duke of Cambridge observing: '. . . As a speculation the Hall seems to be too large and vast, and will never answer. . . .' E. Sheppard, *George, Duke of Cambridge*, 2 vols., London, 1906, I, p. 296.

32. See G. Grove, *Dictionary of Music and Musicians*, 3rd edn., 5 vols., London, 1928, IV, pp. 341–2. *See also* 'An English Opera House', in *The Musical Standard*, 15th February 1868, pp. 70–1.

33. Reginald Allen, *William Schwenck Gilbert, an Anniversary Survey*, p. 3, off-print from *Theatre Notebook*, XV, 4, London, 1961.

34. '. . . We are glad to find that Mr. Sullivan's *Contrabandista* is not to be pushed aside for the *Ambassadress*, but that the two operas will be occasionally played together.' *Musical Times*, 13, March 1868, p. 315.

35. *The Musical Standard*, 15th February 1868, p. 71.

36. *See* p. 55 for reference to Mrs Bouncer.

5

Sullivan without Gilbert

In the light of his further development, and the effect of this on his ultimate reputation, it is not quite easy now fully to appreciate the extent and significance of Sullivan's early achievement. Yet when those works which belong to the time before his close association with Gilbert are reviewed, it will be seen that not only is their intrinsic interest considerable, but that they represented a point of some significance in the history of British music.

Before he was thirty Sullivan had contributed to all the main categories of music, and such was the esteem in which he was then held that Queen Victoria commanded that she should receive presentation copies of his complete output—an honour hitherto conferred only on Mendelssohn. She also laid on him the duty of editing the compositions of Prince Albert.

In more senses than one Sullivan was a great Victorian. During the first part of his life he was eager and zestful in pursuing his aims, confident that the energy, enterprise and sense of adventure that inspired scientific and literary thought could be communicated to music. He also valued the right of the individual to maintain his independence. This independence had two facets. The artist's claim to independence rested on the right to depart from convention; that of the citizen rested on economic security. In Sullivan, as in Millais and Tennyson and many other artists of the period, these two forms of independence came into collision. It is, however, too easy to propose that Sullivan sold out on his ideals; for in attempting to follow a two-fold ambition, and by keeping his ear close to the ground in doing so, he ultimately played a considerable part in shattering merely elitist values. In the end he became the despair of the academicians because of his failure to follow a prescribed pattern of development, and the unwitting agent of the transference of power to the popularists. It may well be that Sullivan is the most popular of all British-born composers. Whether this is absolutely true or not is irrelevant to the fact that he made music *per se* a popular

68

art in Britain, and, at the same time, helped to make the way easier
for future generations of native composers.

> From beginning to end of his career Sullivan wrote nothing
> that was subversive or polemical; the taste of the average man
> was what he sought to meet, and it was in meeting this taste
> that his work in regard to the renaissance [of English music]
> was fulfilled . . . in as much as he was the first Englishman [sic]
> who contrived to excite enthusiasm in his countrymen, he must
> be held to have done much to prepare the way of the revival
> of interest in English music.[1]

In this passage Fuller-Maitland, though one would wish to know
what music he did consider 'subversive' or 'polemical', states the
position justly. A year earlier, however, his attitude had been somewhat different, and less than just (see pages 263–4).

In the course of his career Sullivan accumulated enemies who
showed their feelings after his death. This was due in part to the
quality of his following. Before he was thirty he enjoyed an esteem
that had hitherto been accorded to no British-born musician. Fame,
of course, is relative; but those who at that time supported Sullivan's
claim to at least potential greatness were by no means deficient in
knowledge, nor in experience, nor (if the word must be used) in
taste. Nor was he backed by those whose views and opinions were
merely insular. Manns, Smart, Hallé, Grove, the Goldschmidts, for
instance, were well aware of the virtues of great music, and they were
prepared to find some of them in Sullivan.

Concerning the music of Sullivan's apprenticeship there are
certain points that emerge at once. He preferred economy of statement to diffuseness. He had a gift for perceiving and expressing the
direct connection between words and music, and a correlative
talent for understanding the principles of melodic design. He was
naturally inclined to reduce rhythmic factors to the elements of
dance. He was intuitive in execution and readily avoided what he
saw in others as pedantry. Hearing rather than seeing what he
composed, he quickly mastered instrumental and vocal sonorities.
All of this goes back to his first environment. The son of a bandmaster, he was brought up to old virtues of craftsmanship. He learned
to arrange music for any combination so that it was practicable and
convincing, without recourse to a priori aesthetic precepts.

Sullivan rarely gave effective verbal expression to his attitudes on composition. There is, however, a letter written to Mrs Ann Bartholomew [2] on 14th September 1871, which gives some insight into them:

> With pleasure I enclose the little bits of the 'Lullaby' [3] as a tribute of respect to one who has every right to claim it from a young musician. With regard to the phrase you quote, I am of opinion that it is one of those cases in which a rule must be broken for the sake of the effect gained, for after all, rules in music are but the means to an end, not the end itself; and although I should be the last to transgress wantonly (indeed, I am sometimes taunted with being too much of a purist) yet slavish adherence to a rule is not less open to stricture, than a reckless disregard of it.
>
> The melody and bass are each moving independently in a sort of fixed progression; if 5ths turn up it doesn't matter, so long as there is no offence to the ear, and I confess that the phrase you quote doesn't hurt me. [4]

So Sullivan bears out Fuller-Maitland's conclusion that he had neither subversive nor polemical instincts.

Sullivan's innate musicality was, no doubt, mistaken too soon for genius, with the result that he was not often enough compelled to extend himself. Whether at the Royal Academy in London or at the Conservatorium in Leipzig, he was encouraged to retain his energy within the conventions. The substance of what he composed was taken to be of less importance than the mode in which it was expressed. Neatness in exercises counted for a lot. From the start Sullivan was a scrupulous composer, whose capacity for developing the potentialities inherent in his first thoughts was sometimes seen to be limited. Nevertheless there is an obverse to this: Sullivan's simplicities frequently carried their own kind of profundity. At a distance of a hundred years and across at least two major musical revolutions, one perceives how Sullivan may now appear to be on the side of some of the angels.

The first extant composition was a 'sacred song' (a good many more of this genre were to follow). O Israel, a thinly disguised waltz, is hardly more than a creditable exercise by a schoolboy, and unless one takes notice of an effective use of hemiole (at the words, 'Lord, say unto him'), and a not quite expected transition from G major to B minor across the dominant of the latter which immediately succeeds a G major triad, there is not much to stir interest. Yet, in succeeding works, it is precisely this kind of timing of effect that catches the listener unawares to compel attention and to assert individuality.

Although he composed songs in his student days, only *O Israel* and the Schubertian serenade written in Leipzig for Rosamond Barnett (see page 21) have survived. Soon after his return from Leipzig, however, he composed the settings of Shakespeare on which much of his early reputation was established. Emboldened by his previous successes in the Shakespearian field (an overture at the Royal Academy, and *The Tempest*) he undertook this task no doubt with an eye on the coming tercentenary celebrations.⁵ The most successful of the set, *Orpheus with his lute*,⁶ is a clean, extravert example of a conventional type of superior ballad similar to songs by Henry Bishop or to those in Sullivan's *The Tempest*. But it is by no means the best. Much more meaningful are the *Willow Song* and *O mistress mine*, both of which illustrate Sullivan's innate ability to convey lyrical impulses through melodic phrases.

In the first of these examples there is a poignancy in the siting of the notes, in the emotive use of the interval of the seventh, and in the gentle decoration of the cadence. In the second, from which the accent of Thomas Morley is not far distant, there is an echo of folk-song and an engaging and characteristic flexibility within the rhythmic structure. The quality of English song is deeply embedded in these pieces. Unconsciously, they reach back to the Jacobean air and, by-passing the 'English Renaissance', look forward to Warlock and even Britten. The pure liquidity of these melodies distinguishes others of the early phase, which also show features of an unusual order for the period in which they were composed. There are, for example, the pentatonic opening of the setting of George Herbert's *Sweet day, so cool, so calm, so bright*; the shaping of the phrases of Bishop Heber's *The moon in silent brightness* around the minor triad; the pert thirds of Tennyson's *What does little birdie say?*—an enchanting children's song; and the easy flow of the voice in *There sits a bird on yonder tree*—a solitary selection from *The Ingoldsby Legends*: all of these represent a freshness in song-writing that for more than half a century had been almost entirely absent from English music.

At this time of his life Sullivan was not concerned with the question of 'English music' (although some twenty-five or so years later he had something to say on the subject), but with finding his own style. In the end, no doubt, this was an eclectic style. But if he borrowed from familiar sources he also had a knack of anticipating what might happen in music. Thus, in *Oh! ma charmante*, he comes, melodically speaking, within earshot of Fauré with a tune made bitter-sweet by reason of the modified leap of the seventh in the third bar:

In melodic invention Sullivan showed not only his mastery but also his versatility at an early stage. His problem was one of adjustment. Acclimatized to the tradition of ballad-opera song (to which tradition Sullivan was later to return), the English had missed out almost entirely on that of the fully developed *Lied*. In this one field of music the Germans had been repelled. The dominating feature of 'domestic' music in the nineteenth century was the 'drawing-room' ballad—something of a misnomer for that ill-starred offspring of the true ballad and the 'Gardens' song (itself often the result of miscegenation between Italian aria and folk-ballad). In the drawing-room ballad, designed for the star singer, there was very little for the accompanist to do; indeed in many cases the accompanist could quite well have extemporized a perfectly acceptable background. By the 1860s the principal publishers in London had discovered that the combination of an ever-broadening but not always educated musical public, a set of highly publicized singers, and a group of compliant composers, presented them with a gold-mine. Song-plugging is no new exercise.

The composer-accompanist did as he was told. Benedict, for example, 'every evening went from one aristocratic soirée to another'.[7] The singer was no more than 'the servant of the publisher'.[8] Fresh from his German experiences, Sullivan promoted propaganda for modern German music, but took care to exercise discretion in putting into practice what he had learned. At first, then, he did his best to infiltrate English song with Schubert-Schumann idiom, in so far as piano accompaniment was concerned.

In *The snow lies white* and *What does little birdie say?* a tremulous calm is represented by undulating eighth notes (quavers) and sixteenth notes (semiquavers) respectively, set above a double pedal—a device much used by Sullivan. In the *Arabian love song* the double pedal is put to other use; vitalized by percussive repetition it enlivens an oriental ritornello with a flavour of Bartók.

The character of this item runs through a number of exotic pieces, like the quick dance in *Kenilworth* and the 'Moresque' in *On Shore*

and Sea, and the interaction between song and dance is revealed in the rhythmic accompaniment in such songs as *The moon in silent brightness*, *Sad memories*, and the *Venetian Serenade*. In these songs atmosphere is created by allusion. In others definite description, more or less discreet, is introduced. *Will he come?* is not among Sullivan's best pieces, and its interest lies mainly in its biographical reference (see page 59). It should, however, be noted that the employment of triplets, taken from the *Erl-King*, in mid-course might have indicated to a keen-eared worshipper at St Peter's, Cranley Gardens, on St Peter's Day 1867, that the Lord Bishop was on his way on horse-back (see page 52). In *I heard the nightingale*—the melodic contours growing from Sullivan's Italian inheritance—an obvious device of tone-painting is rendered rather the more charming by some rhythmic side-play.

Sullivan's immediate contribution to English music was recognized as the quality of gracefulness, the term applied, for instance, by the *Musical Times* to the anthem *O taste and see* (December 1867, page 220) and to the piano pieces of *Day Dreams* (January 1868, page 261). In November 1868 (page 574), the same journal welcomed *The long day closes*, remarking that it was 'extremely melodious, and harmonized with a freshness and absence of pedantry in perfect keeping with the theme'. These opinions collectively add up to a tribute to Sullivan's originality, which lay in an ability to refine procedures and techniques within certain lyrical contexts. In his earliest works he looked away from the main-stream conventions. In addition to melodic patterns already cited, there may be mentioned the gentle contour, nocturnal in the manner of Field, of *Twilight* (one of Rachel Scott Russell's pieces), the 'andante' motiv from the *Duo Concertante* with its Elgarian triplets, and the 'allegro moderato' motiv from the same work, hinting at the remoteness of a fundamental 'gapped scale'.

Neither *Twilight* nor the *Duo Concertante* live up to the promise of the best of their fugitive thoughts. Nevertheless they represent a wider view concerning *materia musica* than was general among Sullivan's contemporaries. This is even more evident in his explorations of tonal contrariety. In the 'Allegretto' of *Day Dreams*, a delightful piece with the character of a carol, the general atmosphere of G major is infused with a new and unexpected radiance from F sharp major midway through. The 'Valse' in D major—somewhere between Johann Strauss and Tchaikovsky—also moves to a triad of F sharp major (ostensibly as the dominant of B minor) but then

neatly side-steps to the dominant seventh of E flat major. In the second of *Thoughts* (see page 75) there is a nice delicacy, the point of aural interest being the incidental and ambiguous D sharp.

In an opposite direction, one occasionally finds Sullivan testing the rigours of a colder climate. In his setting of Scott's *Joy to the victors* for male voices (a piece held together by a rhythmic intensification learned from Beethoven), the words 'war-axes wielding' provoke a harmonic pile-up of A natural, D, B flat and A flat. Such audacities were rare, and there were plenty of Beckmessers about to denounce them. When the anthem *We have heard with our ears* was reissued in 1873, the harmonic infelicities (as they seemed) were torn apart:

> ... An incident of prominent brightness and some novelty in the modulations from the key of E minor with that of C, upon a second inversion of the tonic chord, at one of the repetitions of the opening words. Far less agreeable, but little less startling, is the combination of $\begin{bmatrix} E \\ D \\ C \end{bmatrix}$ upon a D pedal, the top note rising to G, while the lowest (for the tenor) descends to B, at the word 'heard'. . . . We protest, however, against the consecutive 7ths $\begin{bmatrix} D\ C, \\ E\ D, \end{bmatrix}$ between treble and bass, at the words 'hast destroyed' for the upper voice; how strange it is that the composers who would shrink with horror from writing two 5ths in succession with some two parts, as from a foulest sin, write the infinitely worse sounding progression of two 7ths in cool blood . . .[9]

Apart from songs, small-scale choral works, and piano pieces (of which he wrote very few), Sullivan's main hope, if he wished to establish himself on a sure foundation, was in church music. In the end his contribution to the repertoire of the anthem was slender, but one or two items suggest what Sullivan might have done had his ideals not been subjected to such unfriendly scrutiny as is shown above. The difficulty was that there was a frontier between 'secular' and 'sacred' which was not to be crossed. On the few occasions when he did appear to cross this frontier, he was recalled and reminded of his proper duty. The severe indictment of *We have heard with our ears* indicated the accepted limitations on harmonic freedom. In a notice of the quite innocuous *O taste and see* a reviewer found the work 'rather secular in style, perhaps, considering the purpose of the composition'.[10]

The reference, no doubt, is to the then unusual move from F major, by way of a dominant 7th chord of G and a resolution of this on the second inversion of a chord of G flat major, to D flat major, at the words 'Come, ye children, and hearken unto me': Sullivan, it would seem, had hearkened to some of the audacities of Samuel Sebastian Wesley.

We have heard with our ears, dedicated to Helmore and appropriately based on a plain-song motiv ('8th Gregorian tone, 2nd ending'), was Sullivan's nearest approach to the authentic tradition of English church music. When he was a choir-boy the works of the old masters were sometimes resurrected, and he certainly sang in one Orlando Gibbons anthem at a Festival of the Sons of the Clergy Service in St Paul's Cathedral; but his polyphony was founded on the more orderly procedures of the school of Boyce, and, of course, on Handel. Sometimes this led to perfunctory conclusions, as in the fugato conclusion—'O that men would praise the Lord'—of *The Prodigal Son*. In the final section of *We have heard with our ears*, on the other hand, Sullivan captures the vigour of Samuel Wesley in this free-flowing spread of parts.

In another expressive verse anthem, *Sing O heavens*, dedicated to Francis Byng, Sullivan again emulates the younger Wesley, the emancipator of organ accompaniment. About the 'secularity' of the opening of this piece there is no doubt—Byng, as may be deduced from his occasional comments, was no puritan—but it is as original as it is simple. It is also highly attractive in its Pre-Raphaelite brightness. A brilliant and mobile high melody, for boys' voices, is kept going in continuous quarter notes (crotchets), against which a bright counter-tune, also in quarter notes, runs on the choir manual, while a chordal background is sustained on swell and pedals. This too is within an area more recently occupied by Britten. A similar interplay of the simplest elements, worked out with marked effect, occurs in the concluding section of *I will worship towards Thy Holy Temple*, built from the motiv, *d, r, m, f,* and from the development of this motiv against its diminished inversion. Although not an anthem, but rather a kind of sacred glee, 'I sing the birth' (Ben Jonson) may be classified as such. An imaginative setting for *a cappella* singing, it contains in the melody a particularly haunting descent of 5ths: F sharp—B; E—A; D sharp—G sharp; C sharp. . . .

Sullivan's historical sense was slight, his interest being in what was contemporary. But he was not unaware of the aesthetic significance of history at second-hand; of the age of Elizabeth I through Walter Scott, of Renaissance Venice through the pen of Tom Taylor, and of music of that period through such intermediaries as John Stafford Smith and Robert de Pearsall. As a schoolboy Sullivan had tried his hand at madrigal composition. One of the pieces salvaged from *The Sapphire Necklace* was a madrigal, and if there are traces of Wilbye in the figuration, the disposition of the parts and the changes of mood, there are also habits acquired from the prolific glee-writers of the later eighteenth century. The bass line especially betrays a somewhat indolent attitude towards counterpoint.

Sullivan's 'madrigals', the familiar examples being in *The Mikado* and *Haddon Hall*, are, of course, not madrigals at all. At one time, however, a certain excess of approval was bestowed on them by critics whose glands were stimulated by a Pavlovian reaction to the term madrigal and a frill of fa-la-las.

What may be termed the immediately marketable works of Sullivan's first decade as a composer show both his qualities and his defects in a clear light. He wrote easily, often casually, and without much sense of self-criticism. The dividing line between charm and elegance—virtues generally attributed to him by contemporary critics—and banality, was (and remains) thin, and to put certain works on one side or other of the line is a matter of personal opinion. From time to time warning voices were to be heard. So in 1872, on the appearance of *None but I can say*, a critic of *The Musical World* observed that, 'whether it is likely to help the composer's reputation may . . . be open to doubt'.

There have been composers who have been able to overcome the handicap of indifferent texts. Sullivan was not among them. Sensitive as he was to the values inherent in fine poetry (for example that of Shakespeare), and capable of transferring these values to music, he was even more sensitive to bad poetry, the shortcomings of which he was also masterly in exposing. Often this came down to a kind of nescient neutrality; to a type of melody which dominates and destroys *Thou'rt passing hence*, *In Memoriam*, and considerable areas of the oratorios, and which may be found later also in *The chorister*, *Edward Gray* and *The lost chord*, as well as in many hymn-tunes. The impotence of Sullivan's worst melodies may be best illustrated by the opening motivs of *In Memoriam* and *The chorister*, which are hardly redeemed by any contention that they are 'sincere'. This kind of thing is the *reductio ad nauseam* of the tenets of the philosopher-musicians of the early eighteenth century who suggested that music should be 'natural' and that it should be 'affecting'. Indeed the beginning of *The chorister* reads like a parody, which in a sense it was—a parody of the current sentimental idiom. It was only when Sullivan consciously realized his capacity for parody in an appropriate context that he began to expose his unique gifts. What applies to melody also applies to harmony. Sullivan was capable of producing highly individual, even impressionistic, harmonic statements, and of delicious sleights-of-hand in respect of tonality; he was equally capable of thudding through an accompaniment with no more than reiterations of dominant and tonic. The *Duo Concertante* is a case in point. This over-long piece also shows Sullivan's irresolution in development. It is the kind of piece which may be described as 'well-constructed' because the mechanical details of formal design are so evident that they effectively prevent any coherence of idea.

The environment in which a composer operates is the chief determinant of his style, if not of the quality of his music. Up to a point a society gets the composers it wants, or deserves. England in the Victorian era was strewn with composers whose ambitions contradicted credibility, in that they presumed to invade areas for which they were, by common opinion, unlicensed. The broad acres of classical music were reserved to Germans; the territory of opera was an Italian preserve. Cipriani Potter (whose ten symphonies are far from negligible) and Sterndale Bennett attempted invasion of the former, Michael Balfe, William Wallace, Edward Loder and John Barnett of the latter. The one faint hope of achieving some degree of immortality lay in the province of choral music, where, however, Handel and Mendelssohn were still supreme.

Sullivan set out to become a 'great composer', and spent most of his life listening to the complaints of those who considered that by not pursuing a more 'noble' end he had been guilty of some kind of moral impropriety. In fact Sullivan eventually made the best use of his talents, which were of a particular order: they were those of a miniaturist. He had a great sense of epigram, and an appreciation of the passing moment; he had little interest in musical dialectics—in the consideration of thesis and antithesis, in argument, or in 'development'. He was, in fact, no Brahms.

However, both in Leipzig and after his return he was encouraged to believe that he was something he was not. His first extant abstract work is the string quartet movement composed in 1859. Neatly contrived in ternary form, based on G minor-major-minor, this piece is unremarkable. However, there may be noted the *féerique* implications of the principal rhythmic pattern, and the illuminating effect of the opening of the interlude in major tonality (characteristically settled over a pedal). The model is Mendelssohn (with slender suggestions of impulses from the Scherzo of the Octet), but the apprentice accomplishment is far distant from that of the master. With *The Tempest* the case is otherwise. This is a masterpiece, albeit a minor masterpiece, in its own right, and it certainly challenges comparison with the prototypical *Midsummer Night's Dream* music, with Schumann's incidental music to *Manfred*, and with Henry Hugh Pierson's (1815–73) score for *Faust* (Part II). Pierson, an English expatriate who flourished in Germany during the period of Sullivan's residence there, is a composer whose merits were considerable—greater than those of most of his British contemporaries. In the fairy music in *Faust* Pierson also illuminates the general territory occupied by Mendelssohn in *A Midsummer Night's Dream*, and from his deeper perception it may be thought that Sullivan drew occasional inspiration. The 'aria con coro' for the Elves in Act I of *Faust*, with its evocative harmonies and fluttering orchestration, seems particularly to support this supposition. On the whole Sullivan avoided the more mystical qualities of *The Tempest* and, conditioned by the same kind of pictures that caught the youthful fancy of Dante Gabriel Rossetti, kept to the lighter side of fantasy. He was, as Johnson wrote of the play, attracted to the 'humorous and frolick controlment of nature, well expressed by the songs of Ariel'.

At the same time, in *The Tempest*, Sullivan now and again expressed himself in terms which amount almost to pessimism. The Introduction, which has no precedent in British music, is restless as Tchaikovsky was often restless. The melodic germ (which, together with the passage quoted below, reappears as a *Leitmotiv* in Scene 2, when the Banquet vanishes) is disturbed by an almost Asiatic feeling; the extended accompanying chord given melancholy purpose by the deep reverberations of double-basses and bassoons.

Bass drum

Following the 'andante con moto' a wild rhapsody for first and second violins in unison catches the Celtic strain noted in the Symphony (page 86), and represents Prospero's invocation of the elements. It runs directly into a section which, if inspired by Beethoven, has a keenness of its own in the disposition of the strings and wood-wind.

There are many hints of Schumann, in rhythmic variety, in occasional details of counterpoint, and in a frequent sense of aspiration. As for example in this fragment from the prelude to Act III, which recalls the fifth piece of *Kinderscenen* in the contour of the middle-register tune. This is also used again, in the prelude to Act V.

As has been pointed out many times, Sullivan was not unaware of the idiom of Mendelssohn. But at this stage of his career he was by no means overawed by it, even though some of his critics may have been. Just as he could appreciate Schumann without servility, so could he relate the felicities of Mendelssohn to the matter in hand without in any way providing carbon copies. (One piece by Sullivan which is pure, unadulterated Mendelssohn is the *Allegro risoluto* of 1866—a straightforward 'song without words' for piano. This, however, remained unpublished.) The bucolics of *A Midsummer Night's Dream* were transmuted by Sullivan into the barking dogs of

Ariel's 'Come unto these yellow sands' (behind which song
Mendelssohnian figuration often runs in the strings) and into the E
minor episode of the 'Reapers' Dance' in Act IV.

In this episode—a waltz—the dominant is nicely picked up by
bassoon, horn, and flute, at different octaves, on successive beats of
the bar.

The arrival of the masquers in Act IV is announced by a flutter
of wood-wind thirds that is from Mendelssohn. But the passage
leading into it is not; and how elegantly and fancifully Sullivan
prepares the ground in the nervous tonal divagation of the strings.
This came from paying attention to Spohr.

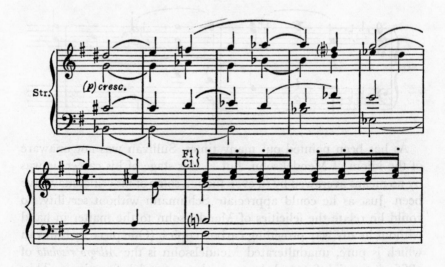

Sullivan's capacity for composing ballet was never really tested.
But in all his Shakespearian music the talent is evident. Often it

suggests an affinity with French music, and the 'Banquet Dance' of *The Tempest*, in particular, lies somewhere between Berlioz and Bizet. It is, of course, improper to review *The Tempest* out of context. It was intended as incidental music and during the nineteenth century such music performed a necessary function—to cover lengthy pauses for scene-changes. In the twentieth century it is not needed for this purpose. It is, therefore, homeless at the present time, but is nevertheless 'both apt and inventive, and a modern producer would be lucky indeed if he was able to commission anything so good'.[11] And it was composed by a boy of eighteen.

Between 1864 and 1870 Sullivan made his strong bid to win a permanent place in the symphonic repertoire. During this period he staked his claim with a full-scale symphony, a concerto and three concert overtures. The symphony was a nine days' wonder, the concerto was a failure, one of the overtures almost completely disappeared from view after its first performance, one remained in suspended animation, the third carved a cheerful path through the nineteenth and into the twentieth century.

The Symphony arrived when Brahms, Tchaikovsky and Dvořák were barely on the threshold of their symphonic careers, and Sullivan's achievement may therefore appear the more remarkable. His work has the essential quality of youth—it is free from inhibition. It begins with a proud statement in the brass, which runs into an extended 'Dresden Amen'.

At this point one may recall Cipriani Potter, who thus represents Imogen at the beginning of his *Cymbeline* overture.

The introduction of Sullivan's first movement leads (as does that of Potter's overture) to an energetic Allegro in E minor, dominated by an extensive first subject, which is developed through confrontations with varied sonorities rather than through the commonplaces of sonata argument. Sullivan found these rather wearisome. So for that matter did Tchaikovsky, whom Sullivan approaches both in the stirring conclusion of his first movement, and in the formal structures (A 2/4, B 2/4, C 3/4, A¹) of the third. The second movement, 'andante espressivo', is ardent, with Schubertian contrasts of major and minor, wide melodic intervals, and, towards the end, a clarinet cry that seems unconsciously to have sprung from the composer's Celtic heritage. In the second and third movements Sullivan exploited wood-wind characteristics superbly—in the scherzo it is the oboe that takes precedence, although there is a fine passage of swirling clarinets, in thirds, in the 3/4 section. In the final movement—an eager, spirited 'allegro vivace e con brio'—it is the alertness of the string writing that predominates.

One critic had a correct view of Sullivan's symphony after the first performance. At least he was not hindered by previous prejudices regarding the nature of symphony.

> The orchestration is very beautiful; like a skilled colourist, our composer has handled his lights and shadows tenderly, and while we are not stunned by incessant blare, bright tints are not wanting whenever they can lend a charm. . . .[12]

In Memoriam, the first of the concert overtures, was precisely the kind of work to catch at Victorian sensibility. It is the musical counter-

part to effusions such as Felicia Hemans's 'Music at a deathbed', or
'The funeral day of Sir Walter Scott', and—a high-class companion
to *The volunteer organist*—fatally moral-theological. *In Memoriam* falls
down on its thematic content, and on its lack of purposeful energy
in thematic development. Like the early *Romance* for string quartet,
this overture is a contrast between major and minor tonalities—C
major, C minor, C major. Just as Sullivan mistook the slowness
of the wood-wind melody in the principal motiv for 'nobility'
so he mistook the repetitious ♩ ♫ ♩ ♫ as an earnest of strife
(through this mortal life). The 'hymn-tune' is first given out by
wood-wind, then repeated by wood-wind, trumpets and horns, and
empurpled string tone—deep chords by divided cellos and basses.
In its transfigured condition at the conclusion of the work, timpani,
bass- and side-drum, and organ are added. It is wonderful what one
organ can do to elevate the pious mind.[13]

Of *Marmion*,[14] which was never published, there remains one
informative critical notice:

> . . . Of what the Germans call 'character-overtures', there is,
> perhaps, but one in existence, and that is Beethoven's *Coriolan*,
> [which] . . . as a musical personification . . . stands alone. . . .
> Mr. Sullivan's *Marmion* has no pretensions to a 'character-
> overture'. Nevertheless, it is eminently picturesque, and has,
> here and there, just enough of the Scottish turn of melody to
> suggest so much of the Scottish element as is an ingredient in
> the story of *Marmion*. It consists of a highly interesting intro-
> duction, in slow measure, and a spirited and well-worked out
> quick movement. The themes are clear and striking; the treat-
> ment is broad and ingenious, and the orchestration masterly.
> In short, Mr. Sullivan has composed a new work calculated to
> enhance the reputation so well earned by his overture, *In
> Memoriam*. . . . The overture . . . was well played, under the
> direction of Mr. Cusins,[15] and received with genuine and
> unanimous marks of approval.[16]

The 'Scottish turn of melody' shows in occasional pentatony—
as in the second part of the second subject.

[*Allegro vivace*]

This North British atmosphere was later to be exploited in *Haddon Hall* (see page 182). The whole work has a consistency of thematic character unusual in Sullivan's extended works, which is grounded on the basic intervals of fourth and fifth. The introduction, for instance, begins thus:

Andante maestoso

The episode following the first subject runs as follows:

All in all, the germinating force of the interval of the fourth puts one here somewhat in mind of Dvořák.

Marmion, having been played at a Philharmonic concert on 3rd June 1867, was repeated at the Crystal Palace on 7th December in the same year. On 24th October it was played again at the Crystal Palace, but in a revised form, and four years later a Scottish audience was given opportunity to hear it at a Glasgow concert.

In *Di Ballo* Sullivan allowed his genius for rhythmic invention and instrumental definition full play. The orchestra is large—including the virtually obsolete ophicleide—but never heavy. Indeed, in the opening 'andante moderato' the textures are gossamer-like. The following Allegro once again shows Sullivan's mastery of the waltz, here treated almost symphonically, with development achieved by subtle variations of note value. The end of the work is a 'tempo di galop' pulled back from E flat to C major, based on a syncopated metamorphosis of the initial waltz theme. It is, perhaps, *Di Ballo* that is the true memorial overture to Thomas Sullivan. *In Memoriam* itself is an English period piece; *Di Ballo* goes back beyond the garish days of the Royal Surrey Theatre of childhood memories and captures another aspect of Irish temperament.

Sullivan in youth had a certain command of magic. This allowed him access to resources of sonority that had hitherto been veiled—from British composers at any rate. It was Shakespeare who particularly stimulated Sullivan to discover the most fitting combinations for the expression of his perceptivity in this respect. It is not surprising, then, that the one memorable section of *Kenilworth* is the passage from *The Merchant of Venice*, 'How sweet the moonlight sleeps'. This naturally urges comparison with Vaughan Williams's *Serenade to Music*, which is among the classics of music for Shakespeare. Poised and serene, the latter is a masterly exposition of lyrical mood. Sullivan perhaps allows us a longer look at the summer night sky, and his arching melody at one moment rides above the evening sounds—of harp arpeggios and divided violas—to the 'floor of heav'n . . . thick inlaid with pattines of bright gold'.

Apart from this moment, one should esteem the two dances from the masque; the quick dance for its exotic liveliness, the slow dance for a contrary homespun quality. In this essay in eighteenth-century style one notes again Sullivan's liking for hemiole.

The Prodigal Son, as Goss suggested, betrays a lack of commitment. In this work Sullivan, like many other composers, was unable to escape from the limitations placed upon him by a God-fearing public which misread respectability for piety. But there are a number of places where the music comes to life, often stimulated by fine details of orchestration. In bar 5 the side-drum enters, followed at a distance of three bars by timpani and wood-wind. Five bars later the double-bassoon is introduced. In the tenor aria 'How many hired servants' (No. 11) there is beautiful colouring by solo oboe, muted strings and delicately shaded flutes, while in 'There is joy' (No. 2)—which was written in D but marked 'a note lower' in the autograph—a background of clarinets, bassoons, four horns and organ effectively gives way to organ only. In 'My son attend to my words' (No. 4) the exhortation to 'trust in the Lord' swings into a broad, confident tune in 3/4 time, cheerfully anticipating the virile measure of Parry. In 'Let us eat and drink' (No. 6) a tiny 'oriental' figure, such as Sullivan frequently used in his operas, flickers across the score. In 'They went astray' (No. 15) there is some splendidly dramatic writing in a gaunt canon—first for soprano and bass, and then for alto and tenor—against an empty orchestral background. Here Sullivan is at his most economical and his most effective, and way ahead of his British contemporaries.

Like all British composers of his generation, Sullivan not unreason-
ably believed that if music for great occasions was to be written it
was best done by paying due regard to Handel. The last fugal chorus
of *The Prodigal Son* is Handelian in outline, but is, alas, too restricted
in movement to carry conviction. In the *Te Deum* of 1872 Sullivan
allowed a good deal more cheerfulness to break in—as well he might
since the work was a thank-offering for the recovery of the Prince of
Wales. There is a fair amount of Handel about it; not least in the
fugal parts. Though once again the subject of 'To Thee all angels'
also has the character of Parry.

This *Te Deum*, scored for very large forces, should have its attrac-
tions for those who enjoy extravagance of sound. In its conclusion
(with military band added to the orchestra) the work is probably

to be included among those defined by under-nourished pedants as vulgar. Whether it is vulgar (in this sense) is, of course, a matter of opinion. There are, however, many passages which have a splendour all of their own. In the second movement, 'To Thee all angels', the scoring for brass and double-bassoon is impressive, and the shifts of tonality (from E flat to G major, and thence through E, C, G, and D major, back to E flat) rich in colour. In the sixth movement the build-up from strings and organ to the entry of the fugal 'Day by day' is finely gauged. The finale surrounds a military march brassily exposed by military band (the proper corollary to 'Onward Christian Soldiers') with the strains of 'St Anne'.

At the time of Sullivan's *Te Deum* the hymn-tune 'St Anne'—a fulcral point in Anglican latitudinarianism—virtually occupied the place of a subsidiary national anthem. Hence Sullivan, in the last movement of his *Te Deum*, by exploiting the stereophonic possibilities of the Crystal Palace (where the work was performed) was, at long range, picking up where the Venetians of the seventeenth century left off. This *Te Deum*, as well as presenting the hungry ear with sonorous splendours of Berlioz proportions, has the ring of truth: this is the English people in the high summer of Victorian optimism.

NOTES TO CHAPTER FIVE

1. J. A. Fuller-Maitland, *English Music in the XIXth Century*, London, 1902, p. 170.
2. Widow of William Bartholomew (1793–1867), known for his English versions of Mendelssohn's vocal works. Mrs Bartholomew, formerly Anne Sheppard Mounsey, was the singer for whom Mendelssohn composed *Hear my prayer*.
3. 'Hush-a-bye bacon', *Cox and Box*, of which Sullivan enclosed the first five bars.
4. BM. 41570, f. 6. In *There sits a bird* consecutive fifths (direct and by contrary motion) turn up more blatantly than in this example.
5. In 1864 the Philharmonic Society performed 'Shakespearian' works by Beethoven, Haydn, Arne, Mendelssohn, Henry Bishop and Nicolai.

6. This was not, as Arthur Jacobs states, 'significantly . . . also written for the theatre' (*A History of Song*, ed. Denis Stevens, London, 1960, p. 154). The song (with orchestral accompaniment) was, however, included in the incidental music for *Henry VIII* in Manchester in 1878 (*see* p. 282).

7. Hanslick, *Aus dem Concert-Saal*, p. 589.

8. *Ibid.* p. 268.

9. *Musical Times*, 15, February 1873, p. 758.

10. *Musical Times*, 13, December 1867, p. 220.

11. Roger Fiske, 'Shakespeare in the Concert Hall', in *Shakespeare in Music* (ed. Phyllis Hartnoll), London, 1964, p. 227.

12. *The Musical Standard*, IV, 93, 24th March 1866.

13. cf. 'The definition of the introductory movements suggests the melody it comprises may be intended for a kind of hymn. . . . The introduction of the organ at the end is a novelty in a purely orchestral piece, and this, with the employment of the subdominant harmony for the penultimate chord in pursuance of old Church use, tends to strengthen the religious impression to which reference has been made.' G. A. Macfarren in programme of the Philharmonic Society, 2nd June 1870.

14. Scott's poem, published in 1808, was at once immensely popular.

15. William George Cusins (1833–93), sometime professor at the Royal Academy of Music, was conductor of the Philharmonic Society from 1867 to 1883. In 1870 he became Master of the Queen's Music. A well-known pianist, he also composed a number of large-scale works among which are a Piano Concerto in A minor (1866), and Overtures to *King Lear* (1862) and *Love's Labour's Lost* (1875).

16. *The Musical World*, XLV, 25, Saturday, 22nd June 1867.

6

Sullivan, Gilbert and D'Oyly Carte

In 1871 Sullivan's position as the leading composer in England was unassailable, though, to be truthful, at this time the competition was hardly keen. The older men, through disillusionment or pressure of other duties, had virtually abdicated. Potter died in 1871. Sterndale Bennett, now knighted, was largely precluded from composing by the burden of his duties as Principal of the Royal Academy. Benedict—also made a knight in 1871—was busy conducting. Goss, in his seventies, was given his passport to honourable oblivion in 1872 when he became Sir John. On 24th April of that year he was entertained by the College of Organists to a celebratory banquet at the Albion Inn in Aldersgate Street. Sullivan, who went to everything, was there, and so were some of his old friends—Helmore, George Cooper and Captain Ottley. There were also present Benedict, John Stainer (Goss's successor at St Paul's Cathedral), Sir George Elvey (1816–93), organist of St George's Chapel, Windsor, and other celebrities in the profession. Unless he was careful Sullivan was going to find himself saddled with an official appointment. Worse still, he would be invested with pedagogic duties for which he lacked the temperament; musicians in England were expected at that time to undertake academic work as a guarantee of respectability. Most of them, of course, had to teach in order to live.

In the 1870s Sullivan, under persuasion, made several forays into the narrow world of academic music—and hastily withdrew. In 1870 he had ventured into adult education, to deliver a series of twelve lectures at the South Kensington Museum on *The Theory and Practice of Music*, which were illustrated by examples of part-singing. He had also cursorily glanced at elementary education. The Forster Education Act of 1870 called for protest from a number of musicians, Sullivan included, since it seemed likely at first that the conditions under which grants were to be made to schools would exclude class-singing (then the sum total of musical instruction). For four years, during which his name remained on the list of Crystal

Palace professors, Sullivan remained on the educational side-lines, but in 1875 he agreed to join the staff of the Academy as a professor of composition. An unwilling teacher (his pupils included Eaton Faning, Myles Foster, Tobias Matthay, Goring Thomas and the American, G. S. Tracy), Sullivan stayed at the Academy for two years, towards the end of which period he pleaded ill-health and took extensive leave of absence. His place was supplied by Ebenezer Prout. In fact at this time Sullivan had become involved in matters of some contention, and his position had been made somewhat delicate. Because of Bennett's death, on 1st February 1875, two vacancies were created, and rumours began to fly. *The Athenaeum* of 22nd February opined that while the Management Committee of the Royal Academy wished Mackenzie to succeed as Principal, the Directors were all for Sullivan.

This was naturally embarrassing, not least because *The Athenaeum* added some snide remarks about the Board of Directors being 'composed chiefly of aristocratic amateurs'. Sullivan wrote a letter of rebuttal to *The Musical World* on 24th February, and on 13th March made clear his position regarding Cambridge (with which his name had also been linked) by joining Benedict, Goss, Joachim, Manns and Grove in a letter of support for Macfarren's candidature. But behind all this simmered a general unrest regarding higher musical education.

During the last years of Bennett's direction of the Royal Academy an opinion had been growing that the time was ripe to replace that establishment with one that was more fitted for the purpose of a national school of music. In 1873 an idea first mooted by the Prince Consort began to be realized. A site in Kensington having been granted by the commissioners of the 1851 Exhibition, building operations for the erection of a new school of music commenced. Under the presidency of the Duke of Edinburgh a hard-working committee raised an endowment fund, and on 17th May 1876 the National Training School for Music was opened. The Principal was Arthur Sullivan, who, having first refused the appointment, was pressed to reconsider his decision by the Duke of Edinburgh.[1] Sullivan remained Principal of the National Training School for five years, and during this time rendered one signal service to the cause of musical education. He made a point of encouraging students to play stringed instruments and founded a student orchestra. Nevertheless, if Sullivan disliked teaching, he was kindly disposed

to the young student, as Landon Ronald testifies.[2] It is of further
interest that in encouraging Ronald as composer Sullivan directed
him closely to study Mozart's G minor symphony (K.550)—the
work that Elgar and Sibelius also took as their early ideal. By 1880,
however, many calls on his time made it necessary to up-grade
Stainer from the post of Professor for Organ to that of Acting
Principal. A year later Sullivan resigned, and in 1883 the National
Training School was re-formed as the Royal College of Music, of
which Grove was the first Director.

During this time Sullivan (who ceased being organist at Cranley
Gardens in 1872) had other daunting experiences in the general
field. In 1871 a Royal National Opera was installed in the St James's
Theatre, and the undertaking was launched with a revival of Balfe's
The Rose of Castile. Sullivan was the conductor. The enterprise lasted
but a few weeks. From 1874 until 1876 he was musical adviser and
conductor at the Royal Aquarium Theatre, Westminster, this
activity overlapping his direction of the Glasgow Choral Union
which began with the first of the season's six orchestral concerts on
10th November 1875, and lasted until 1877. Such was Sullivan's
reputation that he was offered (but refused) the conductorship of the
Liverpool Philharmonic Society, while at the end of 1874 certain
dissidents in Manchester were in favour of a Free Trade Hall
revolution by means of which Hallé should be deposed and Sullivan
put in his place. When the idea was put to Sullivan he honourably
refused to have any part in the conspiracy.[3]

Sullivan also conducted an amateur orchestral society, 'où . . . le
duc d'Edinbourg tenait sa partie au premier pupitre des premiers
violons'.[4] This brings us to the centre-point of Sullivan's life and
career. He was a 'royal favourite' in a way unknown in English music
either before or since.

Alfred, Duke of Edinburgh (1844–1900), second son of Queen
Victoria, who had been elected King of Greece in 1862 but compelled
to refuse the election for political reasons, was able, attractive and
cultivated. Educated for the Royal Navy, he retained a life-long
interest in a service in which he insisted on being very much more
than a nominal figurehead. He was, perhaps, the first high-ranking
English naval officer since the time of Drake to take to sea with him
a group of chamber musicians.[5] Two years younger than Sullivan,
he appreciated to the full Sullivan's talents and capacity for friendship. From 1873—in which year the Duke was betrothed to the

Grand Duchess Marie Alexandrovna, daughter of Czar Alexander II—Sullivan was a frequent guest at the ducal residence at Eastwell Park, Ashford, Kent.[6] There is a touching reference to this period in Sullivan's Will, in which he left to the Duke (then Duke of Saxe-Coburg) [7] the autograph score of *The Light of the World* (which was dedicated to the Duchess) 'in remembrance of the many happy hours which he spent with His Royal Highness while he was writing it, also the music stand which belonged to his friend Joseph Barnby'. If the Duke of Edinburgh was effective in ordering the affairs of the Navy he was hardly less so in respect of English music. The result of his sponsorship of Sullivan has already been shown.

Sullivan, of course, was thereby put in an immensely strong position: royal approbation was a powerful asset in the age of Victoria. That this stimulated envy in some quarters is, perhaps, to be understood from a gossip note:

> Sir Michael Costa is not the only musical composer who has received honours from the hand of English Royalty. Mr. Arthur Sullivan is a great favourite in the happy family of 'the Edin-burghs'. He hangs in his study a memento of the Duchess's kindly feeling for him. It is not a very elegant article—only a rough and ready 'butterfly catchet'; but it is highly prized, for the royal and Imperial Princess made it herself. It came into Mr. Sullivan's possession in this wise. He formed one of a party of moth-hunters down at Ashwell Park. He went out with the intention of being a mere spectator. The Duchess noticed his empty hands. She challenged him. 'I have no net,' Mr. Sullivan pleaded. Bidding the party wait, she returned indoors, impro-vised a net with her own fingers and presented it to the English maestro. If Arthur Sullivan ever becomes great, the net will be historic.[8]

Sullivan's connections with royal personages were widespread, and provided a powerful antidote to any sense of rebellion that might have sprung from his origins. Sullivan was a strong Tory (see page 258) and, flattered by the attentions of the great, made it his business to cultivate the ennobled and also some of their less agreeable qualities. Of revolution he had his fill when caught up in the rising of the Commune in Paris in May 1871, as he had written to his mother.[9] During their exile Sullivan met Napoleon III and the Empress Eugénie, and added them to his list of superior acquaintances, which also included the King of Denmark, the Czar and Czarina of Russia, the Kaiser and Prince Henry of Prussia.

In May 1873 Sullivan went to Oxford as a guest of the Liddells, whose daughter had become 'Alice in Wonderland' by the publication of Lewis Carroll's masterpiece in 1865. A few years after Sullivan's stay with the Liddells, Carroll (i.e. Rev. C. L. Dodgson) wrote to Sullivan asking him to consider setting the songs in *Alice*. Sullivan was unenthusiastic, explaining that his terms would be too unfavourable, but that he might be prepared to consider a dramatized version of the story.[10] In May 1873, more important than an introduction to the eponymous little girl was that to Prince Leopold (at whose christening Sullivan had sung). Sullivan met the Prince, now an undergraduate, at one of Ruskin's lectures. 'He and I,' wrote Sullivan, 'walked back to the Liddells and had tea. We chummed together, and he gave me his photograph.' [11]

At the end of 1871 the Prince of Wales contracted typhoid fever. His recovery was seen by other members of the royal family as due to God's intervening with the purpose of discomfiting those with republican sympathies—and particularly Sir Charles Dilke who had lately been delivering public lectures on the unnecessary expense of a monarchy to the nation. On 27th February 1872 a Thanksgiving Service took place in St Paul's Cathedral. To nourish still further the loyalty of the British people a fête was organized at the Crystal Palace on 1st May, under the auspices of the Duke of Edinburgh 'and other members of the Royal Family'. Sullivan's *Te Deum* was first performed on this occasion, and was thought by those present to be a masterpiece of the first order. Since there were 2,000 performers taking part it could hardly have failed to make an impression.

On 18th July there was another jamboree at the Crystal Palace at which the *Te Deum* was given a second performance. Carl Rosa's wife, Mme Parepa-Rosa, was the soloist, Manns the conductor, and the work was going well until

> . . . the arrival of the Royal party in the middle of Madame Parepa's solo, 'To thee, Cherubim', when the audience, regardless of time or place, uttered a cheer which, however, complimentary to His Royal Highness, evidenced such a thorough contempt for art and artists as to make it too evident what, in the majority of those who attended the fête, was the real attraction . . .[12]

On 1st March 1873, the *Te Deum* was again performed at the Crystal Palace. The concert was otherwise memorable for the first performance at these concerts of Schumann's *Concertstück*, Clara being the soloist.

On 9th September 1872, Sullivan wrote to Katie Helmore complaining of an 'appalling amount of work'. Not only was there *The Light of the World*, on the book of which he was working hard with Grove, but he was also busy with '2 new songs for Titiens & Sims Reeves for the Norwich Festival', where he was also to conduct the *Te Deum*.

It was confidently anticipated by his closest friends that *The Light of the World* would turn out to be a masterpiece comparable with *Messiah* and *Elijah*. Having written the music at customary full speed Sullivan made several visits to Birmingham, where—as William Pountney recalled—he made a good impression on the choristers.

> I well remember the rehearsals of this work. The composer came several times to try over the choruses, and his firm but gentle manner soon made him a favourite with the choristers, who seemed to vie with each other in the desire to make the oratorio a success. . . .[13]

The Duke of Edinburgh hurried down to Birmingham for the first performance on 27th August, in which the principals were Tietjens, Trebelli, Sims Reeves and Santley. The work was received with considerable enthusiasm and the President of the Festival, the Earl of Shrewsbury, created a precedent by publicly congratulating the composer.

> Sullivan used to say that when the lull in the cheering came and he heard Lord Shrewsbury's voice calling out 'Mr. Sullivan' a sudden dread came upon him, lest the religious prejudices of the noble President should have been wounded by the treatment of the libretto, and that he was going to hear a protest. He was soon relieved, however, and Lord Shrewsbury's eulogy was warmly supported by the audience.[14]

The Light of the World was soon installed in other places—in Bootle on 5th January 1874, Nottingham on 21st January, and Manchester on 19th February.

It being understood that the composer found the composition of oratorio a profitless occupation the music-lovers of Manchester, led by J. H. Agnew, clubbed together and, at a complimentary dinner, presented Sullivan with a 'handsome silver cup and a considerable sum of money'.[15] It is only fair to Cramers, Sullivan's publishers, to add that according to their contract with him, dated 4th September 1873, a payment of £300 in respect of all rights was then available.[16] The Manchester Testimonial added £200 to this sum.

In the meantime Sullivan had been strengthening his claim on the loyalties of the religious by augmenting the repertory of spiritual song. The music for 'Onward, Christian Soldiers'—Sullivan's most famous contribution to hymnody—was composed in 1872, and like most of his works has a social connotation. On 5th July 1901, Herbert Sullivan wrote as follows to F. G. Edwards:

> When [Sullivan] wrote 'Onward Christian Soldiers' he was staying with Mr. and Mrs. Clay Ker Seymer at Handford [=Hanford, Stoke-on-Trent] and he named it after his hostess Gertrude Clay Ker Seymer.[17]

While all this was taking place, however, the future direction of Sullivan's talents was being determined by another set of circumstances, and by two men of complementary genius. The one was Richard D'Oyly Carte, the other W. S. Gilbert.

Richard D'Oyly Carte had a picturesque background and upbringing, with an inheritance of both Welsh and French blood from his mother's family. His maternal grandfather, Thomas Jones, a clergyman and sometime Reader in the Chapel Royal who claimed descent from the Norman D'Oylys, was a connoisseur of art and literature and a friend of Lamb and Coleridge. He was also passionately devoted to most forms of French culture. He hoped that his daughter, Eliza, would in due course make a satisfactory marriage. As so often in such cases this hope was not fulfilled. Eliza eloped with Richard Carte, a flautist, whose father had been a sergeant-major and adjutant in the Life Guards Blues, and (like Sullivan's grandfather) had seen service in the Napoleonic Wars. After having been educated partly in England and partly in Germany, Richard Carte established a musical-instrument business to supplement his earnings as a player. After his marriage, however, life was difficult, until his wife's father relented and undertook to subsidize the household. Richard D'Oyly Carte was born in Greek Street, London, on 3rd May 1844.

During his childhood Richard enjoyed unusual privileges. Because of the interest which his mother had acquired from her father, French was spoken at home two evenings a week. Mrs Carte was also enthusiastic about painting, in which D'Oyly's two sisters developed a considerable proficiency, and he himself a lively and informed interest. His father, who had a taste for nonsense and practical jokes, was a keen theatre-goer, and he frequently took the children to entertainments considered to be within their grasp. D'Oyly enjoyed particularly the dioramas—as of the battles of Napoleon, views of the Holy Land, etc.—and other shows which the German Reeds put on at the Gallery of Illustration. He developed a taste too for plays in general, and particularly for French plays. His father, it was said, not only bequeathed to him a general taste for the theatre but also 'his strong predilection for the macabre, combined with a sardonic sort of humour'.[18]

D'Oyly Carte was educated at University College School, where he first began to compose music, of which some was dedicated to Kate Terry. After a brief experience of working in his father's business he decided that this offered too little scope for his talents. He branched out on his own, therefore, providing music for entertainments, conducting it on occasion, and generally making himself useful in the music-dramatic world. Widely experienced in the ways of the world, possessed of reserves of both charm and tact, a generous host, and a more than shrewd business man, D'Oyly Carte set up a theatrical and lecture agency in Charing Cross Road in 1870. Of a small, neat build, with black curly hair, a dark complexion and brilliant dark almond eyes, he was not easy to forget.

William Schwenck Gilbert (1836–1911), whose career had already lightly touched that of Sullivan in 1867, was as various in his early activities as D'Oyly Carte. The son of a naval surgeon who was also a minor author, he was educated in France and England. Having graduated as Bachelor of Arts from London University he served as a civil servant and then, appalled at the eternity of boredom that such an occupation threatened, read for the Bar, after which he opted for independence. His heart being in writing, however, in 1861 he joined the staff of H. J. Byron's *Fun*. He had already invaded musical territory, for in 1857 he wrote a translation of the 'Laughing Song' from Auber's *Manon Lescaut* for Euphrosyne Parepa to sing at one of Alfred Mellon's Promenade Concerts. In 1869 Gilbert published his *Bab Ballads* (they had appeared in *Fun* over the previous three years), by which time he had also established himself as at least a minor influence in the theatre. Some of his contributions to the German Reed repertoire have already been noticed, but he had other connections which were to assume some significance in his relationship with Sullivan and D'Oyly Carte.

In 1868 John Hollingshead (1827–1904), who, among other things, was one of the fraternity of *Punch* contributors, became the manager of the Gaiety Theatre. For the opening of that theatre on 21st December he commissioned a burlesque, *Robert le Diable*, from Gilbert, who then proceeded to other commissions for other theatres. Hollingshead meanwhile turned his attention to comic opera and lighter musico-dramatic entertainment, running in close competition with the Opera Comique. In 1871 Lortzing's *Czar and Zimmermann*, Balfe's *Letty, the Basket-maker*, and Offenbach's *Grand Duchess* and *La Belle Hélène* represented the higher quality in the Gaiety repertoire. In contrast to these was Alfred Thompson's *Cinderella the Younger*, with music by Emile Jonas, which was played—in the presence of the Prince of Wales—on 30th September. At the Opera Comique the one notable piece for this record was an operetta entitled *Marie*, performed as a curtain-raiser to *Le Médecin malgré lui*. The music for this piece (no longer extant) was by Richard D'Oyly Carte, who also conducted the performance. Towards the end of the year the Opera Comique management brought a German *opera bouffe* company to London, but it was a dismal failure. Hollingshead therefore, with the pressure of competition thus reduced, was in a position to try a new line of entertainment. In Manchester Sullivan's music for Charles Calvert's production of *The Merchant of Venice* had just been playing, and in looking for notices of his own productions in *The Musical World* Hollingshead could hardly have failed to have seen a quotation from the Manchester *Sphynx* in the issue of 14th October. Referring to the 'Lorenzo Masque', the writer commented on

> . . . the rollicking sort of hide-and-seek horse-play of a band of masked revellers, wonderfully shown by the odd bits of quaint notes dodging one after another all over the orchestra from unusual instruments. . . .

In 1871 Gilbert's star in the theatre was also in the ascendant. At the beginning of the year he had written *A Sensation Novel* for German Reed, who had composed the music, and the opening piece for the

Court Theatre. In April his *Creatures of Impulse*, for which Alberto Randegger (1832–1911) provided the score, was also performed at the Court. During this same year Gilbert prepared an English version of Offenbach's *Les Brigands* for Boosey (published 1889), and sketched an independent and 'entirely original grotesque opera in two acts' entitled *Thespis, or The Gods grown old*. The text of the latter he speculatively sent to Hollingshead, who promptly dispatched it to Sullivan. He took on Hollingshead's commission, but with muted enthusiasm since there were in the intended cast

> comparatively few actors or actresses who could sing, and of those who pretended to, hardly any could be said to compass more than six notes. Naturally I found myself rather restricted as a composer in having to write vocal music for people without voices.[19]

Thespis, the first Gilbert and Sullivan collaboration, was duly given its first performance at the Gaiety on 23rd December 1871. It was, of course, inadequately rehearsed (Hollingshead offered 'Operetta, Drama, Extravanza, Ballet, EVERY EVENING'), and anyway was far out of range of the intelligence of many of the patrons of the Gaiety. The *Daily Telegraph* registered a mild protest on the part of the Boxing-Day audience. *The Sporting Life* complained that the show was 'over their heads'. *Vanity Fair* remarked that Sullivan's music was as good as that of Offenbach, while *The Athenaeum* observed that Sullivan had not written but merely arranged the tunes. *The Standard* accused him of plagiarism—citing the similarity of the overture tune to Molloy's *Paddy O'Flynn*. The *Pall Mall Gazette*, on the other hand, was impressed by Sullivan's extended orchestration 'including . . . the employment of a railway bell, a railway whistle, and some new instrument of music imitating the agreeable sound of a train in motion'.

Thespis was stamped with royal approval, for the Duke of Edinburgh attended the performance on 9th January 1872. At the end of the month, however, it was taken off. Both Gilbert and Sullivan had other matters to attend to, and they attended to them. Of the cast, the most interesting member was Sullivan's brother Frederic, who, having exhausted his interest in architecture, had decided to invest his real talents in a theatrical career. Later that year Fred appeared in Suppé's *Die schöne Galatea*.

From *Thespis* Arthur Sullivan extracted one song, 'The Maid of

Arcadie', to make the rounds of the ballad market, while the opening chorus was later to be used in *The Pirates of Penzance* for 'Climbing over rocky mountains'. Busied with other matters, and still chasing immortality through oratorio, Sullivan took no further part in theatrical projects until 1874, when Hollingshead persuaded him to write the incidental music for *The Merry Wives of Windsor*, for the Gaiety. Two days before the performance he wrote to Joseph Bennett:

> . . . All the music is new, but (and this is not necessarily for publication) if you remember a ballet called 'L'île enchantée' which I wrote for the Italian Opera, Covent Garden, many years ago, you will recognize two themes, the 1st in the Prelude —[in E major, see page 160] and the second in the scene between Anne Page and the children [in E minor, also see page 160]. I wouldn't write an overture because I didn't care about competing with the very pretty one of Nicolai.
>
> Your masterly judgment, my dear Joseph, will at once enable you to see that as the fairies are not *real* fairies (if such exist), but only flesh and blood imitations I have endeavoured to indicate this, and have not written music of the same character as I wrote for the 'Midsummer Night's Dream', or that Mendelssohn wrote for the 3rd Act of the 'Tempest'.[20] I have only had 3 weeks to do the whole thing in, but I don't think you will find it scamped . . .[21]

Behind the façade of assurance the solid Victorian was often insecure. His imagination, stimulated by a bifurcated Anglo-German Gothic romanticism, and the allurements of the popular theatre, often uneasily busied itself with the supernatural. The supposition that unreality was reality, or reality unreality, was strongly, and not always surreptitiously, maintained. Fairy-tales were not thought to be quite incredible. Sullivan, Carte and Gilbert were brought up within this tradition, which they variously modified. Gilbert, his style becoming increasingly efficient for this purpose, became more and more interested in the thesis that reality and its obverse are in some cases the same, and in others interchangeable. He went on developing his talent for satirizing institutions, thereby making them both more and less real. Gilbert is to be found somewhere between Wilde and Shaw, a social realist with an epigrammatic pen and a contempt for the commonplace. Before his association with Sullivan,

Gilbert was very active and not unsuccessful. But his genius needed the catalytic force represented by music. By itself it was insufficient.

Before and after *Thespis* the patterns that later became definite in the Gilbert-Sullivan tapestry were shaping. Right back in 1867 ideas that were later to be refined for *Iolanthe* appear in the study of the parliamentarian, Peter Bowindo, M.P., entitled *Highly Improbable* (Royalty Theatre, 5th December). Bowindo, in order to make provision for his six daughters, proposes the introduction of a 'Member of Parliament Matrimonial Qualification Bill'. At one point in the farce the ladies' maid Cocklethorpe is 'dressed in absurd combination of ladies' maid and footman's dress'—'a footman down to the waist and a ladies' maid from thenceforth', observes Oates the groom. In *Our Island Home* (1870) Gilbert introduced Captain Barry—who had been apprenticed to a pirate instead of to a pilot by his nursemaid.

A few months after *Our Island Home* Gilbert wrote *The Palace of Truth*, in which for the first time he indulged in unchivalrous wit at the expense of ageing beauty. So Chrysal announces the Queen:

> My Lord, she comes—
> A perfect type of perfect womanhood.
> The dew of forty summers on her head
> Has but matured her beauty, by my life!
> For five and thirty years, a bud—and now
> A rose full bloom.

Aristaeus (with Jane and Katisha in view) observes:

> Say over-blown.

After *Thespis* Gilbert wrote a dozen or so burlesques and similar pieces, of which, in the long view, the most significant were *Happy Arcadia* and *Topsyturvydom*, the first performed at the Gallery of Illustration on 28th October 1872, the second at the Criterion on 21st March 1874.

Happy Arcadia opens with this pretty glimpse of 'existence à la Watteau':

> *Exterior of Strephon's Cottage . . . Pretty Arcadian Landscape . . . Strephon and Chloe discovered. Strephon seated beneath tree, playing on flageolet. Chloe dancing with a pet lamb, decorated with ribbons. . . .*

The relevance of this to *Iolanthe* and to *Patience* is clear, while the text (at some points anticipating the comedy of Wilde) itself has the sense of mockery soon also to be exploited operatically. So Lycidas 'the handsomest man in the world' applauds the rural life:

> This is the life for me. I see plainly this is the life for me. I will be a simple shepherd and come and live with you. Oblige me with the addresses of a house agent, a field, a fold, a flock of sheep and a list of local charities.

In a letter to Charles Plumptre Johnson [22] Lady Gilbert said of *Topsyturvydom* that it was 'above the heads of the general public', which is exactly what was said about *Thespis*. *Topsyturvydom* is in the Utopian line of descent—at any rate from as far as Swift—and has observations on parliamentary democracy and free elections that are by no means without present point. In Topsyturvydom, where the second scene is laid, the King's birthday is being celebrated. Crambo, a court functionary, is by no means sure that things are going in the right direction, saying:

> ... medicines are to be served out gratuitously to the poor— ten pence in the pound will be put upon the income tax, and all the operating theatres of the Hospitals will be thrown open to the public.

'It is well,' says his colleague, 'in a country where folly is honoured.' Not surprisingly some of the Utopian ideas in *Topsyturvydom* turn up later in *Utopia Limited*.

In 1873 Gilbert had a look at the law, and having produced a libretto out of an old ballad he had published in *Fun*, offered it to Carl Rosa on the understanding that it should be set to music and that Rosa's wife should star in it. The death of Mme Parepa-Rosa, at the age of thirty-seven, on 21st January 1874, put an end to this intention.

A year later D'Oyly Carte, now managing the Royalty Theatre for a season of Offenbach directed by Selina Dolaro, ran into Gilbert in the theatre one night during a not very successful performance of *Giroflé, Girofla*. According to an interview with Carte published in *The Umpire* on 2nd February 1890, he asked Gilbert there and then if he had a suitable fill-up piece to hand. Gilbert suggested a 'breach of promise' piece before that evening was over. Carte intended that the music should be by Sullivan, and when the proposition was put to him Sullivan obliged with the bulk of the music in a fortnight. *Trial by Jury*, notable for the fact that it was *durchkomponiert* and for the precedent set by an active chorus, was painted from life. Gilbert had in mind the Clerkenwell Session House where he had once worked as a barrister. *Trial by Jury* was immediately used in the hope of pulling Offenbach's *La Périchole* out of the red, and so well did it succeed that *La Périchole* faded from view.

A great deal of the credit for the success of *Trial by Jury* went to Fred Sullivan, who played the part of the Judge and never allowed 'the audience to miss a single syllable in four or five verses'.[23]

Among those who applauded the music was the Lord Chief Justice, Sir Alexander Cockburn—one of Sullivan's acquaintances—who, however, wondered whether the action of the operetta was not likely to bring the Law into contempt. In June *The Zoo*, a 'musical folly' with words by B. C. Stephenson and music by Sullivan, was put on at the St James's Theatre, after which Sullivan, as a guest of Sir Coutts and Lady Lindsay (who was a poet and played the violin), turned his face to the south and went to Italy for a holiday. During that summer a gratifying article appeared from the United States, from *Watson's Art Journal* of New York. On 21st August the visit of a troupe known as the Bohemians to Tarrytown, New York State, was reported:

> The great speciality of the programme was, of course, the farce *Cox and Box*, which, in its new musical dressing, is far more funny than ever. Arthur Sullivan has written music to this farce, which is not only beautiful and masterly, but brim full of the very spirit of fun.

As with all such transatlantic performances the material was pirated. This was a familiar hazard, and one which had caused Gilbert too optimistically to insert a 'Caution to American Pirates' in the sixpenny word-book of *Thespis*.

The Gilbert and Sullivan partnership began at the point in history at which British prestige (in the eyes of the British) was at its zenith. In 1875 Disraeli bought the shares of the Khedive Ismail in the Suez Canal, and Sullivan, *il primo dei compositori inglesi viventi*, was honoured with a testimonial from the Royal Conservatory in Milan when he visited the city to produce some of his compositions in response to an invitation from Alberto Mazzucato, Director of the Conservatory and sometime leader of La Scala orchestra. Two years later Queen

Victoria was proclaimed Empress of India, and in South Africa the Transvaal was annexed. The rich had never had it so good, and their capacity for appreciating the worst in art had never been so abundant. In the theatre the ephemeral reigned supreme. But if industry boomed, and imports with it, sounds of distress were heard from the increasingly impoverished farm-lands. If the established social order appeared impregnable, its bastions were under assault from women in pursuit of their rights and Trades Unionists in search of justice.

In that era of free enterprise competition was cut-throat, and no sooner had D'Oyly Carte effectively staked his claim in the market with *Trial by Jury* than Hollingshead counteracted by establishing a new *opéra-comique* company at the Gaiety. It is interesting that, in reply to Gilbert's innovations in stagecraft and in respect of the chorus, Hollingshead deemed it expedient to tighten the disciplines of production. He insisted that his French agent should provide him with 'a company so generally efficient as to enable him to offer a constant succession of operas, carefully rehearsed, and presenting an *ensemble* . . .' and a chorus that was 'well acquainted with the repertory, and, therefore, effective'.[24] The repertoire, kept up 'with unflagging spirit', comprised works which had long proved box-office draws—by Halévy, Boildieu, Hérold, Donizetti, and others of less note.

In 1876 D'Oyly Carte took a lease of the Opera Comique Theatre (where the Aldwych now is) with the intention of founding a Comedy Opera Company for the main purpose of producing operas (yet to be written) by Gilbert and Sullivan. He enlisted support from the publishing houses principally interested in Sullivan, and Frank Chappell and George Metzler, together with A. D. Collard and E. H. Bayley, joined Carte in setting up the company. By the spring of 1877 Carte was ready to put a proposition to Gilbert and Sullivan.

In the meanwhile Gilbert had kept his hand in, as far as comic opera was concerned, with *Eyes and no eyes* and *Princess Toto*. The former, with music by German Reed, was played at St George's Hall on 5th July 1875. It opened with Clochette alone at her spinning-wheel singing 'As I at my wheel sit spinning', which provided an idea used again in *The Yeomen of the Guard*. *Princess Toto*, which starred Kate Santley, was set to music by Frederick Clay that had a distinctly Danubian quality—there is a splendid waltz-song, 'Banish sorrow', for the Princess.

In the summer of 1876 Sullivan was made an honorary Doctor
of Music at Cambridge, on which occasion he dined with W. H.
Thompson, the Master of Trinity. In 1879 Oxford followed suit,
and the degrees in music then bestowed on Sullivan, G. A. Macfarren
and Herbert Oakeley were the first honorary degrees of this kind to
be awarded in that university. A few months after receiving his
Cambridge degree Sullivan was shattered by the death of his brother,
which occurred on 18th January 1877. Arthur was at his bedside.
He left a large family whose interests were then and ever afterwards
a prime concern of Arthur; and this devotion, first to his parents
and then to his brother and his brother's wife and children, is one
of the most attractive sides of Arthur Sullivan's personality. On this
theme Hesketh Pearson makes an illuminating comment, to be set
beside those on pages 42, 130 and 139: 'Sullivan's feeling for his
family was essentially un-English. It was the feeling of a stranger in
an alien land for his kin.' [25]

Sullivan's feelings on the death of his brother found expression
in *The lost chord*, and a somewhat odd light is thrown on them by a
letter to Arthur Boosey written on 21st April:

> My dear Boosey:
>
> I will take 3d a copy for the P.F. arrangement of 'The Lost
> Chord'. I hope it is doing well. I have protested against
> Metzler's dishing up old songs of mine with new words, and
> advertizing them as 'new songs' by me.
>
> Yrs.
>
> Arthur Sullivan.

Grief was a saleable commodity. So too was comedy, and after
Sullivan and Gilbert had thoroughly discussed Carte's proposition
their decision was as follows:

> 9 Albert Mansions
> S.W.
>
> 5 June, 1877
>
> My Dear Carte,
>
> Gilbert and myself are quite willing to write a two act piece
> for you on the following terms.
>
> 1. Payment to us of two hundred guineas (£210) on delivery
> of the MS. words and music—that is to say, before the piece is
> produced.
>
> 2. Six guineas a performance (£6.6.) to be paid to us for the

run of the piece in London. From this will be deducted two hundred guineas paid in advance so that the payment of the six guineas a performance will not really commence until about the 33rd or 34th performance.

3. We reserve the country right. Your right to play it in London on these terms to extend only to the end of your season.

The piece would be of a musical comedy character and could be ready for performance by the end of September. If this outline of terms is agreed to we could prepare a proper agreement upon this basis.

Yours very truly,
Arthur Sullivan.[26]

Gilbert had by this time already sketched the libretto of the piece, which was based on his *The Elixir of Love*, but Sullivan, whose determination to arrange a satisfactory contract before undertaking a work was only equalled by that which he showed in fulfilling it, was not yet ready to start. In fact—Sullivan worked best nearest to his date-line—he left his contribution very late and only finished the opera, *The Sorcerer*, with a day or two to spare before the first performance on 17th November. According to precedent there were two pieces on the bill, *The Sorcerer* being prefaced by Arthur Cecil's *Dora's Dream*, the music by Alfred Cellier. During the summer Sullivan, acting on instinct, approached George Grossmith (1847–1912) and asked him to take the part of John Wellington Wells which, had he lived, would have been allotted to Fred Sullivan. Grossmith, sometime newspaper reporter, lecturer, sketch-writer and entertainer, was surprised and flattered. He had played at the Gallery of Illustration (where, when he was a boy, his father used to take him to see the shows) and was popular in the provinces. But he doubted his capacity to fill a Sullivan role. Others doubted it too, and Sullivan's directors, hearing of his intention, telegraphed the instruction: 'Whatever you do, don't engage Grossmith.' After he had sung 'My name is John Wellington Wells',[27] however, Grossmith was assured by the composer that he would do. Indeed it was Grossmith who really made *The Sorcerer*, which enjoyed a six-month run. Apart from Grossmith, the cast included Mrs Howard Paul, Alice May, Miss H. Everard, Richard Temple, Rutland Barrington, Frederick Clifton, and Giulia Warwick and George Bentham who were hired from the Carl Rosa and Her Majesty's (Haymarket) Opera Companies respectively.

After the launching of *The Sorcerer* Sullivan went to Paris, officially
to confer with the President of the Exhibition Commission but in
fact to enjoy an environment increasingly congenial to him. Two
days after Christmas he had a letter, together with a draft for a new
piece, from Gilbert. It was to be about the Royal Navy (memories
of the Surrey Theatre burlesque, *Blue Jackets*) and Gilbert was at
once anxious to assure his colleague (whose loyalty to the Navy was
ensured by his friendship with the Duke of Edinburgh) that although
the production should be realistic, with the uniforms being made at
Portsmouth, its satire should not be taken as directed at any one
person. 'The fact that the First Lord in the Opera is a *Radical* of the
most pronounced type,' he wrote, 'will do away with any suspicion
that W. H. Smith is intended.' [28]

Although *The Sorcerer* was doing splendid business Carte was anything but satisfied with his business partners, who were beginning
to gang up against him. The preliminaries to a sorry, squalid business
that was to end in the law courts were being assembled, and Sullivan,
now at the Hotel Chauvin in Nice, and in indifferent health (see
page 203), alluded to them in his letter to Carte of 5th February 1878:

> My dear D'Oyly,
>   Thanks for your letter. Don't be under any apprehension
> about the 'Company'. They can do nothing without us, and I
> certainly shall not deal with them unless through you. And I
> shan't deal with them at all unless they make up their minds to
> settle your business quickly. They ought to have done it long
> ago. Is the 'Sorcerer' seriously on the wane. I mean is business
> bad? I hope not, for I am not on very good cue yet for writing
> anything fresh and bright.
>   I think the new piece [*Pinafore*] ought to be very funny. I see
> you are doing Cox and Box at the Philharmonic [Theatre,
> Islington]. I suppose you arranged with [H.] Blackmore [later
> Secretary of the Theatrical Managers' Association] for it. When
> is Cellier's piece coming out? [29] I thought it was due a fortnight
> or three weeks ago. I wrote to Gatti's [30] on Saturday, and tele-
> graphed yesterday, to say I had no wish to withdraw from the
> engagement, but wished the terms reconsidered. I hope they will
> do so, as my holiday will be entirely broken for the Concerts.
>   I am going to see the Danseuse today to see what sort of
> terms she wants. She is more graceful than anything I have seen
> for years and has made a tremendous success here.
>   Keep [George] Power, and send [George] Bentham into the

country. Furneaux Cook [31] is not a great favourite of mine I confess, and I wish you could find someone else amongst your Baritone list.

What I remember of 'Rosetti', I like—but she ought to change her name to something English. Are her terms high?

There will be no part for Mrs. Paul I believe in the new piece. Where does 'Sorcerer' tour begin. Good bye my dear D'Oyly. Keep good and virtuous. I shall be at home at the end of the month, and have received nothing yet from Gilbert. I have lost all my money gambling—a regular facer.

Ever yours,
A.S.

P.S. Don't leave any letters for me to attend to when I return. Settle straight off or send to me.

Gilbert has been given credit for his reforms in theatrical production. Sullivan's contribution in this respect has received less attention. Already the importance of a chorus adequate in every respect was obvious to him in respect of *Pinafore*, and on 23rd April he wrote to Carte:

Dear Sir:

The men chorus play such an important part in the new piece, that the present chorus must be strengthened. I shall therefore advise your making up the number to 6 tenors and 8 basses.

Pray see that everyone is present tomorrow to begin at 11.30 and that the Stage is ready with seats and Piano.

Also Mr. [Edouard?] Silas.

Yours very truly,
Arthur Sullivan.

The first performance of *H.M.S. Pinafore* (prefaced by Grossmith's sketch, *Cups and Saucers*) took place on 25th May. It was a brilliant social event, but, as Gilbert had feared, there was a good deal of concern that W. H. Smith had apparently been held up to ridicule. Gilbert, of course, had denied that this was his intention; nonetheless the idea that a Cabinet post might be made the subject of comedy was by no means congenial to the political die-hards who packed the Opera Comique. After the first night sell-out audiences fell away, and every so often the directors of the Company announced their intention to take the piece off, only to go into reverse when the receipts showed signs of picking up. Carte himself was no party to this vacillation and no one was better pleased than he when Sullivan himself gave the fillip necessary to keep *Pinafore* going on an even keel. As conductor of Gatti's Promenade Concerts he agreed one night to include a selection from *Pinafore*, arranged by Hamilton Clarke. Having heard the music the promenaders decided to see the opera—and business rolled merrily on. In the June issue of the *Musical Times* (page 329), however, a sour note appeared: '*Pinafore* confirms us in the opinion we expressed in noticing *The Sorcerer*; that this firmly cemented union between author and composer is detrimental to the art-progress of either.' Sullivan was not good at taking criticism (who is?), but at least his public position was absolutely unassailable. He was the great master.

While preparing for *Pinafore* Sullivan was also busily involved in the preparations for the Exhibition in Paris in July. So he wrote to Henry Leslie shortly before it was time to leave for France:

> 9 Albert Mansions,
> S.W.
> Tuesday
>
> My dear Leslie,
>
> (1) Have you received the patterns of tickets? I have applied in vain for them.
> (2) Mad: Goddard *will* play.
> (3) I can get *no answers* from anyone about anything in Paris. I am in despair.
>
> Yrs. ever
> Arthur Sullivan

> Orleans Club (Town House),
> 29 King Street,
> St James's,
> Friday night
>
> My dear Leslie,
>
> I go over tomorrow night, as I must have a quiet hour with the Orchestra on Sunday afternoon.
>
> Shall you come then? I have a cabin & have ordered a coupe lit for myself. If you want the same telegraph in the morning to Thornsett, Calais, & tell him to secure you one with mine.

[Edouard] Colonne writes to say that he has 'convoqued' the accompanying band for 11 on Wednesday.

Today's 'Figaro' has a notice of the approaching concerts.

Ever yours
Arthur Sullivan [32]

In Paris Sullivan conducted movements from *The Light of the World*, Macfarren's *Chevy Chase* overture, an *Intermezzo* by J. F. Barnett, and Sterndale Bennett's F minor Piano Concerto (Arabella Goddard being the soloist). *La France* and the *République Française* of 19th July were loud in their praises of Sullivan, both as composer and conductor. He could be content that he had done his part for the *entente cordiale*.

All this time Sullivan's mother was deeply worried about Arthur's health. He was not, as she knew only too well, of a robust constitution, and he was doing too much. There were also frequent periods in which he suffered intense pain, caused by his kidney complaint. In the summer of 1879 Mary Sullivan wrote to J. W. Davison of *The Times*, saying that because he was 'suffering from a very painful disease' Arthur was compelled to give up the Covent Garden concerts.

However, his association with Gilbert and Carte meant that in their joint interests he had to concentrate on their affairs wherever he might be and whatever else he might be engaged on. After the Paris Exhibition he went to Switzerland at the end of July 1878, but a month later he was back in London, and on 12th September he wrote a sharp note to Carte. It was always possible to skimp on the musical side of comic opera—but not when Sullivan was around. His suspicion that Gilbert was not over-concerned on this head was one of the causes of later disagreement (see page 152).

My dear Carte,

I regret to say that on my visit to the Theatre last Tuesday I found the Orchestra both in number and efficiency very different to what it was when I rehearsed the 'Pinafore'.

There seemed two second violins short and the whole band is of very different quality. I beg to give you notice that if the deficiencies are not supplied by Saturday and the efficiency of the orchestra increased by engaging better players both of the

wind and the stringed instruments I shall withdraw my music
from the Theatre on Monday night.

You know perfectly well that what I say I mean.

Kindly inform the Directors of this and oblige.

Yours very truly,

Arthur Sullivan [33]

per A & M.W.

Meanwhile another company had been on tour with *The Sorcerer*,
and it being summer-time and the place being Yorkshire, the chorus
challenged the principals to two cricket matches. The one was
played in Hull, the other in Sheffield. But, commented the *Sheffield
Independent* of 10th August after the chorus had beaten the principals,
in the evening performance of *The Sorcerer* 'Messrs W. S. Gilbert
and Arthur Sullivan bowled all the crickets out of remembrance'.

As has already been seen Sullivan was by no means unknown in
the United States. After *Cox and Box* had established itself there its
successors were greeted with enthusiasm, and by the middle of 1879
Pinafore was making huge profits—but not for Sullivan, Gilbert or
Carte. There being no effective law generally to protect British
copyright interests in the U.S.A., theatre promoters were able to
put on such works with a minimum of expenditure. Piracy was
rendered somewhat less profitable by the number of operators following this occupation.

Boston put on the first production of *Pinafore*, the 'FAMOUS
NEW MUSICAL ABSURDITY . . . Another Great and Attractive
Novelty . . . The most MIRTHFUL AND MUSICAL YET' at
the Boston Museum on 25th November 1878. An extra matinée was
arranged for Thanksgiving Day, for which the sensitive American
might not have felt a piece in honour of the British Royal Navy
entirely suitable. However, there was some satisfaction in practising
large-scale piracy (even if not on the high seas). Manager Field of
the Museum had, it was said, needed 'laborious painstaking in the
preparation of the piece'. The fruits of his labours were the word-
book available from the ushers or at the coat-room for 10 cents, and
the music (published by Louis P. Goullaud) to be had at the coat-
room for 25 cents.

The *Boston Advertiser* opined that: 'It is a long time since any
entertainment at once so novel, droll, decent and delightful . . . has
been presented in Boston.' The satire at the expense of the First

Lord of the Admiralty (the Boston newspapers were agreed that it was a deliberate sending-up of 'newsdealer Smith') was an expression of sentiments to be heard in the U.S.A. concerning the Secretary of the Navy. The 'By Jingo' ditties, 'which, under the express patronage of the queen, did so much political business for Beaconsfield', were not found to be offensive. Sullivan's music carried all before it: the *Advertiser* found it

> . . . extremely good. It is as funny as possible, to begin with. It burlesques almost every sort of serious and emotional composition known to the world of music; the opera, the oratorio, the ballad simple and sentimental, are all presented with an extravagance which is peculiarly funny, because it is so exactly in the line of the originals themselves. As for familiar musical authors and their works they appear in kaleidoscopic variety, a touch here, a flash there, yet always amusingly recognisable. . . .

The Boston production bore some relation to the original work: none of the eight performances which were soon running simultaneously in New York bore any resemblance to the authentic version. In April 1879 Baltimore succumbed to the Gilbert and Sullivan contagion with performances of *Trial by Jury* and *Pinafore*, of which the most remarkable was an 'oratorio style' presentation by the Baltimore Independents, with 'symmetrical characters'. In Baltimore soon

> there were as many breeds of *Pinafore* as auditoriums: a children's operetta; marionette shows, and many others which did not keep Ford's [Theatre, Baltimore] from advertising theirs was the 'only original travestie, with the most original minstrel in the world'.[34]

Carte decided to reconnoitre, to discover in what way his and his collaborators' interests could best be served in the U.S.A. He sailed to New York in July 1879, leaving Michael Gunn to keep the affairs of the Comedy Opera Company under control.

While Carte was away the Company's lease of the Opera Comique ran out and Carte's fellow-directors saw an opportunity of practising a major act of piracy on their own account. While Gunn continued to superintend *Pinafore* in its original form, the dissidents determined on setting up a production under their own, independent management. A long, complicated series of adventures and misadventures (as when the directors unsuccessfully sent along a gang of toughs to remove the scenery from the Opera Comique) led to a law case before the Master of the Rolls. This process was reduced to précis form by Carte some years later when he had other and similar worries in the U.S.A.

> The Comedy Opera Co. (the company formed by the break-away directors) who had no right to the Pinafore announced that they would play the opera. We applied for an injunction which was granted, but which was reversed the same day on a trivial point. They therefore played the piece (first at the Aquarium and then at the Olympic). The case came on in the ordinary course later on. We won it of course and obtained a perpetual injunction, damages, and costs. But in the meantime the Company had gone bankrupt, we got no damages and had to pay our own costs.[35]

Having arrived home Carte apologized to Sullivan for not having written immediately. He knew that he would understand, and continued

> . . . I cannot tell you how grateful I am to you for having stuck out as you did for my interests . . . I have signed to open in N. York at the Fifth Avenue on Dec. 1st and to play a 12 weeks season during which we ought to do the New Opera, Pinafore and perhaps Sorcerer. Boucicault [36] most strongly advises our opening with Pinafore and reserving our trump card the New Opera . . . But we must be prepared to open with the New Opera if necessary. I have arranged to follow this in March with Chicago, St. Louis etc., and Cincinnati is pending. I have *splendid terms* 60% in N. York, 65 in Chicago, and 75 in St. Louis, and I hope to close at 70 for Cincinnati. . . .
>
> The oratorio business is well in hand. I shall send you the Handel and Haydn's people's proposition for *Prodigal* [*Son*]. They won't do the Light of the World—they say they can't get it up. I hope to fix the L. of the W. for N. York and we have in hand a great 'Sullivan Festival' in Philadelphia. The orchestral concert business is very doubtful and can be done nothing with until we get out.
>
> Now as regards cast—our people must all be *strong* singers. The people there are nearly all splendid singers, but have not got the business of Pinafore at all. But it is quite necessary to give a much more 'prononcé' performance than we do here.

They like 'emotional' singing and acting. The placid English style won't do and I assure you that if we took out such a company as the Opera Comique we should make a big failure as likely as not. . . .

For the next six weeks or so negotiations for an American tour—for which it was decided to take principals from London and recruit singers for minor roles and chorus in New York—continued. During this time Gilbert provided Sullivan with the libretto of *The Pirates of Penzance* (Carte's 'New Opera') and Sullivan composed some of the music of Act II. On 4th October he wrote to Carte conditionally accepting Carte's terms for America.

My dear Doyly

We agree to your proposition, subject to your giving us in addition one sixth of your net profits . . . your net profit to be calculated over the whole tour. I think you had better close with this and save all further bother and negotiation. I will only answer one point in your letter. The America scheme did not originally emanate from you, it came from *me*, in consequence of offers I had from America to go over and conduct the 'Pinafore' whilst the rage was still on. Ford [37] offered me *one thousand pounds* to conduct it in Philadelphia for a few nights. If I had gone over alone on my own account, I should have probably made a large sum without any bother. As it is, I have suggested that others share it with me.

Pray say you agree to our amendment and the thing is off our mind.

Yours sincerely,
Arthur Sullivan.

A month later Sullivan and his colleagues sailed uncomfortably to the United States.

NOTES TO CHAPTER SIX

1. 'Such is the national mania for establishing schools of music that a few years ago some £200,000 was collected for establishing a new musical academy with, for the most part, the same professors as those already-employed at existing academies; and an attempt moreover, was made to shelve Sir Arthur Sullivan . . . by placing

him at the head of this quite superfluous establishment.' J. H. Mapleson, *The Mapleson Memoirs, 1848–88*, 3rd edn., 2 vols., London, 1888, II, p. 272.

2. *See* Landon Ronald, *Variations on a Personal Theme*, London, 1922, pp. 32–4.

3. 10th January 1875; *see* Michael Kennedy, *The Hallé Tradition*, Manchester, 1960, pp. 84–5.

4. F. J. Fétis, *Biographie des musiciens (1835): Supplément II*, Paris, 1880. Sullivan carried out many commissions for the royal family, as is shown by his letter of this period (but undated) to Henry Leslie, the well-known choral conductor.

> *Private*   9 Albert Mansions
> My dear Leslie,
>   The Prince of Wales has asked the Duke of Edinburgh to ask your choir to help the Amateur Orchestral Society at their last Concert at the Albert Hall on the 17th inst. The Prince was very keen indeed about it.
>   The Duke asked me if I would find out from you *confidentially* what you thought about it, so that he might not officially ask you & be refused perhaps.
>   Perhaps you will kindly tell me frankly whether you think it feasible, and desirable. I will then tell H.R.H.
>   They are both very desirous to have your assistance I know.
>   Yrs. sincerely
>   Arthur Sullivan

(R.C.M. MS. 4090, f. 120).

5. 'H.R.H. The Duke of Edinburgh told me that he had a complete string quartet amongst the officers on board his ship . . .' Arthur Sullivan, *About Music*, lecture given at the Birmingham and Midland Institute on 29th October 1888, Birmingham, 1888, p. 11.

6. Writing from Eastwell Park at the end of 1873 Sullivan gave this account of life there: 'I had a lot of musical letters to write for H.R.H. today, so missed the post for you. This morning we were to have gone out shooting, but it was wet. The Duchess and I played some duets after dinner—Schubert's marches. She plays extremely well. Princess Christian (of Schleswig-Holstein) asked me to try to help a protégé of hers at Windsor. I wish I had a quarter of the influence that folks think I have. To-night is New Year's Eve in the Russian calendar, so there was service in the chapel.' H. Saxe Wyndham, *Sullivan*, p. 126.

7. The Prince of Wales having relinquished his title to the Dukedom of Saxe-Coburg in 1863 it was transferred to his brother. On the death of his father's brother in 1893 the Duke of Edinburgh, renouncing his privileges as an English peer, succeeded.

8. *The Musical World*, LIII, 45, 6th November 1875.

9. Letter quoted in A. Lawrence, *Sir Arthur Sullivan*, London, 1899, pp. 78–9.

10. Sullivan and Flower, *Sir Arthur Sullivan*, 1950 edn., pp. 85-6.

11. H. Saxe Wyndham, *Sullivan*, pp. 125-6.

12. *Musical Times*, 15, August 1872, p. 565.

13. *The Mercury*, Birmingham, 3rd August 1895.

14. *The Manchester Guardian*, 23rd November 1900.

15. J. H. Agnew (1830-91), prominent industrialist and Liberal, was a friend of Hallé and Santley. He was for some time Honorary Secretary of the Gentlemen's Concerts in Manchester. See *The Manchester Guardian* for 28th February 1874, and Obituary of Agnew in the issue of 31st December 1891.

16. A further sum of £100 was to be paid when the sales (of the vocal score) reached 2,000, and a similar sum at 4,000.

17. BM. Eg. MS. 3095, ff. 217-18. 'She [Gertrude] was a daughter of Ker Seymer and his heiress and married Ernest Clay, Fred Clay's eldest brother . . .' H. Sullivan to F. G. Edwards, 4th August 1901. Gertrude was a novelist, her works in this *genre* including *The Black Patch* (1894), a 'sporting novel', and *Since first I saw your face* (1899). For Clay Seymer, *see also* F. C. Burnand, *Records and Reminiscences*, 2 vols., London, 1904, II, p. 363.

18. From notes on Richard D'Oyly Carte prepared by his cousin, and now in the possession of Miss Bridget D'Oyly Carte.

19. Quoted in Baily, *The Gilbert and Sullivan Book*, p. 81.

20. The unconscious interchange of personalities expressed by this slip of the pen indicates, perhaps, the role which Sullivan envisaged for himself.

21. Bennett, *Forty Years of Music*, pp. 68-70.

22. 31st May 1931. BM. g. 27.0.132.

23. *Punch*, quoted by *The Musical World*, LIII, 24th April 1875, p. 17. This issue also gave complimentary excerpts from *The Times* and other London newspapers, as well as from the leading provincial press in Manchester, Liverpool, Sheffield and Newcastle upon Tyne.

24. *The Musical World*, LIII, 14th August 1875, p. 33.

25. Hesketh Pearson, *Gilbert and Sullivan*, London, 1935, p. 99.

26. On 4th July Carte's agreement concerning his salary as manager and his percentage of the profits was outlined by him to George Metzler, after which a contract between the Comedy Opera Co. Ltd and Gilbert and Sullivan was ratified in the same month.

27. *See* George Grossmith, *A Society Clown*, Bristol, 1888, pp. 91 and 93-125, for a full account of Grossmith's association with Sullivan and Gilbert.

28. William Henry Smith (1825-91), who acquired a fortune through the development of his father's newspaper and book distribution business, became a politician. He was M.P. for Westminster and in 1877 was appointed First Lord of the Admiralty by Disraeli.

29. Nb. note on first programme for *The Sorcerer*: 'Messrs. James Albery and Alfred Cellier are engaged on a New Musical Piece,

which will be produced as soon as may be practicable.' It was entitled *Bella donna*, and produced in Manchester.

30. Messrs Gatti, the firm of restaurateurs, maintained Promenade Concerts at Covent Garden Theatre. Refreshments were an important feature of these concerts. The music varied in quality from Hervé's Choral and Heroic Symphony, *The Ashantee War*, to Beethoven's Choral Symphony, which Sullivan boldly introduced.

31. Furneaux Cook took the part of Samuel in *The Pirates of Penzance* at the New York première on 31st December 1879.

32. R.C.M. MS. 4090, f. 44.

33. Regarding Sullivan's musical discipline Grossmith wrote: '. . . Sir Arthur Sullivan is strict with the music. Every member of the chorus has to sing the exact note set down for him or her; and often, in the midst of the rehearsal of a full chorus *double-forte* we have been pulled up because a careless gentleman has sung a semi-quaver instead of a demi-semi-quaver, or one of the cousins, sisters, or aunts has failed to dot a crotchet.' *A Society Clown*, pp. 100–1.

34. Lubov Keefer, *Baltimore's Music*, Baltimore, 1962, p. 242.

35. R. D'Oyly Carte to John Stetson, 13th June 1885.

36. Dion Boucicault (1820?–90), actor and dramatist, retired to the U.S.A. in 1876.

37. John Thomson Ford (1829–94) built the Grand Opera House in Baltimore and three theatres in Washington. The first of the Washington theatres was destroyed by fire and its replacement, known as Ford's Theatre, was where Lincoln was assassinated. Ford, manager at the time, together with his brother, was imprisoned for more than five weeks and the theatre seized by the Government. Ford also managed theatres in Alexandria and Richmond, Virginia, and in Philadelphia. He was the only American manager who paid Gilbert a royalty on *Pinafore*. He leased the Fifth Avenue Theatre, New York, for *The Pirates of Penzance*.

7

Fame abroad, discord at home

Gilbert, Sullivan and D'Oyly Carte, fortuitously brought together in an alliance that was profitable to each, soon found that personal incompatibilities and differences of temperament placed a strain on their relationship. Gilbert, a dictator in the theatre, was often assailed by a sense of insecurity that prompted him to make outrageous, sometimes unforgivable, remarks. Not unnaturally, he assumed that he was the fountainhead of success since he was the author of the plays that fed the prosperity of his partners. At the same time he preferred to think that his talents could be better used, that he was, at least potentially, a great dramatist and a great poet. It is, of course, frequently so with a master of comedy. By the same token, Sullivan was loth to believe that his music for the operettas represented the best of him. Nevertheless he was quite certain that so long as he was in association with Gilbert he was, as shown in his letters on pages 111, 113 and 152, in supreme control so far as musical matters in the theatre were concerned.

D'Oyly Carte's relationship with Sullivan was warmer than that with Gilbert. The two of them shared similar tastes, especially in food and wine. They enjoyed being cultivated by the great and they enjoyed the voluptuous life that this afforded. Gilbert's was a more withdrawn personality, through which ran a strong vein of suspicion. All three men, however, had no reason to doubt that their chief end in life was to accumulate wealth. So long as he maintained his profits Carte was content to do his best to oil the wheels of his creative colleagues. In the end, however, he ran out of oil.

Gilbert's eyes, and ears, were opened when he went with his companions to America. The hero of the tour was Sullivan, whose music permeated the polite drawing-rooms and, by courtesy of the organ-grinders, the streets of the cities. The words of the plays could be altered out of all recognition in the theatres, but the melodies at least remained intact. (Which is not to say, however, that the same

was the case in respect of harmony and orchestration.) Gilbert began
to feel twinges of jealousy in the autumn of 1879.

The *New York Herald* of 23rd October reminded its readers that
'one need hardly name Sullivan's songs to a generation which hears
"The Snow lies White", "The Lost Chord", and "Sweethearts"
echoing in a thousand drawing rooms'. Gilbert and Sullivan had
arrived in the Cunard steamship *Bothnia* the previous day. The
reporters were at them before they had finished breakfast '. . . delightfully ensconced amid a bevy of charming American young ladies'.

Sullivan, who explained that he had been 'seriously ill and often
in great pain' while writing *Pinafore*, and that he had had to have
an operation during the summer, made an appealing figure '. . . with
a face of wonderful nobility and sensitiveness, in which the slightest
emotion plays with unmistakable meaning, with eyes which only
the Germanic adjective of "soulful" would fitly describe, and the
full, sensuous, lips of a man of impassioned nature'.

Neither Gilbert nor Sullivan had any cause for complaint at their
reception. Two days after landing they were entertained at the
Lotus Club, where Chauncey Defew, John Hay, Robert B. Roosevelt
and other notables made pleasant speeches of welcome, and where
Sullivan's songs were sung well into the small hours. Gilbert made
a speech, and drew attention to the loss suffered by him and his
colleague through the copyright situation. Sullivan also made a
speech to the same effect. They were to go on plugging this motiv
for a long time to come. Their main immediate purpose, however,
was the superintending of the rehearsals of *Pinafore*, which was to
open at the Fifth Avenue Theatre on 1st December. The Americans
thought they knew *Pinafore*, but 'the *Urtext*, brought to New York
by the D'Oyly Cartes, was unrecognisable'.[1] Sullivan wrote to his
mother of the magnificent opening performance, but then gloomily
drew her attention to declining receipts. He worked every minute
of every day that could be taken off from social and extraneous
musical functions [2] to finish *The Pirates of Penzance*. Alfred Cellier,
conductor of the D'Oyly Carte company (Sullivan himself conducted
on special occasions only), and Cecil Clay, who had preceded the
main party to New York, helped to copy parts. The overture was
finished at five o'clock in the morning of the day of the first performance. In the meantime parts had been sent back to England so that
an English performance could as near as possible be made to coincide
with the American première as a precaution against piracy. On 30th

December a company touring Devonshire with *Pinafore*, still for the most part dressed *Pinafore*-wise, and reading their parts, gave a bizarre performance (in fact *the* first performance) of *The Pirates* at the Royal Bijou Theatre, Paignton.

Sullivan's diary entry for 31st December shows his condition:

> . . . No rehearsal, except Band at 11 for Overture. Home at 1.45 to breakfast. Too ill to eat. Went to bed to try and get sleep, but could not. Stayed in bed till 5.30. Gilbert came. Got up feeling miserably ill. Head on fire. Dressed slowly and got to New York club at 7.30. Had 12 oysters and a glass of champagne. Went to Theatre. House crammed with the elite of New York. Went into the orchestra, more dead than alive, but got better when I took the stick in my hand—fine reception. Grand success. Then home [3]—could not sleep, so did not go to bed till 3.30. Felt utterly worn out.

As Boucicault had opined, the retention of *The Pirates* until after *Pinafore* had had a preliminary run paid off. It played only to full houses. It was possible for even the dimmest American theatre-goer to appreciate that the music as performed under Sullivan's surveillance was quite different from what he had previously heard. The *New York Herald* drew attention to the fact, like the *Boston Advertiser* underlining the fine quality of Sullivan's parodistic skill:

> The humour of the music lies in fact in its serious imitation of grand opera, the most outrageous perversions of common sense in the text being treated with the utmost solemnity. This application of serious music to the absurd situations of the text beggars description. . . .

Success in New York warranted the sending of other companies to other cities, preparations for which were beginning to get under way when Sullivan went off to Baltimore for a New Year Festival arranged by the Wednesday Club, the Peabody Institute and the Academy Theatre.

When it was learned that Sullivan was to spend some days in Baltimore, J. T. Ford (see page 120, n. 37) tentatively proposed that he should be invited to a reception at the Peabody. Not expecting the directors of this institution to be ready officially to honour a non-serious composer, Ford was surprised to learn that Asger Hamerik,[4] the Danish musician who was now established in Baltimore, was

even eager to welcome Sullivan at the Conservatory. At the Festival
concert on 8th January Sullivan made a great impression, not only
as 'the conjuror of the most enjoyable nautical opera' but also as a
'gracious, firm, but sensitive conductor and pianist'. He was delighted. 'They can't,' he wrote home, 'do anything of this sort in
New York.' Next day he went out of town. Two days later he returned
from Berryville, Clarke County, Virginia, and the newspapers
reported that he was

> . . . invited to dinner at Mr. Robert Garrett's . . . It was
> understood that he was to be present afterwards at the Peabody
> Students' Concert at night, as he had been cordially invited
> to attend by Professor Asger Hamerik, with whom he had been
> on cordial terms since his arrival in Baltimore.[5]

As often, Sullivan was in difficulties. The Wednesday Club [6]
wanted a visit from him as well as the Peabody. In the end he
decided to go to both. The Peabody came first and since he was an
hour late the programme had already started. It was

> . . . during Miss Belshoover's programme of some charming
> variations on a theme by Mendelssohn . . . that [Sullivan] came
> to the door of the hall, and after waiting outside for fully five
> minutes . . . he walked in, accompanied by several friends, all
> in evening dress. The concert took place in the old library hall,
> which is rather small, and Dr. Sullivan, not wishing to attract
> attention to himself, begged to be allowed to remain standing
> near the doorway, where he would be scarcely noticed. Mr.
> Hamerik would not hear of this, and the unwilling little gentle-
> man was taken up to the other end of the hall and seated in full
> view of all. He came just in time to hear Miss Lizzie Kruger,
> an ex-student, sing two of his songs—'Let me dream again',
> and 'The lost chord'. She sang them sweetly, albeit she was a
> little frightened. . . .[7]

Sullivan enjoyed Baltimore, especially its 'German' tone, and
left the town oblivious of the fact that Ford's, who claimed to be
'the sole owners of the *Pirates* south of New York' [8] were at war over
this work with the Academy.

D'Oyly Carte sent Cellier to Philadelphia to rehearse a new
company. Sullivan continued to make speeches and to give inter-
views to the press on a variety of topics. He also dealt with the matter

of the Leeds Festival—of which he had been invited to become conductor—at long range. Having sent his acceptance of this post to England (see page 206) he went with Carte and Gilbert to Buffalo to inaugurate a company there, and then on to Niagara. While Carte and Gilbert returned to New York (where an 'Irish Famine Matinee' performance of *The Pirates* on 25th February brought in $394 to this charitable cause), Sullivan crossed the border into Canada. His coming was heralded by this notice in *The Daily Globe*, Toronto, on 17th February 1880:

Mr. Arthur Sullivan is quoted as saying that at the end of the year, in October probably, Mr. Gilbert and he will produce another piece in New York. Work, however, has not commenced on it. Mr. Sullivan will, at the end of this month, return to London to fulfil his many professional engagements there. He is going to Ottawa before he sails, as the Princess Louise has written to say that she and the Governor General hold him to his promise to visit them, made some time ago.

In honour of the Canadians Sullivan composed his *Dominion Hymn*, which takes its place among those works that are best forgotten.

On April 8th *The Pirates* was produced in London at the Opera Comique, and began a run of 400 performances. On 12th May Sullivan acknowledged the cancellation of the existing agreement with Carte and the substitution of a revised version. For the authors of the operas this was by no means unprofitable, for Carte was to pay £2,900 for the sole rights in *The Sorcerer*, *Pinafore* and *The Pirates*. For the time being at least, amateur performances were not to be licensed. Apart from this, Sullivan was collecting royalties from his publishers. For each vocal score he received 6d, for each separately issued number, 4d. Similar terms obtained in respect of the 'sacred musical drama', *The Martyr of Antioch*, which he was due to present at the Leeds Festival in the autumn.

During the summer the long-drawn-out case between Carte and his former business associates kept a spate of correspondence flying round among the 'triumvirate', and while *The Pirates* was happily engaging public support, Sullivan was able temporarily to dissociate himself from what his critics took to be an unworthy occupation. Having also disengaged from the in-fighting of the educational world, he was free to concentrate on nobler ends. On 29th July he attended a function in the banqueting room at St James's Hall, at which Grove was presented with a 'handsome gold chronometer, and a purse of 1000 guineas'. Sullivan made a speech remarking on Grove's encouragement of young musicians (in this connection he also chivalrously noticed Manns), and his devotion to the twin cause of Schubert and Schumann. In October Sullivan conducted the Leeds Festival for the first time, and if his own new work was in some quarters damned with moderate praise, he had by now grown accustomed to a certain amount of critical sniping. He was, of course, well protected by his immediate entourage of patrons and sycophants. Nevertheless he may well have secretly agreed with the critic of the *Musical Times* who, complaining that the 'sacred drama' was in no sense 'dramatic', said that 'Mr Sullivan knows best where his strength lies'.

He was soon reminded of where his strength lay by Gilbert's informing him that he was preparing a new work for Carte. He had in train a kind of comic counterpart to George Eliot's *Scenes of Clerical Life*. Whether he was encouraged towards this project, or dissuaded from it, by his ecclesiastical associations through *The Martyr of Antioch*, is not known. But not liking the context of parochial life, he transformed his plot so that what had been two Anglican curates—Messrs Clayton Hooper and Hopley Porter—in the poem *The Rival Curates*, became, in the persons of Bunthorne and Grosvenor, high priests of the cult of aestheticism. Aesthetics generally had been in the process of readjustment at the hands particularly of Whistler and Oscar Wilde. Whistler, a protégé of Sullivan's friend Sir Coutts Lindsay, had lately won a *cause célèbre* (although awarded only a farthing damages) against John Ruskin, who had accused him of 'flinging a pot of paint in the public's face'. Whistler, indeed, was a close friend of Carte, and helped to decorate his apartments at 4 Adelphi Terrace. Here he mixed the paints for the 'yellow room' and brightened up the billiard room by painting the walls to match the cloth of the table.

Whistler, naturally, was talked about in philistine circles. But the spotlight of suburban disapproval was beginning to focus more closely on Oscar Wilde, whose 'lank, languid, limpidity' was, for instance, increasingly capturing the attention of *Punch*. Gilbert's *Patience* is, of course, a comment on the aesthetic movement in general as well as on Wilde-Bunthorne in particular. It is not certain, but it is possible, that one effect of *Patience* was to prejudice Wilde's candidature for election to the Beefsteak Club. On 25th May Sullivan, who belonged to this as to a number of other clubs, noted in his diary: 'Then to Beefsteak Club. Committee for election. Oscar Wilde the only man pilled. . . .'

Sullivan went off to Nice at the end of 1880 and came back, after staying briefly in Paris, at the end of January. *Patience* was produced at the Opera Comique on 23rd April. Among those present was the critic Vernon Blackburn (*d.* 1907), whose memory of the occasion reanimates the spirit in which this new work was received. He refers first to *Trial by Jury*.

> Well do I remember the surprise and delight of those who, going to that haunt of amusement to see a somewhat dull play, happened to arrive a little too soon, and were perforce compelled to see the curtain-raiser. Settling down with boredom (there are few curtain-raisers which do not compel you to settle down to boredom), one was suddenly made aware of a brilliant, an engrossing, a captivating piece of work which set the whole theatrical table, as one may say in parody, in a roar. . . .
>
> [*Patience*] seemed to me like a new planet which had swung into my ken. It was all new, all fresh, all fascinating, all captivating. When the curtain rose upon 'Twenty love-sick maidens' I thought that, despite the burglary from Wallace's 'Hark those chimes so sweetly stealing', a fine goal of beauty had been reached. As the piece went on, culminating in the first act with that exquisite sestet, 'I hear the soft note', I assumed an all-reverential attitude, and, when the end came, I bowed my head in recognition of an artist who, like the flowers in the Song of Solomon, had appeared in the land. 'Flores apparuerunt in terra nostra.' [9]

A month after the first performance of *Patience*, it would seem that Sullivan was taking a fresh look at his career, and that the impulse to write more 'serious' music was again being active. Carte, who had many ideas in mind at this time—particularly since the action against the Comedy Opera had at last been settled in March—wrote a letter to Sullivan which hints at unease.

> I look upon the operas by you and Gilbert as my mainstay. And I want to remind you that I rely on your promise to let me have under any circumstances another piece to follow Patience —if necessary for the opening of the new theatre—, I want to record now my conviction that notwithstanding the present

rush, the duration of the run of Patience is most uncertain, and I *want strongly to urge you in all our interests to be looking ahead and preparing the new opera.*

In view of further arrangements would it not be desirable now to tell Gilbert that after the next piece you will probably not be able to write another work with him for a long time— always supposing that your plans respecting Covent Garden are unchanged.

The 'new theatre' referred to here was the Savoy Theatre, which was Carte's considered response to the by-now established popularity of the Gilbert and Sullivan productions. A man of vision, Carte also brought an orderly mind to bear on all questions of the theatre. Thus he was insistent that actors should be accommodated and treated in a civilized manner. He saw no reason why the costs of programmes should not be absorbed in charges of admission—so those who went to his new Savoy Theatre, after its opening (with *Patience*) on 10th October 1881, had their programmes free. Interested in technological change, Carte had electric light installed in the Savoy, which thus became the first theatre in the world to be illuminated by electricity. He also persuaded those who sought admission without having previously bought tickets to form up in queues. Thus he became a great benefactor of the English people.

Carte was concerned not only about the expansion of his interests in Britain but also about his prospects in the U.S.A. (where the running battle over copyright continued), and in order that the American public should be enabled to know what they were laughing at, purposed sending Oscar Wilde on a lecture tour. Sometime soon after the English production of *Patience* (his letter is undated) he wrote to his efficient secretary Helen Lenoir—who was a powerful voice in all D'Oyly Carte affairs—that

there have been stupid paragraphs in the Sporting Times, one saying that I am sending Wilde out as a sandwich man for Patience, and another one afterwards stating that he was not going as 'D'Oyly Carte found that he could get sandwich men in America with longer hair for half the money', and he is slightly sensitive although I don't think appallingly so. I however suggested to him that it would be a good boom for him if he were to go one evening to see Patience and we were to let it be known beforehand and he would probably be recognised. This idea he quite took to. . . .

At the beginning of 1882 (probably in January) Carte was again in New York. Writing from 1,267 Broadway to Sullivan, who was in Egypt at the time, he noted the first serious rift in the affairs of the triumvirate. Gilbert, taking advantage of Carte's absence (as had previously the dissentient directors of his company), raised strong objections to the rental of the Savoy. Carte tried to placate him and wrote a conciliatory letter. To Sullivan he wrote:

> I have suppressed my feelings as I want to avoid a storm being raised in my absence, but I feel 'boiling over' when I think of it. I cannot conceive how Gilbert can go back on me, to use the American phrase, in such a way. . . .
>
> It seems that Oscar Wilde's advent here which has caused a regular 'craze' has given the business a fillip up.
>
> I hear there are some wonderful speculations in Florida in the way of *orange* groves. Shall I buy you one???

Sullivan did not invest in an orange grove; two years later another English composer, Frederick Delius, did—or at least his father did on his behalf. At the time Sullivan was somewhat too deeply committed on too many fronts, and there was the successor to *Patience* to consider. He duly fulfilled his contract with Carte, and *Iolanthe* [10] was produced at the Savoy on 25th November 1882. At the back of his mind—and this indeed is somewhat reflected in the music of *Iolanthe*—was the wish to write another kind of opera. What Carte had hinted at in 1881 came out into the open two years later.

> Speculation has been busy of late with regard to Sir Arthur Sullivan and opera. We have seen it stated that the successor to *Iolanthe* is finished and waiting to be produced. The truth of this is open to question. We believe that the new comic opera—rightly described as suggested by Tennyson's *Princess*—is not yet complete and, consequently, that *Iolanthe*, which still draws a profit, must continue to keep the boards awhile. It is further said that Sir Arthur will shortly set to work upon an opera called *Marie Stuart*, to be produced at Covent Garden next season. We shall not be far wrong in stating that, as to this, rumour is playing her believers false. It is true, no doubt, that Mr. Gye applied to Sir Arthur for an opera, and that the composer had a fancy to the subject named. But a libretto is not at hand, and we very much question whether Sir Arthur would write an opera in Italian. A serious lyric drama in English may be expected of him sooner or later.[11]

On the surface Sullivan's life was one of comfort and contentment; but beneath there were tensions and psychological conflicts. These arose in the first place from his origins and his relationships within his family, in the second (as has been indicated) from an incapacity properly to use the whole range of his creative talent. The period lying between *Patience* and the publication of the article in *The Lute* referred to above, was critical in more ways than one.

The most endearing feature in Sullivan was his loyalty to, and concern for, the members of his family. In his own success he saw their justification and emancipation. His grief at the deaths of his father and his mother was intense. His understanding with his mother —to whom he used to write almost daily when away from her—had always been especially deep, and with an access of fortune he had taken pleasure in setting her up in her own home in Fulham, where, after Frederick's death, she had also given sanctuary to her daughter-in-law and grandchildren. Meanwhile Sullivan himself had moved into a new establishment, 1 Queen's Mansions, Victoria Street, which was to be his home for the rest of his life. Towards the end of May 1882, Mary Sullivan, now in her seventy-second year, suddenly fell ill after lunching with Arthur. Two days later, on 27th May, she died. On 1st June the funeral, conducted by Helmore, took place at the Brompton Cemetery. Sullivan made a note in his diary: 'Home, feeling dreadfully lonely.'

The particular intensity of his feelings for his family, especially for his mother, had proved something of an impediment to any durable relationship with other women. In his student days Sullivan had flirted with the Barnett (and other) girls. At the beginning of his professional career a brief affair with Rachel Scott Russell— more passionate on the girl's side—had exploded in his face without apparently doing much damage. This was succeeded by a shadowy connection with an unknown Irish girl. At the time of his initial success as Gilbert's co-partner, when he was much talked about in Society, Sullivan was natural prey for the predatory instincts of the socially ambitious. He was captured, and captivated, by an American adventuress, Mrs Mary Frances Ronalds.

Mrs Ronalds, a Carter of Boston, separated since 1867 from her husband Pierre Lorillard Ronalds (*b.* 1828) whom she had married in 1859, joined a lengthening queue of wealthy American ladies anxious to achieve social eminence in Europe. First she tried France, where she became attached to the Empress Eugénie. When the

Empire fell Mrs Ronalds came to London in the wake of the French royal family. She established herself at 7 Cadogan Place, and also in the favour of the Prince of Wales, by whom she was described as 'my good friend'. She was well known in high society for her beauty and as an amateur singer with a talent for rendering the songs of Sullivan in an expressive manner. In order fully to observe aristocratic protocol Mrs Ronalds held 'musical afternoons' at her house,[12] which differed from those maintained by the English ladies of fashion in that guests were expected not to talk while music was being performed. In spite of this they were very popular. Their popularity was largely caused by the array of distinguished personages assembled by Mrs Ronalds, for 'great artists from the Royal Opera House who charge millionaires and other folk $1,000 a song at private entertainments, sang without price and for friendship at Mrs. Ronalds's' (*Boston Transcript*, 3rd June 1910). Sullivan was very attached to Mrs Ronalds, to whom he wrote daily for the last twenty years of his life. She it was who in 1882 took over the maternal role. She may have fulfilled another, but that is no more than a matter for speculation. Occasional diary entries for the year 1881–2, in fact, indicate that Mrs Ronalds at that time, at least, was more likely to have been confidante than mistress.

> 6. June, 1881: at Luton Hoo. All went to Luton. Mrs. Leigh opened a Bazaar. I gave £5, and accompd. Mrs. R[onalds] in the 'Lost Chord'—in the middle of the Bazaar! Great enthusiasm.
>
> 9 May, 1882: . . . then to Her Majesty's to see 'Götterdämmerung' with Mrs. R. and Fanny—got the most splitting headache from it, played a little loo at Tom Chappell's—won £18.[13]
>
> 10 June, 1882: Mrs. R. returned from Ascot and went to Claremont. L.W.[14] came at ¼ to 3 to lunch, stayed till 5.45.

This, it will be noticed, was a few days after Maria Sullivan's funeral, when Sullivan was acutely aware of his loneliness. That L.W. had particular feelings in respect of him is clear from the other diary notes. It has been inferred by a reliable authority who had access to the Sullivan diaries before they were made inaccessible by their transatlantic purchaser that L.W. was pregnant and that she underwent an operation for abortion. All in all it appears that Sullivan's encounters with women on the level of natural intimacy were not entirely satisfactory.

During the latter part of 1882 Sullivan was also undergoing other trials. In the course of a few years he had made a great deal of money, enough to make a good deal more by judicious use of the stock market. He chose as his adviser E. A. Hall, of the broking firm of C. Cooper Hall & Co., 46 Lombard Street. He did not, as it happened, choose wisely. Hall, however, was useful in other ways, and a note from him to Sullivan, written before their association ended, gives another insight into the way of Sullivan's life. The letter is undated.

> 131 Piccadilly
> Monday
>
> My dear Arthur,
>   I find the claret comes to [£]69.10.0 so that added to what we made the champagne £127.8.0 is, in toto, £196.18.0. I have told Silva [Sullivan's valet] to deliver it at once to you.
>
> Yours ever,
> E. A. Hall

On 2nd October 1882 Sullivan received a note from Hall that made him somewhat apprehensive.

> You shall have your account in a day or two ... the ledger-keeper has mixed up $20,000 of N.Y., Penn & Ohio 1st Mort. Bonds which I bought a long time ago.

Two days later all seemed well, Sullivan's securities, Hall said, being presently worth more than £6,000, viz.

> 14 January 1881, $2000, Atlantics 1st Mort. Bonds—£2560
> $9000, Galveston & Harrisburg Railway—£2000
> 1 June 1881   £2500 5% Debentures, Quebec Central Railway—£2127

On 25th November, the very day of the first performance of *Iolanthe*, Sullivan had the following letter delivered to him by special messenger.

> 131 Piccadilly
> 25 Nov.
>
> My dear Arthur,
>   Perhaps you have learnt by this that I am hopelessly [messed?] and that you must for the present look upon your money as lost.

God knows how it will all end but I have seen it coming for ages.

Thank God my friends stick to me and believe me honest. I am afraid Cooper is not the man we have always thought him. I have been weak and he has exerted a fatal influence and power over me. My mother and family are awfully kind though they have suffered cruelly. Come and see me my dear boy though I feel you will hate me.

Yours always,
Edward Hall

P.S. I went out of my mind on Sunday but am better.

Sullivan, recovering from the strain of conducting *Iolanthe*, replied next day in a more considerate tone than many would have used under similar circumstances.

My dear Edward,

I am deeply grieved at the terrible news which I learnt first from your letter yesterday.

I of course knew from what you had told me that you were passing through critical times, but I did not anticipate such a speedy and lamentable end. As a friend, and one to whom I am so much attached, you have my deepest sympathy, for I know what you must be suffering.

[One question I must ask you. When you speak of my money being lost, do you refer to money I have lent you alone, or to securities of mine which you hold? Money I have lent you would probably include the Galveston and Harrisburg securities. Before I can talk the matter over, I must know this. Send me a line at once, and I will try and see you tomorrow, my poor boy.] [15]

One thing I must ask you to do without delay—that is to send me back the securities you hold of mine, or tell me where to send for them. The Galveston and Harrisburg securities are I suppose gone with the thousand pounds. Send me a line at once, and I will try to see you tomorrow, my poor boy, and talk over the disaster.

Yours ever sincerely,
A.S. [16]

On 13th December Hall wrote again, saying

The meeting is fixed for next Tuesday. Come if you can and the statement will be I think satisfactory. You have I think Ingles report of the Colorado Mine in your rooms, it must have dropped out of the book, as I did not find it in the book. I daresay Smyth[e] [17] can find it. . . .

P.S. I received a note from Dicey [18] which expressed the kindest sympathy, but I think he doesn't wish to see me at present, at least I gather that from the expressions in the letter.

Life, however, had its compensations. During this time of tribulation Sullivan had a congratulatory letter, dated 6th December, from the Prime Minister. Sullivan, after reading in *Punch* on 9th December that his *Iolanthe* music was 'very far from his best' replied to the Prime Minister on the next day:

Dear Mr. Gladstone,

I am much gratified at your valued praise of 'Iolanthe'; but, that in the midst of all your work and anxious occupations you should bethink you of writing to me on the subject, is even more flattering to me, and I cannot refrain from thanking you for such kindly and gracious thoughtfulness.

I am
Yours very truly,
Arthur Sullivan. [19]

However many irritations came his way during this period Sullivan could always rely on the support of the famous. It may be supposed, indeed, that the vast quantities of claret and champagne kept in Queen's Mansions were for the casual entertainment of royal personages who had a habit of dropping in from time to time. Particularly, of course, the Duke of Edinburgh, who in the summer of 1881 took Sullivan and Fred Clay with him in H.M.S. *Hercules* on a semi-official excursion to Russia. This, the first such visit since the accession of Alexander III, was a necessary courtesy visit according to the diplomatic practice of the time. To the politics of the situation Sullivan was oblivious, his faith in the dogma of a divine right being almost as firm as that of the Czar himself. The whole expedition was a source of great satisfaction, both to Sullivan and to his royal host. On the way to Kronstadt the ship put in at Copenhagen where the party was greeted by the Danish royal family. On the return voyage *Hercules* anchored at Kiel, where the Crown Prince and Prince Henry of Prussia paid their respects—and spoke of their enthusiasm for the music of Sullivan.

What made the deepest impression on Sullivan during this mission was the singing of the Russian Imperial Chapel Choir. At almost exactly the same time as Sullivan was remarking on the superb standard of performance of this body, Tchaikovsky, similarly inspired, was beginning a serious study of Russian liturgical music.

At the end of 1881 Sullivan went to Egypt, staying there for three months. Like Bartók and Holst at a later date Sullivan was greatly interested in the Arab music that he was able to hear, and it even began to be rumoured that he was writing an 'Egyptian' Symphony. But it was a period of rest and recreation (more recreation than rest), and finding that the folk-music that he heard defied precise notation he contented himself with absorbing the atmosphere. His recollections came in usefully to relieve a rather dull lecture that he once gave:

> ... I have myself witnessed the extraordinary effect of their rhythmical music on the Arabs in Egypt, more especially at the great ceremony of the departure of the Sacred Carpet for Mecca. In one tent there were nearly a hundred dervishes swaying their bodies in all kinds of movements and contortions, and singing the same monotonous measure over and over again, until they got maddened, and fell down, some senseless, some in furious fits, when they were really dangerous.[20]

While he was in Egypt Sullivan conducted a concert in Alexandria. Otherwise he spent most of his time at parties. Edward Dicey, a member of the Anglo-French dual control commission then administering Egyptian finances, was in the country and able to give Sullivan useful introductions. He met sheiks and pashas, Wilfrid Scawen Blunt and his wife, and the Duke of Clarence (Albert Victor) and Prince George, sons of the Prince of Wales, with whom he played 'riotous games' at a party at the home in Cairo of Sir Edward Malet, Consul-General in Egypt.[21]

A few months later a nationalist revolt broke out in Egypt. It was suppressed by the British, which gave some satisfaction to those who had been put out by the 'humiliating' Peace concluded with the Boers in South Africa a year earlier.

While Sullivan was away in Egypt progress towards the foundation of a new school of music was being made. On 28th February the Prince of Wales presided over a fund-raising meeting held in the banqueting hall of St James's Palace. The scheme came to fruition a year later, and a few days prior to the opening of the Royal College of Music the Prince of Wales dropped a broad hint to Sullivan that there was something significant in store for him. On 13th May Sullivan gave a birthday party in his house. The guests were the Prince of Wales, the Duke of Edinburgh, Lords Hartington and Kenmare, Ferdinand Rothschild, Millais, Gilbert and Burnand. Nine days later Sullivan was knighted at Windsor.

Although he enjoyed the grand life, Sullivan nonetheless had his reservations about the cultural health of those who often helped him to enjoy it.

> . . . there is no doubt that Music has had to suffer much from the lofty contempt with which she and her votaries have been treated by those who professed to have a claim to distinction in other walks. . . . At any great meeting on the subject of music, archbishops, judges, politicians, financiers—each one who rises to speak will deprecate any knowledge of music with a smug satisfaction, like a man disowning poor relations.[22]

Similar words were used by Elgar during his Birmingham lectures. At heart both men held a secret contempt for those by whom they were often flattered. Sullivan beat the philistines at their own game. He made money and spent it ostentatiously. Of this ostentation a note, dated 15th January 1883, from one Thos. E. Dawes of Victoria Yard, Broadway, Westminster, is amusing evidence. Mr Dawes respectfully undertook

> to supply . . . a double Brougham or Victoria Carriage (when you are not using your own Brougham), with Horse, Harness, and Coachman at any time you may require it . . . for £20.

The philistines wanted entertainment. Sullivan supplied it; but it was not what they had at first expected.

Patience, at the expense of artists, was well within the permissible limits of ridicule. Whether *Iolanthe*, holding Parliament and particularly the hereditary peerage up to ridicule, would be so was a matter of concern to Gilbert. He had experienced more than usual trouble with this libretto, and of some parts at least Sullivan had been critical. However, *Iolanthe* not only escaped condemnation but, as shown, was approved in the highest political circles. The popularity of the work can be gauged from the fact that on one day alone Chappells were happily able to report to Sullivan the sale of 10,000

vocal scores. It is sometimes suggested that the works of Gilbert and
Sullivan depend for their popularity more on Gilbert's words than
Sullivan's music. The demand for the music suggests otherwise; as
also does the Gilbert and Sullivan vogue then prevalent in the
U.S.A., and the imminent conquest of Europe.

In 1883 Sullivan conducted at Leeds and, intermittently, worked
on the score of *Princess Ida*, which was performed on 5th January
1884. Grievously overworked and racked with pain, he completed
this music with difficulty and conducted the first performance with
even greater difficulty. In order to do so at all he had to be given
injections of morphine. A few days beforehand Fred Clay had suffered
a stroke, and this sad news added to his depression. Throughout the
early part of 1884 Sullivan underwent a severe course of self-exam-
ination during which he continually felt that he had written himself
out—at any rate in the field of comedy: however he looked at it,
this was a side-issue. His duty was to the main tradition. In 1884 he
was put in mind of this by the replacement of Costa at Birmingham
by Hans Richter. They should, he observed with some asperity, have
appointed an Englishman.[23] Certainly no one was going to take
English music seriously while its most distinguished exponent limited
himself to comedy pieces.

He tried to explain himself to Carte and to Gilbert, neither of
whom, however, were willing to prejudice their prosperity by giving
way to the unreasonableness, as it seemed to them, of its author.
Indeed, Sullivan was bound by contractual agreement, but when he
was brought round to realize that his commitment was virtually
inescapable, he took great exception to the variation on the theme of
The Sorcerer which Gilbert had begun to sketch for a new libretto.[24]
He properly observed that by inducing people to fall in love with
one another *à tort et à travers* by means of a magic 'Lozenge', and
producing this plot together with a projected revival of *The Sorcerer*,
he would be inviting unfavourable comparisons. He wished to be
rid of 'topsy-turvydom' and to 'set a story of human interest and
probability'. And then when the impasse seemed absolute the fates
made their own Gilbertian intervention.

In May, 1884, it became necessary to decide upon a subject
for the next Savoy opera. A Japanese executioner's sword
hanging on the wall of my library—the very sword carried by
Mr. Grossmith at his entrance in the 1st Act—suggested the
broad idea upon which the libretto is based. A Japanese piece

would afford opportunities for picturesque scenery and costumes, and, moreover, nothing of the kind had ever been attempted in England.[25]

If anyone had thought twice about likely themes for an opera the provocative influence of the executioner's instrument would not have been necessary. Everybody, so to speak, was at that time talking about Japan, which had recently become very much more than a far-away country. In 1867 the Japanese government signed trade treaties with fifteen countries, which was an effective means of opening up the empire to international inspection, and since the Japanese themselves were anxious to Westernize there was an increasing reciprocity between East and West. The Japanese ruling class rejected the long tradition of the Ukiyo-E print in favour of cheap Western lithographs; but in the West Japanese prints were highly prized, influencing the French Impressionists and also Whistler. The fact that when Gilbert was working on the libretto of *The Mikado* there was a 'Japanese village' exhibition taking place in Knightsbridge was further indication of a widening interest in Japanese affairs. The vogue for 'Japonaiserie' in Germany is shown by the character of the playbill and the word-book for performances of *Der Mikado*, both shown between pages 146 and 147. *The Mikado*, which cost both Gilbert and Sullivan much labour and worry, was performed for the first time on 14th March 1885, and it settled down to a run of more than 600 performances.

As usual Carte was disturbed about the situation in the U.S.A., where in one action concerning copyright an American judge was to observe: 'Copyright or no copyright, commercial honesty or commercial buccaneering, no Englishman possesses any rights which a true-born American is bound to respect.'

On 13th April Carte wrote to Gilbert:

We were speaking some little time since about America and the possibility of getting something out of that country with the Mikado. It is of course not practicable to do anything this season, as the hot weather comes on in May. But I propose to make arrangements to produce the piece there next autumn ... but if the pirates attempt to play the piece ahead of us, which they will probably do, as it has been cabled there to the papers as being a marked success, we shall try conclusions with them if they are in an accessible district and in a state in which there

is a fair chance of getting such justice as is dispensed in America
. . . If the Tracy scheme fails, of course it will *not* be an advantage
but very much the reverse, as we shall lose a good deal in law.
If it succeeds we shall hold the rights of the music but at a cost
of possibly £1000 or more.

The 'Tracy Scheme' was further outlined in the letter of 13th June
which Carte wrote to Stetson in New York, in which he observed
that he had been legally advised by A. P. Browne, the Boston
attorney.

    . . . Our position is this, *Sir Arthur Sullivan's music* is not
published. All that is published is an arrangement from Sir
Arthur's orchestral score made entirely from beginning to end
by an American citizen, Mr. G. L. Tracy [26] of Boston. Of this
publication Mr. Tracy has acquired the entire copyright for
the United States. If any person attempts to play the Mikado
they will be infringing Mr. Tracy's rights and I as his assignee
shall proceed to stop them under the statute laws of the United
States.

On 20th June 1885 Sullivan, partly urged by private business,
once more sailed to the U.S.A.—Carte followed on the next boat—
to do battle with J. C. Duff who was proposing, without warrant, to
produce *The Mikado* at the Standard Theatre in September.[27]
Sullivan, content to leave matters of litigation to Carte, stayed in
New York only a few days before travelling to the mid-west. Hardly
had he reached his hotel room in Chicago before a reporter from
the *Chicago Tribune* came to see him.

    A cheery 'Come in', and 'I am very glad to see you', followed
a rap at Room 24 at the Grand Pacific yesterday morning. The
speaker was a typical Englishman between five-feet five and
five feet six in hight [*sic*], a picture of good nature and good
health, and must have tipped the beam at 175 pounds. His
beard was worn close-cut, and his hair was parted exactly in
the middle . . . 'I am going really to Los Angeles,' he said,
'where I have six [surviving] nephews and nieces ranging from
6 to 21 years. They are children of my brother who died some
years ago. They went West and invested in some property, but
two months ago their mother died, when they wrote for me to
come out. . . .' [28]
    . . . 'There seems to be an endless muddle about *The Mikado*.'

'Yes: and it is extremely annoying to have it put in the way it must be here [Chicago] by this fellow [Sydney] Rosenfeld, who got all he knows about Japanese customs and everything else from a dollar score book . . .'

'You know that Pinafore is running this week in Chicago.'

Mr Sullivan appeared to be astounded, remarking that he did not think it could be tolerated at this late day . . .

The interview went on at considerable length, Sullivan having warmed up to the subject of copyright infringement. He would, he said, have liked to have remained in Chicago longer.

. . . but this *Mikado* you have here rubs the wrong way. You know what I mean. This Rosenfeld is such a—— ——, but don't publish those words, for he could bring a libel suit against me.' . . .[29]

. . . 'No: I do not yet know how long I will remain in the West until I learn how much time it will take to straighten out the affairs of my brother's children.' [30]

Next day the *Evening News* of Chicago commented as follows on Sullivan's interview:

Sir Arthur Sullivan appears to have come to America to teach people a thing or two. We know that Sir Arthur could handle a tuning-fork with considerable éclat, but we do not find him quoted as a legal authority in the revised statutes.

Lower down in the same column the *Evening News* saw Sullivan out of the city, reporting how

. . . he boarded a train for the sunset shore and the baggage was checked for Los Angeles. We have no positive information on the subject, but we suspect he has gone to Los Angeles for legal advice.

Sir Arthur, in fact, did a grand tour; to Denver, Salt Lake City, San Francisco—where, he said, he 'saw the theatre, and went into the vilest dens'—and, from Los Angeles, with his relations, through the Yosemite Valley.[31] Meanwhile Carte had lost his action against Duff before Judge Wallace of the United States Circuit Court. Carte was represented by Joseph H. Choate and Causten Brown, Duff by ex-Judge Dittenhoefer and Aaron J. Vanderpoel. It is clear that

the judge did not entirely approve what was taking place, and that
he had sympathy for Carte and his colleagues. But it was his duty to
interpret the law as it stood. The concluding part of his delivered
opinion, as reported in the *New York Mirror* of 26th September 1885,
runs as follows:

> Both upon reason and authority, therefore, it must be held
> that by the publication of the whole opera, except the instru-
> mental parts, the authors abandoned the entire dramatic
> property in their work to the public. The right to represent it
> as a dramatic composition thereby becomes public property,
> although they still retain the sole right of multiplying copies
> of their orchestral score. If the orchestration of an opera is not
> a dramatic composition, certainly the pianoforte arrangement
> cannot be. In recording the title of Tracy's pianoforte arrange-
> ment the Librarian of Congress described it as a 'musical
> composition'. Although it had been by correct description a
> dramatic composition, the action of the Librarian would not
> be conclusive as to the character of the copyrighted work; his
> opinion as an official interpretation is entitled to respectful
> consideration. No doubt is entertained that his judgment is
> correct. While it is much to be regretted that our statutes do
> not, like the English protect the statutes, author or proprietor
> in all the uses to which literary property may be legitimately
> applied, it is not the judicial function to supply the defect.
>
> In view of these conclusions it is not necessary to consider
> whether a valid statutory copyright for the pianoforte arrange-
> ment of Tracy has been obtained, or whether there was a non-
> compliance in any particulars with the statutory requisites.
> These questions may be more properly reserved until an attempt
> is made to infringe the copyright by an unauthorised multi-
> plication of copies. Of course the defendant could not be per-
> mitted to produce the opera as though it were containing the
> orchestration of Gilbert and Sullivan. He would not be per-
> mitted, by deceptive advertisements or representations calcu-
> lated to mislead the public, to enter upon an unfair competition
> with the complainant. He does not profess to employ their
> orchestration, and the case is free from any element of actual
> fraud. The motion for an injunction is denied.

Regarding the actual authorship and rights in the orchestration
('their orchestration') the judge appears to have been somewhat
hazy. Otherwise he said enough to ensure a full house at the Fifth

Avenue Theatre on 26th September when Sullivan himself was 'in the conductor's chair'. The *Mirror* observed:

> There has been a great demand for seats, and there appears to be a disposition to make this occasion a testimonial of the esteem in which the famous composer is held by our public. The audience will partake of the brilliance of a gathering on an important first-night. A great many professional and social dignitaries will be in attendance. It will be a method of showing to Sir Arthur that the authorised Mikado is the only Mikado that possesses any attraction for the representative, right-thinking portion of the community.

From New York Sullivan went down to Philadelphia for the production of the opera at McCaull's Opera House. As had been announced in the *New York Mirror* on 25th July McCaull had the sole right to *The Mikado* in Philadelphia by arrangement with Carte. On 3rd October Sullivan gave a long interview to the same journal in which he expressed surprise that Judge Wallace had decided against Carte and his partners. Sullivan had expected a favourable decision since in Massachusetts a judge had held in respect of Gounod's · *Redemption*, and *Iolanthe*, that where these works were given other than as intended by their composers the performances were not justifiable. In the same interview Sullivan paid graceful tribute to Gilbert:

> . . . Have you noticed what an extraordinary polish there is to his versification. There is never a weak syllable or a halting foot. It is marvellous. He has a wonderful gift, too, of making rhythms, and it bothers me to death sometimes to make corresponding rhythms in music.

He also told how a troupe of Japanese girls from the 'Japanese village' in London had spent hours teaching the D'Oyly Carte Company authentic dance steps, and how Mr [Algernon] Mitford [later Lord Redesdale], sometime Secretary at the British Legation in Tokyo, had been their authority on Japanese dress. He even had in his possession 'one of the original dresses worn by the Mikado'.

By now the fame of Sullivan (and Gilbert) was as considerable in parts of Europe as it was in the United States. Already, on 25th June 1881 (a remarkably short time after the London première), the Hungarians, as token of their anglophilia, had transferred *H.M.S.*

Pinafore from the Thames to the Danube. It was played at the Népszinhás (the Folk Theatre) as *A Pannifor kapitánya*, in a translation by Jenő Rákosi. *The Mikado*, as *A mikado* (translated by Rákosi and Jenő Molnár), was given its first performance at the same theatre on 10th December 1886. *Patience, Fejő leány vagy Költőimádás* (translated by Lajos Evva and Béla J. Fái), followed almost a year later (15th November 1887). The last of the Gilbert and Sullivan pieces to go into the Népszinhás repertoire was *The Yeomen of the Guard*, *A gárdista* (translated by Evva and Imre Ukki), on 26th April 1889. It had been a long time since British music had been so warmly welcomed in that part of Europe. *The Mikado* was the rage in Holland, and it was introduced into Australia by Alfred Cellier. But its influence was felt most powerfully in Germany.

Preconceived ideas as to the nature of British humour, and British music, were violently upset in Germany as Sullivan (and Gilbert) swept imperiously across the Reich and into the Austro-Hungarian Empire. The D'Oyly Carte Company played *The Mikado* in the Wallner Theatre in Berlin from 2nd to 28th June. Performances followed in Hamburg, Leipzig, Dresden, Breslau, Vienna, Stuttgart, Karlsruhe, Baden-Baden, Strassburg, Mainz, München, Mannheim, Frankfurt (Main), Wiesbaden, Bremen, Düsseldorf, Darmstadt, Kassel, Erfurt, Braunschweig and Hannover, before the company returned to Berlin to play again through most of December and after the New Year of 1887. In the spring a second European tour was undertaken, and on 9th April the season opened at Kroll's Opera House in Berlin where *The Mikado* and *Patience* were performed. Both works were given also in Vienna, München, Leipzig and Dresden; in Breslau *The Mikado* only was given. The *Neue Musik-Zeitung* (page 150) reported 'a striking success', and on 2nd July Siegfried Ochs wrote a long article in the *Allgemeine Musik-Zeitung* on the first Berlin performance, in which he said:

> The attempt to put on a piece in English, the content of which was unknown here and which depends on fine points of dialogue, at first met with a not unreasonable doubt; and despite the first performance being brilliantly successful the house for a time stayed empty. But gradually as people had the privilege of actually seeing the production their testimony led to the fact that the Wallner Theatre is now sold out practically every day more than a week ahead. . . .
> Beneath the masque played in the Japanese town of Titipu

the libretto deals with an entirely inoffensive love story, and shows a delicious persiflage about the political and social condition of England . . .

The music, said Ochs, holds memories of the 'opera-factory' of Suppé or of Karl Millöcker, while there are traces of Auber, and Offenbach—of the 'good' one-act period.

> . . . Those numbers of a quite extraordinary richness and of a fine quality heretofore absolutely unknown in our [German] operetta are Yum-Yum's song in the second Act,[32] the 4-part madrigal which is happily modelled on Morley and Dowland,[33] and the male voice trio characterising the three high dignitaries with old-fashioned counterpoint.[34] . . . The orchestra is handled throughout with the greatest skill and discretion; it is at no time noisy—but, on the contrary, instrumental effects are contrived to the best effect (e.g. the low-lying flutes of the trio mentioned above, and the tone-painting of the Execution speech [35]) . . . A few words about the production. It is, in brief, distinguished, refined, and full of life, and we have not seen anything in any way similar for a long time.[36]

It was Hanslick's turn, among the more celebrated critics of the day, to comment on *The Mikado*. In the course of a long article he made the proper observation that:

> the success of *The Mikado* depends neither on the libretto nor the music alone, nor indeed on the combination of the two: the quite original—of its kind unique—presentation by the English performers must be taken into account . . . The music of Sir Arthur Sullivan strikes one neither by outstanding originality or genius; but, nevertheless, there are features well worthy of notice. . . . [He] shows himself in the ensemble vocal music as a composer trained in the fundamentals of [English] music. The practice of all English composers in madrigal betrays itself, and shows its fruits, in this *Singspiel*. That Sullivan is a trained singer—he began his career as a choir-boy—is also seen to advantage: the vocal parts of *The Mikado* are so intelligible and so modest in scope that powerful lungs and virtuoso techniques are almost as little needed as once was the case in Adam Hiller, Montigny, and Grétry. The orchestra subordinates itself to the voices, but not without lively effects of colour and sharp characterisation at the proper places. *The Mikado* goes

back—to the old style of operetta—it is therefore a move for the better.[37]

Hanslick remarked how *The Mikado* had made its mark not only in England but also in America and Australia and—'what was more wonderful still'—in Hamburg and Berlin. He also noted that for this type of music it had established a record by its (overall) total of 8,954 performances to date.[38]

In Kassel, where the D'Oyly Carte performances of *The Mikado* had taken place on 12th and 13th November 1886, flattery came in its sincerest form. On 26th December a parody version of this operetta entitled *Der Mizekado* was performed. Of this the librettist was Otto Ewald [39] and the composer Franz Beier.[40]

The Mikado having been thus so sensationally sent on its way, Carte held Gilbert and Sullivan to their agreement and required yet another work. This was *Ruddigore*, which Sullivan showed a disinclination to compose, whereat Gilbert was greatly displeased. Nevertheless *Ruddigore* was completed and produced on 22nd January 1887.

As usual the first night was a social occasion. Henry Labouchere, the Randolph Churchills, the Onslows and Lord Dunraven represented political interests. Churchill, who had just resigned ministerial office on account of the heavy bills being sent in by the armed forces, was given a 'mixed' reception by the 'gods'. Leighton, Millais, Whistler, Burnand, Pinero and Albani were the principal delegates for the arts, while the Lord Mayor and Lady Mayoress of London were also present.

But at first *Ruddigore* was thought to be the least successful of the operettas, and after the first performance the joint authors did some quick revision. After this it ran for 288 performances.

But Sullivan all this time had been hankering after higher things. Throughout 1886 he was much occupied with his Leeds commission, *The Golden Legend*, of which the libretto was prepared by Joseph Bennett.[41] The start was somewhat delayed by the last visit of Liszt to London, during which Sullivan, mindful of the old days in Germany, put himself at the old man's disposal. Liszt arrived in England on Saturday, 3rd April, and the boat-train from Dover was specially stopped to put him off conveniently near Alfred Littleton's home, Westwood House, at Sydenham. Littleton entertained a glittering company to dinner, including four or five ambassadors, the Counts Esterházy and Metternich, Lady Walter Scott, Sir Frederick Leighton, Sir George and Lady Grove, Sullivan, Walter Bache, Dannreuther, Goldschmidt, Hallé, Fred Spark (now Mayor of Leeds) and many others prominent in society and the arts.

As far as Sullivan was concerned this was very exciting, but it interfered with his work, as also did the Prince of Wales's command that he should set Tennyson's *Ode for the Opening of the Colonial and Indian Exhibition*. But after this he went more or less into retreat at Yorktown, near where he had lived as a child when his father was employed at Sandhurst. Even here he was not safe from pursuit. On 28th June 1886 the Duke of Cambridge noted in his diary:

> Went to Kneller Hall. There met Sir Arthur Sullivan who had come down from London in my waggonette. Heard the band in the Chapel first and then a fine and powerful band, and was very much satisfied with the whole condition of things, as was Sullivan, who said he had no sort of suggestions to offer for improvements.[42]

The Golden Legend was an enormous success at Leeds (see page 212), as also in London. At the beginning of 1887, soon after the first performance of *Ruddigore*, Sullivan went to Monte Carlo, thence to Naples (where he was taken ill), [43] and from there to Berlin. On 22nd March the King of Prussia, William I, was to celebrate his ninetieth birthday. A Gothic cantata by a British subject would, it was urged, make a fine contribution to the festivities. The Prince of Wales took the good wishes of Queen Victoria to the Emperor, and found time privately to discuss with Sullivan the propriety of the latter renting a house at Newmarket. In Berlin Sullivan pursued a vigorous social round and went to rehearse *The Golden Legend* at the Opera House with a light heart and clear conscience. His only misgivings were in respect of Pattini, the soprano soloist, whom he did not know—and who did not know the music. The performance was pretty disastrous and the music made no favourable impression.

> The performance took place on 26 March and those taking part were Stern's Choral Society,[44] the Philharmonic Orchestra, and some soloists from the opera . . .
> . . . Properly done the music would not be ungrateful to the performers, but it is not what one could have been led to expect from Sir Arthur Sullivan, in view of the fact that his comic

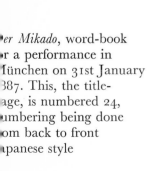

Sir William Schwenck
Gilbert, portrait by
Frank Holl, 1886

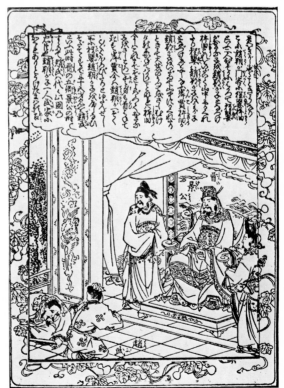

Der Mikado, word-book
for a performance in
München on 31st January
1887. This, the title-
page, is numbered 24,
numbering being done
from back to front
Japanese style

Arthur Sullivan, lithograph,
Verlag Schottlaender, Breslau

'Strange adventure' quartet
from *The Yeomen of the Guard*,
Act IV (autograph)

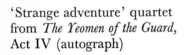

Diese Zettel werden gratis verabfolgt.

Mr. R. D'Oyly Carte's Englische Oper-Gesellschaft.

Kroll's Theater.

DER MIKADO

Japanische Burlesk-Oper in 2 Abtheilungen.

Text von
W. S. Gilbert.

Musik von
Arthur Sullivan.

Kroll's Opera House, Berlin, playbill for *Der Mikado*, 1887

Filey, August 19th 1879.

Part I

Piano Duet — Overture, "Stradella" —	*Misses Delius.*	Flotow.
Song — "How fair thou art" —	Mr. E. J. Spark.	Weidt.
Song — "Ich kenn' ein auge das so mild" —	*Miss Minnie Delius.*	Reichardt.
Piano Solo — "La bella capricciosa" —	*Miss Edith Spark.*	Hummel
Song — Three Sailor Boys —	Mr. Fred. R. Spark.	Th. Marzials.
Duet (Pinafore) — — — — — —	*Miss Spark & Mr. J. Spark.*	Sullivan.

Part II

Piano Solo — Theme Varié — —	*Miss Edith Spark.*	Mozart.
Song — "The Merman" — —	Mr. E. Spark.	Watson.
Song — "Seh on Rohtraut" —	*Miss Delius.*	Schlottmann.
Violin Solo { Cavatina — — — —	Mr. Fritz Delius	Raff.
{ Sonata — — — —		Grieg.
Song — "Sweet Spirit, hear my prayer" —	*Miss Spark*	Wallace.
Piano Duet — Fantasie Nibelungen — —	Mr. E. & Mr. J. Spark. *Miss Delius.*	J. Archer

Pinafore at Filey, 19th August 1879, and début of Frederick Delius

A performance of Romberg's *Toy Symphony*, St James's Hall, London, May 1880, arranged by Lady Folkestone in aid of the Children's Hospital, Great Ormond Street. *From left to right.* BACK ROW: John Stainer, Arthur Chappell, William Kuhe, Louis Engel, Charles Santley, Carl Rosa, Francis Burnand, August Manns, Wilhelm Ganz. 2ND ROW: Joseph Barnby, F. H. Cowen, Albert Randegger, William Cusins, Viscountess Folkestone, Julius Benedict, Hugo Daubert, Jacques Blumenthal. SEATED BELOW: Arthur Sullivan, Henry Leslie.

Leeds Festival, 1880, contemporary newspaper cartoon

'O gladsome light' from *The Golden Legend* (autograph)

The Royal English Opera House, Cambridge Circus, London, 1891

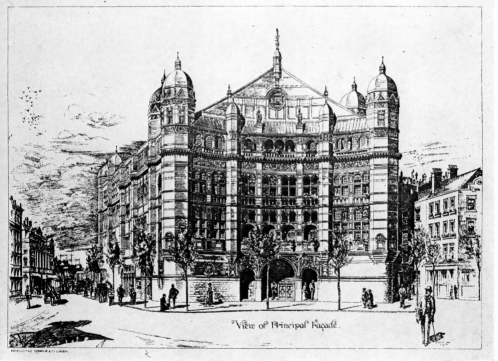

View of Principal Façade.

Friends and colleagues of Sullivan at his memorial in Victoria
Embankment Gardens, London, 10th July 1903. *From
left to right:* Sir George Power, Miss Leonora
Braham, Miss Julia Gwynne, Miss
Jessie Bond

opera, *The Mikado*, left us with the impression of a gifted and
clever composer . . . Sullivan does not here rely so much on the
example of Mendelssohn so far as melody is concerned as on
Mendelssohn's thoughtless followers; there are also some modern
influences, much filtered down, to be remarked. Comparatively
speaking the most important parts of the work are the Prologue
and the Epilogue; the three last main sections of the work are
absolutely feeble and flavourless.

So far as choir and orchestra were concerned the performance
was excellent. The best of the soloists, in voice and interpreta-
tion, were Messrs. Krolop (Lucifer) and Rothmühl (Henry).
Frau Lammert's part lay badly for her, while Miss Pattini was
so inadequate in respect of voice and musicianship that on
many occasions the performance was put in peril by her.[45]

Sullivan was not disposed to leave it at that. He telegraphed to
Antwerp and engaged Albani—who fortunately was free—to come
and save the work at a second performance. This took place on 2nd
April. The critic of the *Allgemeine Musik-Zeitung* found the music no
more agreeable on a second hearing.

> Mrs. Albani was persuaded to take over the principal female
> part, of 'Elsie', which was completely wrecked by Miss Pattini.
> Albani managed a masterly performance which brought some
> warmth of applause for herself and the composer. It was no
> advantage that this singer, who had sung German so effectively,
> as 'Elsa', in *Lohengrin*, performed this role in English. To
> have a mish-mash of languages on the concert platform is just
> as silly and tasteless as at the Opera.
> . . . A duet between Elsie and the Prince, wonderfully sung
> by Albani and Mr. Rothmühl, had to be repeated, but it is a
> movement of disquieting triviality. Nothing that follows is on a
> higher plane than a reasonable level of craftsmanship. The
> performance was not much better, and Mr. Sullivan's conduct-
> ing was uninspiring. What was good only came from the ability
> of choir and orchestra.

Sullivan, however, wrote in his diary that it was a 'very good
performance'.

Sullivan stayed a day or two longer in Berlin, during which he
was entertained by the royal family and by a regimental band
playing selections from *The Mikado*. This, indeed, was all the rage in
Germany.[46] On 31st January there had been a private performance

at Dr G. Hirth's home in München to raise funds for the Künstler-haus.[47] While in Berlin Sullivan was persuaded to supply piano accompaniment to a wax-work representation of *The Mikado*, arranged by the nobility, and for which Princess Victoria posed as Yum-Yum.

Poor Sullivan thus found himself the victim of what he considered his indiscretions wherever he went. At home he was pressed by Carte once more, and after a good deal of haggling over plot with Gilbert, he hoped that Carte might be satisfied with revivals for a period. Naturally the forthcoming Jubilee of the Queen's Coronation could not be without a *pièce d'occasion* from Sir Arthur. His commission was to set an Ode written by Tennyson. With difficulty, so far as finding the time to do it was concerned, Sullivan duly fulfilled the com-mission and then settled down to argue Gilbert out of his intention once more to revive the 'Lozenge' plot. By the autumn, when *Ruddigore* was running out of steam, Gilbert had changed his mind and *The Yeomen of the Guard* came into view. The first title suggested was *The Tower of London*; this was changed to *The Tower Warden*; at the third stage it was *The Beefeater*.

In November C. V. Stanford wrote inviting Sullivan to Cambridge in the following year. Sullivan's reply gives some indication of his frame of mind at that time. He was additionally depressed by the death of Jenny Lind Goldschmidt on 2nd November.

> Brome Hall,
> Scole,
> Norfolk,
> 15 Nov: 1887

My dear Stanford:

I should very much like to accept your kind invitation to come to Cambridge in June.

But I am unable to say definitely now whether I can come or not. I get ill and nervous, and consequently have refused to pledge myself to any public engagements a long way ahead. For this reason I have given up my beloved Philharmonic Orchestra which was the greatest musical enjoyment I had. Will it suffice now, if you express to the Committee on my behalf the greatest pleasure it would give me to accept this cordial invitation, and the desire I have to come to Cambridge—also the hope that I may fulfil this desire?

I quite agree with you about the singers. But I would strongly urge the engagement of Lloyd and *Nordica*, who sings the music to perfection.

She is not expensive.

Ever yours sincerely
Arthur Sullivan [48]

By the summer Sullivan was in better form and duly went to Cambridge to conduct a University Musical Society performance of *The Golden Legend* in the Guildhall on 12th June. The other works in the programme—conducted by Stanford—were Parry's *Blest pair of sirens* and Schubert's 'Unfinished' Symphony.

At this time Sullivan was busy with *The Yeomen*. He had begun work on this at the beginning of the year, but when he went off for his customary winter holiday in the Mediterranean he was certain that he wanted to get rid of comic opera at the earliest moment. His determination to do so was strengthened by the fact that Carl Rosa's recent exertions had apparently injected some life into the frail plant of British serious opera. Operas by Goring Thomas, Mackenzie, Stanford and Frederick Corder had lately been produced, not always entirely unsuccessfully, at Drury Lane; what they could do Sullivan considered he could do better. He had talked with Carte, and the project that was to come to disastrous fruition with *Ivanhoe* was already under review. What Gilbert's place should be remained to be seen. Before he left England Sullivan had promised to write to Gilbert, but he was dilatory in doing so. On 13th February Carte reminded him of his promise:

> ... Now, if you wish the scheme to go through, you will not delay writing to [Gilbert] at once and putting your views with that incisive clearness which is always at your command. ... Gilbert is not fully reconciled to the plan but he is I think in that frame of mind on the subject that a letter from you, such as you proposed writing would probably decide him in favour of it. But *there is not a day to lose* ...

Sullivan was restless and on 26th February he wrote to Mme Arditi:

> ... We are having very bad weather down here, continual rain for the last two or three days. Then there is the usual motley crew of gamblers, cocottes, etc. I shan't stay much longer, as I want to go over to Algiers for a week or two.

But he also wrote to Gilbert, letting him know that while comic opera could be left to Cellier (whose *Dorothy* had chalked up a box-office success at the Gaiety) there was only Sullivan to invest native music with the dignity it deserved, and needed. Gilbert was not impressed. Nothing, he said, could take the place of Gilbert and Sullivan, 'as much an institution as Westminster Abbey'. And what, he noted, was the point of letting go of the Savoy—a veritable gold-mine—for the uncertainties of a new theatre and a new company. In the meanwhile he exploded to Carte, who sent telegrams in quick succession to Sullivan, the first to the Grand Hotel du Louvres, Marseilles, the second to the Hotel de Paris, Monte Carlo.

[22 March:] Serious row with author don't really see how things are to go on You must stick to me present revival [49] artistic success but no money don't believe any other revival will be much better my chance of running present establishment seems to be to rush on new piece if this impracticable must try to let theatre answer Algiers telegram end this immediately.

[24 March:] Row made up all is peace for the moment will write do stay at Monte Carlo till I come hope to start end of next week.

Peace restored for the time being, Sullivan returned to England committed to a continuation of the *status quo*. On 8th May, however, his hardly hidden desire to write a monumental work for the theatre was revived by Queen Victoria. After a performance of *The Golden Legend* at the Albert Hall the Queen, according to Sullivan, remarked: 'You ought to write a grand opera, you would do it so well.' The nearest he got to it that year was in the provision of incidental music for *Macbeth*, for which Henry Irving asked, for his production of the play at the Lyceum Theatre in December. But by now Carte was fully committed and the foundation stone of the new 'Royal English Opera House', at Cambridge Circus, was laid by Helen D'Oyly Carte in the presence of Gilbert, Sullivan and others on 15th December. That this scheme was foolhardy in the extreme was emphasized by Bernard Shaw's reflections on the enormous wastage caused already by the inefficient use made of the three existing opera houses (excluding the Savoy)—Covent Garden, Her Majesty's and Drury Lane.[50] But Carte, dazzled it may appear by the celebrity, and per-suaded by the blandishments of Sullivan, was not to be put off. He is to be commended, if for nothing else, for the fact that his building of 'London's most beautiful theatre' helped to redeem 'what but a few years ago was one of her most unpleasant sights'.

The Yeomen of the Guard, meanwhile, had got off to a good start on 3rd October, in spite of last minute bickering between Sullivan and Gilbert. The latter asked for some cuts to be made. Sullivan finally agreed, but the demand—as it seemed to him—rankled. On 9th January 1889 he once more represented to Gilbert that he wished to compose a serious opera. 'I wished,' Sullivan noted in his diary, 'to get rid of the *strongly marked rhythm*, and *rhymed* couplets, and have words that would have a chance of developing *musical effects*. Also I wanted a voice in the *musical constructions* of the libretto.' Gilbert, it seemed, sympathized with Sullivan up to a point, but could not see why Sullivan should not be able to compose comic opera and serious opera simultaneously. He had, after all, written oratorios with one hand and Savoy pieces with the other. If he wanted a serious librettist Gilbert was not his man; he suggested Julian Sturgis. The fact that *The Mikado* was given its first performance in Salzburg on 22nd February may have been an unconscious spur to effort in the field of serious opera.

A lengthy exchange of views with Gilbert followed through into March, when Sullivan as usual sought the warmth of the south. He travelled as far as Paris with the Prince of Wales—who later went over from Cannes to visit Sullivan in Monte Carlo. Yet running through the pattern of Sullivan's high living was a *memento mori* motiv. He was a very sick man. Just at this time Vernon Blackburn met him.

> [*The Yeomen of the Guard*] was composed, as Sullivan himself told me, amid circumstances of great difficulty. He was ill, he was troubled, he was melancholy; he had taken unto himself some of the gloomy thoughts of the world; and the most famous song in the whole opera, 'I have a song to sing, O!' cost him infinite pains in the construction.[51]

Throughout this time Sullivan was followed by contention. Having been repulsed by Gilbert, he wrote to Carte. It is clear that Gilbert was aggravated by the fact that, in his view, all the credit for their joint work went to Sullivan. Sullivan, on the other hand, felt that for years he had had to submerge his own talents not only for Gilbert's sake, but at Gilbert's command. On 26th March 1889 he wrote to Carte from the Hotel Danieli, Venice.

. . . Gilbert's answer to my letter (the one I wrote to him from Monte Carlo,[52] and the contents of which I related to you afterwards) utterly ignores all my arguments and contentions, and is only a few lines of huffy resentment at one or two of my sentences . . . consequently we are no nearer a solution of the question than before. I cannot reply to it, as it is highly probable I might unwittingly say something which would again be misunderstood and raise fresh difficulties. I was in hopes that he would have met my representations in a more friendly spirit, and that he would have condescended at least to have argued any points whereon he differed from me. As he has not followed this course, I shall take no further steps . . . indeed there is nothing more I can do.

There is one point in Gilbert's letter on which I cordially agree with him. If we meet it must be as master to master, not master to servant. If, in future this could be carried out it would probably smooth many a difficulty, and remove a great deal of unnecessary friction—for *excepting during the vocal rehearsals, and the two orchestral rehearsals I am a cipher in the theatre.* Once the stage rehearsals begin . . . *Gilbert is supreme* until the fall of the curtain on the last rehearsal. . . .

With reference to *rehearsing* the piece I feel very strongly. Day after day everyone is called, and the *chorus and others hang about for a couple of hours* doing nothing whilst two people are rehearsing a long scene of dialogue. When the chorus begin they are tired, and then over and *over again goes the music in order to get an exit or a bit of business right* until the music gets sung so badly and so carelessly that it is impossible to put it right again. Gilbert *of course* has the right to call what rehearsals he likes—and anyone he likes and at any hour. This I am not questioning, my objection is that *I* am the sufferer by this kind of rehearsal that my music gets cruelly murdered. . . .

You had better bring the substance of this letter to Gilbert's notice—if he thinks all I say reasonable, there is an end of the matter. If he is disposed to meet my views in all these matters, we can see about a new piece at once.

Once more Carte acted as peace-maker, and after talking with Gilbert went over to Paris to meet Sullivan who was making a slow progress homeward. Carte then wrote to Gilbert on 24th April.

I went to Paris to see Sullivan and came back with him and after much conversation and negotiation the position is now this.

Sullivan is prepared to write with you at once another Comic Opera for the Savoy on the old lines, if you are willing also, and he says he will write to you to-day to this effect. As an inducement to this I have agreed with him that his 'Grand Opera' shall be produced at my New Theatre later on. I think this is not a bad arrangement. . . .

Sullivan says that he is ready to set to work energetically as soon as you give him the material and I do hope therefore that you will find his letter to you such that you can see your way to write in reply clinching the matter, and then that you can proceed with the New Opera forthwith.

By May Sullivan was aware of the shape of the next piece for the Savoy. Having lately been in Venice he was enchanted by the news that Gilbert had a Venetian setting in mind, which, he said, 'seemed . . . to hold out great chances of bright colour and taking music'. From August Sullivan worked with increasing intensity at *The Gondoliers*.[53] Occasional rehearsals took place at the Savoy Hotel, of which he was a director, and composition was done whenever possible at Weybridge, where Sullivan had a 'summer residence'. Interrupted in October by the Leeds Festival, where *The Golden Legend* was again performed, he thereafter went on to a more or less permanent night-shift. On 7th December *The Gondoliers* was given its première, and a brilliant one it was. Gilbert and Sullivan swopped compliments as they noted the soaring receipts at the box-office. But Sullivan was already deeply immersed in his 'grand opera'.

NOTES TO CHAPTER SEVEN

1. *See* Keefer, *Baltimore's Music*, p. 242.
2. According to Gilbert's diary there were balls at Delmonico's on 8th and 18th December, at Astor House on 11th December, and a masked ball at the Academy of Music on 5th January. On 16th December Sullivan had to hear a performance of *The long day closes* at the Mendelssohn Glee Club.
3. He was staying at 45 East 20th Street.
4. Asger Hamerik (1843–1923), a friend of Hans Christian Andersen, studied with Hans von Bülow and with Berlioz. His *Freedom Hymn* was performed at the Paris Exhibition of 1867 at which Sullivan was present. Hamerik had from time to time included songs by Sullivan in his programmes in Baltimore, e.g. *Birds in the night* at

the third Peabody Concert on 16th January 1875, and *The lost chord* at the seventh Peabody Concert on 19th April 1879.

5. *The American*, 11th January 1880.

6. This largely social club supported amateur drama and music activities. Gilbert's *Sweethearts* was in their repertoire, as also *Trial by Jury* and *H.M.S. Pinafore*, while Sullivan's songs were frequently sung.

7. *The American*, 11th January 1880.

8. Keefer, *Baltimore's Music*, p. 243.

9. 'Arthur Sullivan', in *The Fortnightly Review*, January 1901.

10. On 15th June 1882 Carte agreed to pay Gilbert and Sullivan £3,500 a year for 'sole right of public representation of all their operas . . .' for a period of five years. On the same day he contracted to pay £2,000 for the production rights of *Iolanthe* in the U.S.A. and Canada.

11. *The Lute*, *I*, No. 10, 15th October 1883. Since Joseph Bennett, a friend of Sullivan, edited this journal, this statement may be taken as authoritative.

12. *See* Henry J. Wood, *My Life of Music*, London, 1938, p. 41.

13. *Bedford and Bedfordshire Herald*, Saturday, 4th June 1881:
    Luton Cottage Hospital/ Grand Bazaar and Fancy Fair/ to be held in Whitsun Week/ at the Plait Halls, Luton/ In aid of the fund now collecting for intended new buildings on the site given by the Marquis/ of Bute, in the Dunstable Road . . ./ the Committee have very great pleasure in announcing that/ Mrs. Gerard Leigh (of Luton Hoo),/ Lady of the Manor/ has kindly consented to open the above at 2.0 p.m. on Whit-Monday, 6 June next. . . .
    And on 11th June:
    . . . the Company with Mrs. Gerard Leigh comprised Colonel Frazer, Captain the Honourable A. Walsh, Mr. H. Gerard Leigh, Mr. Arthur Sullivan, Mrs. Ronalds, Miss Ronalds, Miss E. Leigh, Miss Yznaga, Captain John Bastard, Lord Ravensworth and Mr. Hamilton Aide.
    . . . Mrs. Ronalds gratified the company by singing 'The Lost Chord', Mr. Arthur Sullivan playing the accompaniment on the pianoforte. This was well received, and a collection from a few round added 23*s*. to the funds. Mr. Arthur Sullivan liberally contributed £5.

14. Leslie Baily reads 'L.W.' (which is frequently to be found in the diaries) as 'Little Woman', meaning Mrs Ronalds (*Daily Telegraph*, 17th May 1966). But this hypothesis is disturbed by the undisguised use of 'Mrs R.'

15. Paragraph deleted in MS.

16. This is a draft of the letter, in Sullivan's hand, in the possession of Sir Charles Russell & Co.

17. Walter Smythe was Sullivan's secretary. On his death in 1897 he was replaced by Wilfred Bendall.

18. Edward J. S. Dicey (1832–1911), editor of *The Observer* from 1870 to 1889, was an authority on eastern European, South African, and Middle Eastern affairs. He was an old friend of Sullivan, entertained him in Egypt in 1882 (*see* p. 135), and was one of the executors of his Will.

19. BM. Add. MS. 44478.

20. *About Music*, p. 17.

21. Diary entry, quoted in Sullivan and Flower, *Sir Arthur Sullivan*, 1950 edn., p. 122.

22. *About Music*, p. 11.

23. On 15th March 1879, objecting to the German conductors' 'invasion', Sullivan had written to J. W. Davison:

> . . . Why do you encourage these blooming Germans so much. I think the whole business of those Franke and Richter Concerts is an insult to us. Do we require teaching how to conduct the three best known of Beethoven's Symphonies? Give me ten rehearsals and a picked orchestra of 110 musicians and I think I could give a very fair performance of any of Beethoven's Symphonies. . . . (From a letter sold at Sotheby's on 8th December 1959.)

On 19th May he returned to the theme and wrote to Hermann Klein:

> . . . In looking over the 'Sunday Times' I am greatly grieved and disappointed to read your comments on Herr Richter's appointment to the conductorship of the Birmingham Festival.
>
> I think all this musical education for the English is vain and idle, as they are not allowed the opportunity of earning their living in their own country. Foreigners are thrust in everywhere, and the press supports this injustice. If we had no men who could do the work I would say nothing—but we have . . . (Klein, *Thirty Years of Musical Life in London, 1870–1900*, London, 1903, pp. 190–1.)

24. This libretto, *The Mountebanks*, was attempted but not completed by Arthur Goring Thomas (*see* BM. Add. MS. 36739) and fully set by Alfred Cellier (Lyric Theatre, 4th January 1892).

25. Interview given by Gilbert to *New York Tribune* in August 1895, and quoted by H. Saxe Wyndham, *Sullivan*, p. 186.

26. George Lowell Tracy (1855–1921) showed remarkable musical ability as a boy and after tuition in composition in Boston was sent to London, where he became a pupil of Sullivan. Subsequently Tracy was active in Boston as teacher, composer and conductor. He was also manager of the Acorn Publishing Co. (Obituary in *Evening Transcript*, Boston 13th August 1921.)

Tracy was not the only American making transcriptions of Sullivan's music. On 15th July 1884 Sullivan wrote to Mr [J. E.] Perabo:

Allow me to express to you in writing the very great pleasure you have given me by your transcriptions of my lighter works.

They are done with the greatest musicianly feeling, and any composer whose works you might treat in a similar manner, would I should think be satisfied and delighted. Wishing you a safe journey back to America . . . (BM. Add. MS. 41628.)

Johann Ernst Perabo (1845-1920) was born in Wiesbaden, Germany, and was taken by his parents to America at the age of five. He began his musical studies then and within three years he was showing a marked predilection for the works of J. S. Bach. In his teens a group of wealthy Bostonians subscribed to send him to Leipzig where he studied with those who had taught Sullivan. On his return to America Perabo made a name for himself as a pianist. He made transcriptions of works by Rubinstein and Schumann, and of Sullivan's *Iolanthe*. Perabo shared Sullivan's enthusiasm for Schubert, and the autograph of the 'Wanderer' Fantasia in the British Museum (BM. Add. MS. 36738) was once in his possession. (Obituary in *Boston Evening Transcript*, 29th October 1920.) *See* Appendix 1, p. 285.

27. Duff and John Stetson had both visited London to obtain the American production rights in *The Mikado*. At first Duff was favoured as he had a theatre, whereas Stetson had only a short lease. But, to Sullivan's annoyance, Duff insisted on selecting the orchestral players, at the same time trying to get away with minimum terms. Carte and his colleagues would have none of this, whereupon Duff, observing that the work was 'public property', told them that he would produce the opera anyway (see *Chicago Tribune*, 14th July 1885).

28. Frederic's widow married B. C. Hutchinson at the end of 1883. The children of her first marriage were (1) Amy Sophia (*b.* 1863, *m.* Stephens), (2) Florence Louise (*b.* 1865, *m.* Stephens), (3) Edith Mary (*b.* 1866), (4) Herbert Thomas (*b.* 1868, *m.* Elena Vincent, who *m.*, secondly, P. F. R. Bashford), (5) Maude Helen (*b.* 1870, *m.* R. Lacy), (6) Frederic Richard (*b.* 1872), (7) George Arthur (*b.* 1874). Herbert Sullivan lived with his uncle after his mother's departure for the U.S.A., and became his heir.

29. Rosenfeld's *Mikado*, to Rosenfeld's chagrin and surprise, was prevented from taking place by an interlocutory injunction granted by Judge Wheeler. The ensuing civil war between American entrepreneurs is no part of the present study, but it is an entertaining story well worth the telling in its own right. For Rosenfeld's immediate discomfiture, see *New York Mirror*, 25th July 1885.

30. *Chicago Tribune*, 14th July 1885.

31. Perhaps Sullivan remembered how, in November 1872, he had once gone into the Crystal Palace to find John Taylor's exhibition of 'Views of the Yeosemite [*sic*] Valley, and other places in California' on the transept side of the Concert Room.

32. 'The sun whose rays'.
33. 'Brightly dawns our wedding day'.
34. The trio for Ko-Ko, Pooh-Bah and Pish-Tush in Act I is virtually a quodlibet.
35. 'A more humane Mikado'.
36. *Allgemeine Musik-Zeitung*, XIII, 2nd July 1886, Berlin, pp. 276–7.
37. Hanslick, 'Der Mikado von Sullivan', in *Musikalisches Skizzenbuch*, Pt. IV, *Moderne Oper*, Berlin, 1888, pp. 288–95. At the end of this article Hanslick recalls how he himself met Sullivan in the summer of 1862 in the Goldschmidts' garden, when he was watching their children play cricket. 'Take notice of him,' said Goldschmidt to Hanslick, 'he will be talked about. He is far and away the most gifted of English composers and at one blow has become famous through his *Tempest* music.'
38. cf. *Patience*, 5,160; J. Strauss's *Fledermaus*, 3,844; and Offenbach's *Orphée aux Enfers*, 3,194.
39. Ewald, a buffo tenor, had been educated at the München Academy as a painter. He was an excellent producer and had some talent for writing libretti.
40. Beier, a Berliner, succeeded Gustav Mahler as Music Director at Kassel in 1885. The MS. of *Der Mizekado* in the Library of the former Prussian State Theatre in Kassel was lost when the theatre was destroyed during the Second World War.
41. Bennett made over all rights in the libretto to Sullivan for £31 10s. (not £300 as stated by Sullivan and Flower, p. 159) on 22nd October.
42. Sheppard, *George, Duke of Cambridge*, II, p. 153.
43. Carte to Sullivan (undated letter of March 1887): '. . . I fear you have been more unwell than anyone thought . . . capital business with Ruddigore in provinces, but it is dropping right down in New York . . .'
44. The conductor of this choir at this time was Ernest Rudorff, whom Sullivan had known as a student (*see* p. 24.)
45. *Allgemeine Musik-Zeitung*, XIV, 1887, pp. 124–5.
46. On 27th October 1888, W. Bernstein was appointed to act as agent for *The Mikado* in Germany and Austro-Hungary, for a commission of 10 per cent of the profits and expenses.
47. The performance raised 1,848 Marks for the Künstlerhaus. It was conducted by Dr Marsop and produced by Arthur Gordon Weld, who also played Ko-Ko. Several English residents in München took part in the production.
48. R.C.M. MS. 4253, f. 144.
49. Of *H.M.S. Pinafore* and *The Pirates*. An attempt to vary the diet by presenting Alfred Cellier's *Mrs Jarramie's Genie* was unsuccessful.
50. *The Star*, 16th August 1889.
51. Blackburn, 'Arthur Sullivan', in *Fortnightly Review*, January 1901.

52. Sullivan wrote on 12th March and Gilbert replied a week later; both letters are published in Sullivan and Flower, *Sir Arthur Sullivan*, 1950 edn., pp. 187–8.

53. The subject was not unfamiliar, and had previously been treated by Pierre-Antoine Coppola (*Il Gondoliere di Venezia*, Florence, 1859), François Foignet (*Les Gondoliers*, Paris, 1801), and Giuseppe Biangini (*Les Gondoliers*, Paris, 1833).

8

Sullivan with Gilbert

The temptation to apportion the works of any composer to definite 'periods' is considerable: on the one hand, the exercise appears to justify the assessor; on the other, it seems to dignify the subject. To suggest that Sullivan qualifies for the full three-period treatment may seem merely factitious. But in the end it will be found that his effective composing career does indeed clearly divide into three distinct phases. The first and second were each of fourteen years' duration, the third, and last, of eleven. In the first phase, which lay between the first performance of *The Tempest* in Leipzig and the first performance of *Trial by Jury*, Sullivan sought the status of a British classical composer. In the second phase, inaugurated by *Trial by Jury* and ended by the production of *The Gondoliers*, he unexpectedly was accorded this status. He was the first composer to count as a 'national figure' since Handel. Prior to the phenomenon of the collective Beatles he was, perhaps, the only British composer ever to be granted undisputed primacy by popular acclaim. All this reached its climax during the period in which, in the general view, Sullivan and Gilbert became indissoluble. The last phase, which began with the production of *The Gondoliers*, represented Sullivan's attempt to escape from the limitations imposed by the circumstances that had brought his genius to fruition.

Sullivan's middle period, then, is that which contains the main body of what popularly is known as 'Gilbert and Sullivan'. It contains other music as well, but, apart perhaps from *The Golden Legend*, this holds no more than peripheral interest. *The Golden Legend* is left for later consideration so that it may be seen in its proper context.

Gilbert and Sullivan (in the accepted sense) opera is at least a remarkable phenomenon, of which the outstanding feature is its durability. Comedy, expressed in terms of music, must be good comedy or good music—or both—if it is to survive the vicissitudes of changing fashion. In the case of the works of Gilbert and Sullivan there are particular factors, relating to derivation on the one hand and to philosophic attitudes on the other, which will be found to have been responsible for survival. Music that has this kind of survival value becomes in the end part of an extended folk-tradition, because it conveys something of the communal subconscious. There are, however, degrees of survival capacity, which relate partly to historical circumstances, partly to inherent quality. So—to take the obvious case—the most familiar music of Beethoven is the essence of Revolutionary thought and of German feeling at a particular point in time, which also has command of the heights of purely musical perception. The music of Beethoven, therefore, satisfies different aspirations which may or may not overlap. These aspirations, indeed, often conflict, for Beethoven is at the same time the great universal composer, and the great German composer. With Sullivan the case is simpler. Indeed its simplicity makes it the more bewildering. It should have been possible for many composers to have equalled Sullivan's achievement. In truth none did, because Sullivan had certain unique qualities to which he was able to give permanence.

In his first creative phase Sullivan attempted assault on the general broad terrain of European music. He did, however, develop a lyric sense that was set on a narrower base: the best of his songs and dances were purely and recognizably English. The link between his first and second phases was his Shakespearian music. The score of *The Merry Wives of Windsor*, in particular, is a felicitous continuation of the manner of *The Tempest* music (more, in fact, than that of the more balletic *Merchant of Venice*), with more than a hint, however, of Weber in the introductory 'Moonlight' prelude.[1] This is in Sullivan's frequent tonality of E major (cf. the 'Irish' Symphony), warm with wood-wind chords and made romantic by the seductive contours of solo clarinet borrowed from his 'enchanted isle' (see page 103). Sullivan then sends a cold breeze through the night, the resilient opening sixteenth notes (semiquavers) being given within a triad of E minor, and then humanizes the fairies by a hardly disguised can-can reference. (It was a case of making fairies credible in Manchester.) In the second movement—the 'tripping entrance of fairies with Ann Page'—Sullivan uses his second *L'île enchantée* motiv noted on page 103 (wood-wind against *pizzicato* lower strings) and runs it into Ann Page's song, punctuated by a flute and oboe figure that is closely related to that of the Fairy Queen's Invocation in *Iolanthe*.

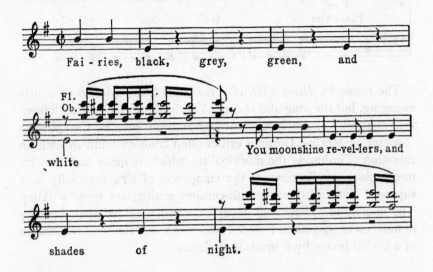

This is followed by a chorus. Another dance—a country dance in D major founded rhythmically on the motivation of the second *L'île enchantée* figure and settled on a rustic's dominant pedal—precedes the finale, a graceful, humourful dance-song with characteristics later to be applauded in the Savoy climate.

The music for *Henry VIII*, of three years later, is less consistently engaging, but the song and chorus 'Youth will needs have dalliance' is as charming as any insouciant and amorous song by Campion or Rosseter or Morley. German critics often credited Sullivan with an intention of imitating the madrigalists, which he never had; but his unconscious recollections of the composers of airs, especially in a supposed sixteenth-/seventeenth-century setting, are quite striking. The melody of 'Youth will needs have dalliance' has that elasticity of movement that stems from an immediate and intuitive realization of a verbal image by a musical analogue:

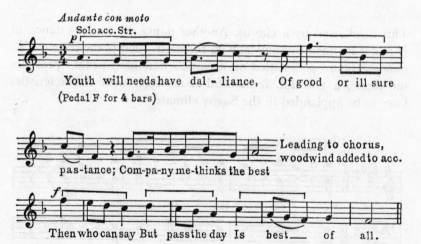

The manner in which words and music also become one under the influence of imminent projection in a theatrical setting is part of the distinctiveness of Sullivan. It is felt especially in a lyric context. The word-music and rhythm-melody amalgam, strongly diatonicized, begins to feel 'English' in a particular sense. Certainly Vaughan Williams would not have disowned 'Youth will needs have dalliance', nor (to anticipate) 'I ask not wealth' and the robust 'The wind blows cold' in *Ivanhoe*. The music for *Henry VIII* also includes an introductory March of a coarseness of which the aptness is only accidental; a charming, mannered 'Graceful Dance' that has the quality of Delibes; and some Mendelssohnian 'Water Music'. In the last piece Sullivan's concentration wandered and the music declines into an unmeritorious tune for solo cornet. Writing to Sullivan from his flagship H.M.S. *Alexander* at the end of September 1888, the Duke of Edinburgh, then Commander-in-Chief in the Mediterranean, remarked that the *Henry VIII* music was the favourite item in the repertoire of the ship's band.

'Sullivan and Shakespeare' is a topic which will one day stimulate a doctoral thesis. It is one which deserves following up for its own sake, for at crucial points in Sullivan's progress Shakespeare would seem to have been at his elbow.

This was one tradition that lay behind the Gilbert and Sullivan operas. Another was the much maligned tradition of English opera, which in its origins was also firmly interwoven with that of Shakespeare. As such, English opera never existed, but what passed for opera was resilient enough to avoid annihilation, even though it increasingly appeared as a poor relation of other forms of opera. Pragmatically, the English started with the play-with-music, and stayed with it. Ballad opera was a popularization of a convention that was, in fact, already popular; and this was developed for a purpose—a satirical purpose. *The Beggar's Opera* was satirical on two fronts, the political and institutional on the one hand, the aesthetic on the other. Ballad opera, like the similar German *Singspiel*, adapted itself to changing needs, but in nature it was the same when Thomas Sullivan played in the Surrey Theatre orchestra as it had been when John Rich discovered that it spelt prosperity. Ballad opera was more often melodramatic than dramatic, while on the other hand its lyrical properties edged near to sentimentality. The tradition, however, was one of some vitality, and both Gilbert and Sullivan drew on it—both consciously and unconsciously. Gilbert himself, for instance, acknowledged that *Ruddigore* was a caricature of 'what used to be known as Transpontine melodrama—a term signifying plays produced at the Surrey . . . and other theatres on the south-side of the Thames'.[2]

Sullivan's connection with ballad opera was indirect, caused in the first place by the way in which melodic impulses (as well as in some cases the melodies themselves) had seeped through into Victorian times. But—because Gilbert on each occasion provided Sullivan with what was in effect the text of a ballad opera—he produced settings which would have satisfied earlier compilers of works in that genre. Similarities between Gilbert and Sullivan opera and earlier ballad opera are not difficult to find.

Sullivan's melodies were simple—deceptively simple—in order to allow free passage to Gilbert's words. Selectivity in respect of rhythm and melodic intervals made for both coherence and artistic credibility. Melodies in the Sullivan style abounded long before Sullivan composed them. William Shield (1748–1829) was a skilled melodist and, whether it is Polly's 'When first I slipp'd my leading string' in *The Woodman* (the 'opera' that so much pleased Haydn) or the Sicilian girls' chorus in *The Mysteries of the Castle*, there is a pertness that is familiar within a Gilbert-Sullivan context.

Stephen Storace (1736–96), a friend of Mozart, was also at home in this field, and Anna's 'The summer heat's bestowing' from *The Doctor and the Apothecary*, a simple, beautifully shaped lyric, and the patter song 'What shall I do', from *The Pirates*, both effectively anticipate the Sullivan manner of inducing theatrical probability by the simplest and most obvious means. There are also the works of Samuel Arnold (1740–1802), whose operas are replete with melodies as direct and humourful as this song of 'enterprise of martial kind' from *New Spain, or Love in Mexico*:

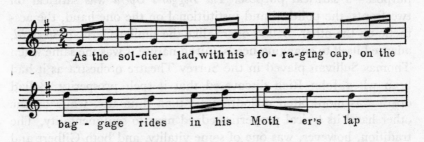

As the sol-dier lad, with his fo-ra-ging cap, on the bag-gage rides in his Moth-er's lap

Those pieces by Arnold of which the libretti were by George Colman the younger were often in a class of their own. *The Enraged Musician*, based on Hogarth's illustration, is a first-rate parody. The subject of the music lesson is exploited operatically by other, more familiar hands, but the Colman-Arnold treatment of Castruccio and his pupils Castruccina and Piccolina is thoroughly deserving of revival. Colman was no bad hand at Gilbertian versification:

> In Air, Serenata, plain song or cantata,
> French, English, Italian or Dutch,
> The sweet liquid note
> That thrills thro' her throat
> A Soul the most savage must touch.

In Castruccio's 'O cease your din', about which street-cries accumulate quodlibet-wise, Arnold puts the contrapuntal instincts aroused in an English chorister to comical use. Both Arnold and Sullivan benefited greatly from the choir-school tradition, but in directions that would not always have been thought quite seemly.

As it developed, English ballad opera made a feature of vocal ensemble. As far as Sullivan was concerned there were helpful precedents, as in the choruses of Shield. These show much variety. There are solid glees, such as 'Hark the Bugle, sylvan strains', in *The Woodman,* and light-weight musical-comedy numbers such as those that open *Marian* ('Three pretty maids') and *The Mysteries of the Castle.* In the latter work there is also a romantic Sicilian boatmen's song, with horns and clarinets behind the scenes, which could fit into a Weber score, or into *The Gondoliers.* As this example demonstrates, Shield, like Sullivan, often found it expedient not to overburden his bass singers with superfluous notes:

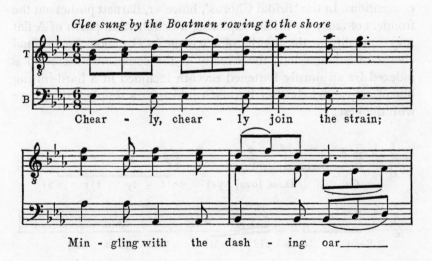

Glee sung by the Boatmen rowing to the shore

Chear - ly, chear - ly join the strain;

Min - gling with the dash - ing oar____

Shield could also manage a neat and obvious parody with a straight face, as for example in the Handelian chorus of Indians in *Omai, or A Trip round the World,* of which the words are:

> Mourn, Owhyee's fatal shore
> For Cook our great Orono is no more.

The chorus is punctuated by rests in the chorus parts, to accommodate affecting 'sackbut' chords.[3]

English operas of this period and of this kind were, perhaps, of no more than minor significance; but as footnotes to the larger and more general repertoire they make at least interesting reading. During the first part of the nineteenth century the challenge of 'grand' opera encouraged some British composers to overtax their strength. The works of Barnett, Loder, Balfe and Wallace—some German, others Italian in manner—enjoyed varying degrees of success. All, however, suffered from the same defects—of sententious plot and intractable libretto. Apart from Balfe's *The Bohemian Girl* and Wallace's *Maritana* the outstanding opera of the first half of the century was Barnett's *The Mountain Sylph*, which surprisingly ran for 100 performances. Thomas Sullivan played in the orchestra for performances of this opera at the Surrey Theatre, and there is no doubt that Arthur's attention was drawn to it by members of the composer's family. Barnett kept his ear close to German ground, and in *The Mountain Sylph* showed some knowledge of the romantic styles of Weber and Marschner, although still obliged to defer to English conventions. In the 'Bridal Chorus', however, Barnett pushes out the frontiers of fancy by briefly exploring a Schubertian patch of A flat major tonality in the middle of a scheme in G major. In the final chorus of Salamanders, the ferocity of the composer's intention is indexed by an unruly flattened seventh included in a hard-hitting line of angry melody. But Barnett could turn a simple lyrical tune with the best:

And he was quite prepared to hold up the action of the play (in the 'Contract' scene) in order to admit a straight part-song—'Now the maiden smiles and blushes'—which, in accordance with current practice, shows a marked disinclination to let the basses stray from the tonic.

While British music was undergoing one of its spasms of dedication to high ideals (exemplified by a rush to compose symphonies and operas) in Europe in general there was a trend (derived from political frustrations) towards a more direct, more popular form of expression. This was especially so in the field of operetta. During Sullivan's formative years the influence of Daniel Auber (1782–1871) and Jacques Offenbach (1819–80) was especially strong. In fact, he picked up operetta precisely at the point to which Offenbach had brought it. 'His [Offenbach's] satirical songs,' wrote Albert Wolff of the *Figaro* in 1879, 'do not, as has injudiciously been said, desecrate sacred institutions, authorities, and functions, but only make merry at the expense of those things that give themselves the appearance of sanctity.'

The invasion of the English theatre by Offenbach was intensive. *Orphée aux Enfers* was played for the first time in English at the Haymarket in 1865; *La Belle Hélène* at the Adelphi and *Barbe bleu* at the Olympic in 1866; *La Grande Duchesse de Gérolstein* at Covent Garden in 1867. By this time Metzler had started his *Opera Bouffe Series* ('for Stage or Drawing Room') and in it had already issued five operettas by Offenbach. Among them was the very popular, and tasteless, *The Blind Beggars*, which Sullivan had seen played by George du Maurier and Harold Power at Arthur Lewis's house in 1865. Offenbach's works, interspersed with those of Lecocq and Suppé and flanked by pieces of less importance by Legouix and Hervé, continued to arrive in London. In January 1875 Offenbach's *Whittington et son chat*, a tribute, Offenbach thought, to English taste, was played at the Alhambra, and it was with the same composer's *La Périchole* [4] that *Trial by Jury* was optimistically coupled two months later. Sullivan was not the man not to notice what it was that made any music function. He took over Offenbach's orchestral preferences (the resources of the theatre pit), normally scoring for double wood-wind (2nd flute doubling piccolo), two horns, two cornets, two trombones, percussion and strings. He noticed Offenbach's habits in instrumentation, such as giving greater definition to phrases in a baritone register by doubling the vocal line with violin two octaves higher.

He perceived the merits of the incisive melodies of Offenbach, and the control of particular dramatic situations which these exercised. This kind of pointillism, in *The Brigands*, is not unfamiliar in Sullivan (see the examples quoted on pages 161 and 161–2 above).

Nor, as a matter of fact, was it unfamiliar in the works of Fred Clay. As has already been suggested (see page 65), it was possible at one time that the partnership 'Gilbert and Clay' might have dominated the light-opera stage in England. Clay was not only an excellent craftsman but a composer of genuine talent. Sullivan was well aware of this talent, and also of Clay's gift for characterization. This was sometimes stated in terms which Sullivan also used, as for instance in *Ages Ago*, where Clay draws the contrast between the busy Mrs McMotherley—

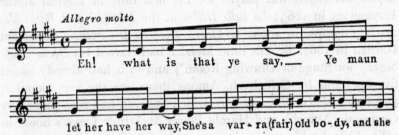

and the languid Lady Maud:

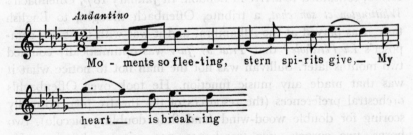

A pupil of Helmore, Clay did not forget his sterner lessons in musical deportment, and in *Out of Sight* (written in partnership with B. C. Stephenson) he introduces Pedro and the Padre ('*stealthily and from different directions*') with a brief *fugato*.[5] In this same work essential geographical information ('*A Roadside Inn, Seville*') is conveyed by a Bolero—a dance-form requisitioned by Sullivan for *The Contra-bandista*. In the end, however, Clay remained on the side-lines of operetta, the place that could have been his occupied by his friend.

Consideration of the list of Sullivan's works shows how completely he was absorbed by his partnership with Gilbert during his second period. Apart from a song for a Pinero play, the only other music he composed for the theatre was the incidental music for Irving's revival of *Macbeth* (see page 150). There was one anthem, *Who is like unto thee?* dedicated to Walter Parratt in token of his appointment as organist of St George's Chapel, Windsor. This anthem deserves passing mention at least on account of the Purcellian accentuation of the treble solo at one point, and of the illuminating character of the organ accompaniment (cf. page 78).

As well as these works there were official Odes, one Sacred Musical Drama and one cantata. The last two works were commissions for Leeds, and they had their pretensions; for they were the outcome of Sullivan's conviction that if he were allowed opportunity to cater only for the really musical, he would qualify for immortality.

The biggest of Gilbertian paradoxes is that he did become immortal (relatively speaking) through conscientious dedication to the purpose of providing ephemera for the ignorant. A secondary paradox is that, by zealously pursuing prosperity he not only achieved it, but also produced an art-form of distinctive refinement.

Sullivan's friends wished him, as he wished himself, to be a great master. He was of course a minor master, if only because he was a miniaturist. What he would have been had he stayed in Germany, or had gone into some other more symphonically or operatically congenial climate than that of England, is anyone's guess. But Sullivan was naturally disposed towards the miniature—a facet, perhaps, of his Irish temperament. Irish composers, at least in the nineteenth century, often had much talent and considerable perceptivity, but not great staying power. Field, Balfe, Wallace and Stanford exemplify the point. But Sullivan had the genius to appreciate the possibilities inherent in operetta for him, and operetta was admirably served by his inspired eclecticism.

It was this which enabled him to transmute Gilbertian situations and texts into music of such vitality that, when detached from its environment, it can still survive. It was formerly suggested that the fact that the Gilbert and Sullivan tradition continued was due to the quality of Gilbert's words. After the passage of almost a hundred years since the first Gilbert and Sullivan production, it would seem that it is the style of the libretti rather than that of the music that appears anachronistic.

On the first level of general appreciation Sullivan is approved for his tunefulness. He was indeed a master of melody and of vocal effectiveness. He was educated as a Chapel Royal chorister and, in so far as composing vocal melodies was concerned, the traditional English training—practical and realistic—paid as handsome dividends as it had in the case of notable choristers of earlier times. Sullivan was not disposed to indulge overmuch in theoretical or philosophical exposition of his views on the technique of composition. In a letter to Helmore, written just after the production of *The Gondoliers*, he did allow himself to make an observation that was more profound than usual—and even prophetic. Helmore apparently had sent him a text for consideration. In response to his old teacher Sullivan wrote:

> . . . It seems to me from the hasty glance I have been able to throw at the book, that the lines require no music—the rhythm

itself is music, and of a most beautiful character. It sounds
paradoxical, but there are times to me when the music would
be more beautiful and complete without notes. I suppose it is
that the diatonic and chromatic scales are so limited. How
often have I longed to be free of fixed intervals. More especially
in the prologue to the 'Golden Legend', I felt myself hampered
by trying to express all I wanted to say by voice and instruments of limited means, and definite interchangeable quality—
After all it is only human to be longing and striving for something more than we have got.[6]

It is indisputable that Sullivan, within his limits, is one of the
most accomplished of melodists. His limits, within the Savoy Operas,
were of course set by Gilbert, and it was in refusing to trespass on
territory which otherwise might have attracted him that Sullivan
showed his artistry. Deep passion, high tragedy, the agonies of
uncertainty—these were not within the prescription and are, therefore, not to be found. But irony, ebullience, mockery and charm—
as proposed by Gilbert—are revealed with particular insight and
sympathy. It took more than melody alone to accomplish this; but
there are at least strong indications of the finer psychological conclusions in Sullivan's lines of melody. The mark of Sullivan's melody
is spontaneity. What sounds spontaneous was not always easily
come by, as correspondence with Arthur Lawrence,[7] the exchange
of letters between Gilbert and Sullivan relating to individual songs,
and Gilbert himself, bear witness. 'You often have some old air in
your mind which prompts the metre of your songs; if anything
prompted you in this one ("I have a song to sing, O!"), hum it to
me—it may help me.' So Sullivan spoke to Gilbert when perplexed
at this point in *The Yeomen of the Guard*. Gilbert then sang 'the chantey
as [his] sailors used to sing it. I found out afterwards that it was a very
much corrupted form of an old Cornish carol'. [8] In fact one may
sympathize with Sullivan's problem in having to give a strophic
appearance to this setting while extending the melody to suit the
expanding verses. Sullivan's feeling for rhythmic flexibility, his
appreciation of the subtleties inherent in repetition of pattern, in
diminution or augmentation of note values, led to many examples
of felicitous word-setting. 'The Sun whose rays' (*Mikado*) shows an
ingenious augmentation of note values in the second part of the
melody. Richard's 'My heart sings' in the trio 'In sailing o'er life's
ocean' in *Ruddigore*, on the other hand, effectively contracts the note

values. The same passage illustrates Sullivan's happy use of a repeated fragment of melody as pendant to a phrase. This is also to be appreciated in Gama's 'P'raps if you address the lady most politely, most politely' (*Princess Ida*), where the effect is as of 3+1 or 2+2 bar-structures. These instances particularly underline the fact that in his songs for the theatre the word-setting was intimately connected with context.

Sullivan's judgment regarding the character of melody required for any given character or situation was invariably correct. He was by no means oblivious of the fact that what in this respect was obvious was generally right.

The allusive properties of particular melodic formulas is an effective means at least of registering interest. Sullivan rifled the general store to good effect. By means of the cachucha [9] he introduced an exotic flavour into *The Contrabandista* and *The Gondoliers*. The gavotte 'I am a courtier' immediately made for courtliness, or a parody of courtliness, in *The Gondoliers*. The shepherd's-pipe motiv in *Iolanthe* effectively establishes a pastoral mood.[10] A triad figure squared to a quick march readily evoked the parade-ground in Bouncer's 'Rataplan' (*Cox and Box*), Plaza Toro's 'In enterprise of martial kind' (*The Gondoliers*), and in many other places. In *Utopia Ltd* Sullivan dispenses with the triad and writes a near parody of 'Onward Christian soldiers' (with Verdi triplets thrown in for good measure) for his 'Knightsbridge nursemaids'. Sullivan certainly picked up verbal rhythms, but within his settings there was often a deeper sense of natural rhythm. Dance lay within song, often patent (as in the frequently used waltz, minuet, gavotte, march, gigue, barcarolle, hornpipe, etc.), but also often latent. *The Sorcerer* (note the 'Wand of Youth' style of minuet of Act I) shows this characteristic in both facets: in the palpable parody waltz 'Happy young heart'—which can, as parody, carry a tonic chord for eight bars on end (cf. the Finale to Act II); and in the subtle variations within the duet 'Welcome joy' between Sir Marmaduke and Lady Sargazwra (Act I). The dance instinct within vocal items reminds one of Sullivan's considerable debt to the French school; the balletic quality beneath his melodies is to be found in Offenbach and, even more, in Auber.[11]

Allusions, when clearly pointed, are one aid to memorability. Repetition is another. In melodic construction Sullivan showed the gifts of a folk-singer in two particulars: in his ready acceptance of commonplace formulas, and in a capacity for variation that seems improvised. In 'The sun whose rays' the activation of the melody springs from the spinning out of the opening gambit, *d*, *r*, *m*. Box's famous 'Lullaby' is built on a four-note figure (*d*, *r*, *m*, *s*), which is also prominent in 'In a contemplative fashion' (*The Gondoliers*), where it is felt in one form or another in almost every bar. The main relieving feature is the octave leap. (In the accompaniment there is an equivalent economy of figuration.) The same figure in minor tonality appears in 'We are warriors three' in *Princess Ida*. Here the vocal melody reverses the opening pattern of the austere instru-mental introduction which continues in quasi-ostinato manner— the whole being stern and masculine. In the Sergeant's song, 'When a fellow's not engaged in his employment' (*Pirates of Penzance*) there are two melodic germs, of which the second, a Czerny-like five-finger commonplace, is amusingly diverted to different conclusions by the chorus, who, no doubt, 'take one consideration with another'.

Sullivan's sleight-of-hand, his gentle shifts of colour to effect an environmental change, and his relation of tune to mood, make the same kind of formulas that are to be found in the more meretricious of the ballads entirely valid. The repeated notes of the Fairy Queen's 'Henceforth, Strephon cast away' (*Iolanthe*), of the 'Love-sick maidens' of *Patience*, or of 'In enterprise of martial kind', have a cumulative value in achieving different kinds of climax or anti-climax. The circulating atoms of the Lord Chancellor's 'When I went to the Bar' (*Iolanthe*), of the 'Peak-haunting Peveril' passage in the Colonel's 'If you want a receipt . . .' (*Patience*), of Point's recitative 'I've jibe and joke' (*The Yeomen of the Guard*), of 'For I'm called Little Buttercup' (*Pinafore*), and many other songs, are cumu-lative in effect; but they are also incentive to counter-thrusts which occur simultaneously at other points in the scores.

Sullivan's lucidity owed a good deal to a firm belief in the basic merits of the one-note-one-syllable principle, which often proved a stimulus to rhythmic inventiveness and diversity. The skill of Gilbert's versification often helped, and in one case that of B. C. Stephenson. At that point in *The Zoo* where Carboys begins his diagnosis of the ailing Thomas, Sullivan indulges in the disequilibrium of 2+3+1 bars for the improbable statement, 'One moment pray— I speak as a physician . . .' In the music for the entry of the crowd in the first act of *The Yeomen of the Guard* a somewhat Slavonic flavour is created by the admixture of Lydian modality, 4/4, 5/4, 3/4 metric divisions, and scoring. The tonic pedal is maintained by violas, horns and cornets, the melody carried by wood-wind in octaves. The virtues of disparate bar-lengths are frequently demonstrated, nowhere more gracefully than in the 3/4—2/4 alternations of 'Thank you gallant gondoliers' (*The Gondoliers*), or in 'In bygone days' (*Ruddigore*). In this ballad-like song, with its fluctuating stresses, Sullivan achieves a true pathos by reason of the rhythmic organization. In the trio 'I am so proud' (*The Mikado*) the varied rhythmic patterns acquire a sardonic flavour, not least because they are also set out contrapuntally. A less well-known example of Sullivan's pleasure in cross-rhythm is an entertaining collision in *The Grand Duke*:

If Sullivan knew how to handle the simplicities of melody effectively, he was also skilled in the art of aptly introducing *melisma* and *fioritura*. There are many examples (after the manner of Handel, Mozart, Storace, Donizetti or Rossini), but few so charming as the nocturnal intermission in the opening section of *The Gondoliers*, with its 'green willow' undulations (see page 175). (see page 175)

More often than not, decorations were introduced as effective gestures in the comedy of manners. There are, for instance, the Handelian flourishes of 'He is an Englishman' (*Pinafore*), the Bellini roulade at the end of Elsie's ''Tis done! I am a bride' (*The Yeomen*

of the Guard), the sentimental runs in 'A wand'ring minstrel' (*The Mikado*), which came from Italy by way of the operas of Henry Bishop. The Finale of Act I of *Ruddigore* carries the sort of cadential embellishments for 'love in merry May' that inspired German critics of the first rank with the conviction that Sullivan came straight out of the madrigalian nest. It will, however, be noted here that Sullivan tested his singing-birds somewhat. He sometimes neglected to consider the matter of comfort in singing by going to an extreme of register.

As has been suggested, Sullivan's melodic contours are in themselves communicative. The most striking examples of this occur in relation to the interval of the sixth, which Sullivan, in mind of Schumann and perhaps Wagner, often sets prominently in a reflective or sympathetic context. The classic instances are Jane's 'Silver'd is the raven hair' (*Patience*), Ko-Ko's 'On a tree by a river' (*Mikado*) and Dave Carruthers's 'When our gallant Norman foes' (*The Yeomen of the Guard*).

The fact that Sullivan's introduction to music was by way of melody (as an early student of wind-instruments and as a chorister) is evident in the operas not only because individual melodies were in themselves important, but because they stimulated collateral activity within the texture of the scores. Part of the charm of the scores lies in the manner in which vocal figures are—almost casually —reflected in, or countered by, derivative or contrasting instrumental figures. *Patience* is rich in this kind of practice. Patience reviewed her earliest love in a passage of sentiment that seems more suitable to Barrie than to Gilbert. Sullivan raised the verse to the level of poetry by an exquisite delicacy and tenderness. The musicianship in this movement is of rare quality.

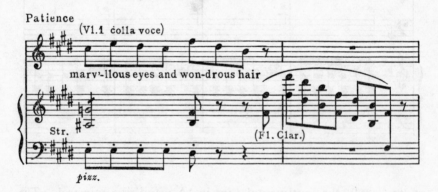

A few bars later comes this diagnosis:

Or, in the same work, there is this beautiful echoing of voice by oboe:

Once again it may be seen how Sullivan's discretion and imaginative perception bring Gilbert's figures to life. In this instance, Sullivan makes Patience credible.

It is injudicious to separate 'melody' and 'accompaniment' in vocal music of this kind: the two are one. In the operas Sullivan shows his Schubertian affinities most of all in this respect. In the act of composition he was, as has been suggested, capable of launching a melody into a particular organic life of its own. The way in which he used orchestral instruments often derived from this fact. In whatever he wrote for the medium Sullivan's technique in orchestration is assured. Within the operas it acquires a brilliance that is the more remarkable for its restraint. Sullivan recognized that he had his permanent responsibility towards the text.

To some extent Sullivan was helped towards clarity of texture by the simple fact that he was always in a hurry. His scores never have passages written out if they occur for a second time—a reference letter or number will indicate the precise detail required. The speed at which he worked (and it seems from his own comments that he spent more time proportionately on shaping melody than in constructing full scores) left its mark in a feeling of spontaneity that also inspires the orchestral parts. A moderate man, Sullivan never asked his players to do what was either uncongenial or impracticable. What the orchestral instruments contribute to a Sullivan opera is realized by most listeners, perhaps, in a negative way. That is to say, the voices are not impeded, and the story comes across. But there is more to it than this. Sullivan had a particular and individual talent for expression through quiet colour, of which a notable example is provided by the two bass drum and cymbal strokes, *pianissimo*, in the eighth bar of the Barcarolle of *Pinafore*. His skill was akin to that of the artist in aquatint or water-colour. Sullivan had something of a Biedermeier sensitivity and purpose.

We may refer to the function of the string ensemble in the operas. Always used more as in chamber music than in compositions of greater dimension, the strings elucidate rhythmic features, but always in characteristic manner. Sullivan learned a good deal from Mendelssohn's example, and the frequent habit of rapid chord repetition was Mendelssohnian. He was also liable to turn to *pizzicato* as a convenient restorative to instrumental textures. In both of the examples quoted on page 161 above, however, there is a singular, beautiful use of *pizzicato* to induce nostalgia. Sullivan's lightest and liveliest *pizzicato*, reflecting well-spent hours of Viennese recreation, is to be found in the waltz-song 'Pretty Elsa' from *The Grand Duke*.

In contrast to this is the sun-drenched arpeggio figuration for violin (against *pizzicato* chords in the lower strings) in the opening chorus of *The Gondoliers*; and the sober organ tone of sustained strings in the ensemble 'In a contemplative fashion' in the same work. In Phoebe's 'When maiden loves' (*The Yeomen of the Guard*) there is a delightful heart-flutter in the viola part, to be compared with the scoring of Rebecca's 'Lord of our chosen race' in *Ivanhoe* (see page 241).

Sullivan's treatment of wood-wind is impeccable. The *Daily Telegraph* noted this in respect of *The Yeomen of the Guard* after the first performance:

> The accompaniments in *The Yeomen of the Guard* are delightful to hear, and especially does the treatment of the woodwind compel admiring attention. Schubert himself could hardly have handled those instruments more deftly, written for them more lovingly, or made them minister so great a share of beauty to the general attractiveness of the work, over the whole of which, let us add, exquisite taste and sound musicianship throw their glamour.

The overture to this opera—one of the few to which Sullivan gave his full attention—is certainly a model of precision in instrumentation. Framed by brilliant string writing, there is a genial parade of wood-wind sonorities. At bar 27 [A] there is a clarinet solo. Four bars later the first violin line is edged by bassoon tone an octave lower. In bars 35 and 37 the chordal texture is provided by clarinets and bassoons, to which horns are admitted two bars later, while at bar 40 the flute appears. At bar 65 the crisp motiv which is to furnish the main material for the Finale of the first act is announced *pp* by the brass chorus. It then runs behind the score from bar 82, while B flat gives way to D minor, G flat major (enharmonically) to F sharp minor, and D major to B flat major, and while clarinet steers the melody towards the oboe, which is soon joined by flute. Sullivan frequently employed wood-wind tone as a midway point between string and vocal sonorities. So in 'Where I thy bride' (*The Yeomen of the Guard*) clarinet and bassoon join the refrain, the colour otherwise present being that of the muted strings. It is, perhaps, permissible to divide Sullivan's wood-wind sonorities into three groups. There is a good deal of the eighteenth century in Sullivan's attitudes. This aspect is summarized on the one hand in the 'madrigal' in *Pinafore*, with its interpolated Handelian bird-song, and on the other in the two-part counterpoint—flute, oboe, clarinet, above bassoons and *pizzicato* cellos and basses—of the introduction to Point's 'I've jibe and joke'. Such nice abstraction in musical behaviour helps to civilize the comedy. In another instance, in the barcarolle ending the first act of *The Gondoliers*, an embellishment of the melody ('When the breezes are a-blowing') by a chain of sixteenth notes (semiquavers), handled by clarinet, oboe and bassoon, induces a romantic atmosphere. This, which also covers certain degrees of pathos, is the second category into which the instrumentation of 'I hear the soft note' (*Patience*) also fits. Of this the ritornello is both index to the sentimentality of the sextet, and its antidote. Sullivan gives this ritornello in turn to clarinet and strings, and then sets it in E major as counter-subject to 'But who is this, whose god-like grace'. Here there is an enharmonic turn to the tonality of A flat, which serves to remind that the nature of the instrumental colours used was intimately connected with, and emergent from, Sullivan's often subtle harmonic scheme. So, still within the category of the romantic, the oboe is found shaping a suitably sickly tune above an indolent vocal melody and an ambiguous fluster of strings in *Patience*:

Such examples of scoring give an insight into Sullivan's wit, which in musical terms he employed with such considerable skill. The art of comic expression through music, as far as the listener is concerned, depends primarily on parody on the one hand, and incongruity in contrasts on the other. Sullivan's range in these particulars was also considerable, but he rarely if ever forgot the virtues of discretion in scoring. From *Patience* may be cited

Bunthorne's 'Am I alone', in which the contrast of wood-wind and brass is effectively shown in this manner:

> This air severe is but a mere veneer [*Woodwind*]. This cynic smile [*Brass*] is but a wile [*Brass*] of guile [*Brass—Wood-wind*].

In *The Mikado* Koko's 'shriek' is written into a rapid descent of first inversion triads for piccolo, flute and clarinet. In a famous reference to Bach, Spohr and Beethoven, in the same opera, the point of the musical quotation is made by a wood-wind frolic with a fugal incipit.

In general Sullivan enjoyed exploiting the highlights of wood-wind colour, a habit which tended to set him apart from many of his British and German contemporaries, who would have thought the private flirtation between flute and piccolo in the duet 'Here-upon we're both agreed' (*The Yeomen of the Guard*) or in 'When you find you're a broken-down critter' from *The Grand Duke* merely flippant. In the latter the orchestration at one point takes on a positively eastern European character:

Sullivan anticipated later tendencies in orchestration by using small instrumental resources. Truly, in the Savoy Operas this was a matter of necessity; but necessity proved in this instance at least a helpful godmother to invention. Sullivan orchestrated descriptively—that was in the unwritten contract agreed between him and his public—but never merely realistically. Just as the plots of the operas are several degrees removed from real issues (although also making constant observation on them), so the music avoids realism. It is indeed impressionistic in its own way, a fact which is emphasized by the frequent originality of Sullivan's harmonies. These, it should be said, are not to be seen (or heard) as having existence apart from their contextual conditions. This is saying no more than that, in absolute terms, there is neither 'good' nor 'bad' harmony; that it is environment that creates the illusion of there being the one or the other. So the alternation of tonic and dominant in 'When I went to the Bar' (*Iolanthe*) is proper to the straightforward, indeed disarming, statement by the Lord Chancellor, and particularly because there is a counterpoint of rhythms that creates its own interest. This type of harmony (cf. reference to tonic harmony on page 183) is the stuff of comic opera and is, of course, basic to Sullivan's technique. It was, however, seldom that he permitted this to become merely mechanical in the works of his middle period. The Finale of the first act of *Iolanthe* is rooted in tonic-dominant progressions, but the harmony is alert to the rhythm and the dynamics, and becomes an adjunct to percussion and wood-wind colour. The distance that Sullivan had moved within the field of comic opera is shown by an excerpt from the Finale of Act II of Auber's *Leicester*. The static bass, the repetition of fundamental chords and the character of the melody (page 183) are also to be found in Sullivan. But Sullivan would not have permitted quite such matter-of-fact behaviour—not, that is, in a middle period Savoy Opera.

Sullivan was as resourceful as he was eclectic. On occasion he walked in the cold climate of pentatonic North Britain (with McCrumbie—in 'Hech, mon!'—of *Haddon Hall*, and with *Marmion*), and he toyed with the modes which he had first heard about from Helmore. A Lydian air is heard in *The Yeomen of the Guard* (see page 173), and Sir Roderic's 'When the night wind howls' (*Ruddigore*) projects a sturdy Dorian motiv at the outset. Otherwise this piece—which Gilbert thought too serious—flashes colours in its Lisztian harmonies and brassy orchestration. Sullivan was often archly simple in harmonic contrasts. The Viennese classical switch from major to minor tended to obsess him, but sometimes he used this

to particularly charming effect—as in the Bridesmaids' chorus in
Ruddigore, where the shadow of passing time is cast by a brief patch
of E flat minor, and as in *Princess Ida*, where a G major passage of
10 bars prefaces Hilarion's 'I am a maiden'. (This latter song also
merits study for its felicitous accentuation.) Sullivan frequently used
the pedal device carelessly. Sometimes, however, he gave it a fer-
menting function, as with the inner pedal shown in the example on
page 180, or as in the last bars of the duet 'The battle's roar is over'
(*Ruddigore*), where Sullivan arrives at a state of ecstasy with a chord
of F major improbably but beautifully set on an A flat plinth. The
latter example also shows the careful organization that distinguishes
those passages which are apparently the most spontaneous. Sur-
rounding the voices hereabouts is a threefold sequence drawn from
the pervasive figure of rising fourth and descending minor third, an
agreeable adaptation of German practice. Enharmony was a conspicuous feature during the period under review. This too Sullivan
employed with discretion, rarely more delightfully than in Dr
Daly's 'The air is charged with amatory numbers' in *The Sorcerer*.

The unique contribution made by Sullivan to *comic opera* was by
way of vocal ensemble, which Gilbert fortunately made integral to
plot and Sullivan to musico-dramatic structure. Commenting on
the lack of individuality in the *characters* of the operas, Gervase

Hughes allows that it was different with the groups: 'They can,' he writes, 'all be *collectively* identified by their music.' [12]

What Sullivan achieves through his expansive ensemble and chorus writing in the Savoy Operas is an indisputable musical dignity. Without exception, German critics admired Sullivan in this genre because he appeared worthy to stand in the great British national tradition. Here his excellence lies less in any direct references back, than in an all-round flexibility. There is a world of difference between the choruses of policemen and pirates, parodies of Verdi opera, and the delicate pointing of the quartet, 'Strange adventure' (*The Yeomen of the Guard*); between the homophonic apostrophe 'Hail Poetry' (*The Pirates of Penzance*) and 'Eagle high' (*Utopia Ltd*), and the swinging pot-pourri that ends the first act of *Iolanthe*. Like Purcell, Sullivan was adaptable and pragmatic. Like Purcell he sometimes reached out to catch the outer edges of the sublime, and sometimes gratefully seized at triviality. In the union of themes in

the double chorus 'Tower warders' (the autumn motiv first sung
by the 2nd Yeoman has the attributes of a chorale) there is a strong
suggestion of Saxon and Thuringian practices of baroque days. The
Finale to *Iolanthe* is straight from Offenbach. In between there are
many subtleties of technique, as in the delicate etching of choral
accompaniment in the waltz-song 'Pretty Elsa' (page 178); in the
marvellous conversation comprised in 'In a contemplative fashion';[13]
in the cohabitation of themes in the chorus 'Welcome gentry', and
the nuptial conclusions to Act I of the same opera. The Bridesmaids'
chorus led in due course to the opening of *The Grand Duke*, where
the wedding music again rings out (literally this time) in E major.

In his Shakespearian music Sullivan worked intuitively, and his
conclusions not infrequently are authoritative in character. In *The
Grand Duke*, unexpectedly, the fragment quoted on the previous page
comes from the same region of fancy.

This is not madrigalian any more than is 'Merrily ring the
luncheon bell' (*Princess Ida*) or the lovely fa-la-la-ing at the end of
Act I of *Ruddigore*—but one can see why Ochs and Hanslick and
others who were not too well acquainted with the idiom thought
it was. In *Haddon Hall* Sullivan provides another splendid example
of a Sullivan madrigal—which is a thing by itself. Tenor members
of 'grand opera' chorus did not often have such entertainment as
Sullivan provided for them. This is the real lesson that Sullivan
learned from the choral tradition. It is possible that the words of
the last line are a fair indication of Sullivan's philosophy. At any
rate they are set with conviction.

NOTES TO CHAPTER EIGHT

1. *See* Sullivan's letter to Bennett, referred to in Chapter 6, p. 103.
2. F. A. Cellier and C. Bridgeman, *Gilbert, Sullivan, and D'Oyly Carte*, London, 1914, p. 217.
3. B. W. Findon's *Sir Arthur Sullivan: His Life and Music* (London, 1904) is based partly on conversations with Sullivan. In some particulars these limited his field of comment, but there are useful points *à propos* of music which emerge directly from first-hand contact. So: 'Sullivan's style in the main is a modernised form of

the English music of the seventeenth century. The folk-songs of the country were the direct inspiration of his ballads, and his concerted music has its paternity in the motets and madrigals of such characteristic composers as Byrd, Morley, and Gibbons. He picked up the broken skein of English traditions and skilfully adapted it to new purposes.' (Findon, *Sir Arthur Sullivan*, pp. 192–3.)

By folk-song Findon (and Sullivan) intended ballad. Hence the relevance of ballad opera.

4. *La Périchole* had been played in French at the Prince's Theatre in 1870. Carboys's attempts at suicide, and the revival of a languishing nobleman, in *The Zoo*, were borrowed from *La Périchole*.

5. cf. Sullivan's canonic writing in *The Grand Duke* 'He has insulted me' (vocal score, pp. 71–2) and 'And Ludwig will as Grand Duke reign' (vocal score, p. 74), and the fugal dance in *Victoria and Merrie England* (*see* p. 248).

6. 26th December 1889; *see* H. Saxe Wyndham, *Sullivan*, p. 208.

7. Sullivan to Lawrence: *see* Lawrence, *Sir Arthur Sullivan*, p. 225 f., and Findon, *Sir Arthur Sullivan*, p. 103 f.

8. *See* H. Saxe Wyndham, *Sullivan*, p. 204.

9. The cachucha was first popularized by Fanny Ellsler, and in England through Pauline Duvernay of *Pauline Duvernay's Cachoucha Dance* (*c.* 1837), and pieces such as C. Czerny's *Rondoletto Brilliant, Sur la dance espagnole, la Cacucha* (op. 475).

10. cf. the 'shepherd's pipe' motiv in Dr Daly's 'The air is charged with amatory numbers' (*The Sorcerer*).

11. *See*, for example, the melodies of 'Mes Chansonnes' (no. 1), 'Le secrét là' (no. 2), and the *Romance terminée en nocturne* (no. 4) in Auber's *Leicester*.

12. Gervase Hughes, *The Music of Arthur Sullivan*, London 1960, p. 143.

13. In an obituary notice (*see* p. 263) J. A. Fuller-Maitland observed of this: 'Perhaps in the whole series no single number excels in all the qualities that are described in light music so completely as the quartet, "In a contemplative manner [*sic*]", in *The Gondoliers*. The efforts of each of the singers to maintain a "tranquil frame of mind", while each is successively moved to animated outbursts of narration, are admirably reflected in the music, which consists of a set of brilliant and ingenious variations upon a sedate theme.'

9

Gilbert versus Sullivan

Sullivan's anxiety to excel in the field of 'grand opera' was only equalled by his reluctance to begin the project when it had come at least into contractual existence. The librettist for *Ivanhoe* was, as Gilbert had suggested, Julian Sturgis (1848–1904), who was responsible for the libretto of Thomas's *Nadeshda* in 1885 and who was later to provide libretti for Stanford and Mackenzie. As soon as *The Gondoliers* had settled down to what proved to be a run of 554 performances, Sullivan disappeared to Monte Carlo. His holiday was interrupted by the necessity of conferring with Sturgis. When he had done this he returned to the Continent: Brussels, Monte Carlo once more, and Milan. In Brussels he went to the Théâtre de la Monnaie to see a new opera. This was Ernest Reyer's (1823–1909) *Salammbo*—based on a *roman* by Flaubert—which had only just had its première (on 10th February 1890). Reyer's work is no masterpiece, as Sullivan, describing it as 'a feeble imitation of Wagner', recognized. It suffered from defects which were to mar Sullivan's one grand opera, being extravagant in respect of setting (in Carthage, in 240 B.C.) but devoid of dramatic force. What Sullivan did not realize was that much of the texture of the music closely resembled that of his own. The orchestral descant to, and the triplets in the melodic line, and the double pedal, of the Slaves' Chorus of Act I, and the easy thirds of the evening hymn in Act II, could well be taken for Sullivan.

When he returned to England at the end of March Sullivan, perhaps inspired by Reyer towards a greater confidence in his own capabilities, prepared to settle down to his already overdue opera (see pages 192–3). But before he could put pen to paper Gilbert, who had returned from a trip to India to discover that things had been happening during his absence, erupted.

On 22nd April Gilbert wrote to Sullivan that he was 'appalled to learn' from Carte that the preliminary expenses of *The Gondoliers* had amounted to £4,500. 'The most surprising item,' he raged, 'was

£500 for new carpets for the front of the house. . . .' Sullivan, always ready to try to extinguish conflagration, wrote gentle disagreement to his partner and then, after Gilbert had disputatiously met Carte, urged a meeting of the three of them. At the end of April, Gilbert offering the outline for a new agreement, it seemed that matters might be put right. On 3rd May Sullivan agreed that a new form of agreement would be generally beneficial, but that it should stand over 'until the necessity or desirability of writing a new piece for the Savoy Theatre should arrive—that in consequence of the great success of the "Gondoliers" this contingency [is not likely] to happen for some months'.

Two days later, Gilbert brusquely responded by stating that the time to dissolve partnership had arrived, that he was instructing Carte not to perform any of his libretti after the coming Christmas. 'In point of fact after the withdrawal of the Gondoliers, our united work will be heard in public no more,' he concluded.

At this juncture Gilbert's behaviour showed distinctly paranoiac traits, with which Sullivan was ill-equipped to deal. 'I learned accidentally,' wrote Gilbert on 12th May, 'that Miss Cameron had been playing the part of the Duchess since Monday last . . . I assume that I may take it for granted that this studied slight was not inflicted upon me with your consent or approval.' Sullivan patiently replied next day that Gilbert had apparently forgotten that the matter of Miss Cameron's substitution had been discussed and agreed. On 13th May Carte confirmed the accuracy of Sullivan's statement in a letter to him. The journalists were beginning to enjoy themselves by this time, and information of varying authenticity and partiality was diffused. *The Observer* of 11th May noted the end of the Gilbert-Sullivan collaboration 'for good and sufficient reasons'. *The Star*, which on 13th May printed a denial of a story that Carte had engaged Eugene Field of Chicago to write a libretto for the Savoy, two days later summed up the general situation as follows:

> . . . When Mr. Gilbert does quarrel with anybody they know it. It is a whole quarrel . . . Sir Arthur did not want to quarrel with Mr. Carte or any one else. He declined to quarrel with Mr. Carte. Consequently he got into a quarrel with Mr. Gilbert . . .

Meanwhile both Carte and Sullivan were concerned about their new commitment. Carte knew that a work by Sullivan would be a safe opening gambit, but the question of what should follow presented

him with the problem that had plagued promoters of English opera
since the days of Purcell. He decided to approach Frederic Cowen
(1852–1935), Sullivan's successor as conductor of the Philharmonic
Society, whose *Thorgrim* had been lately produced at Drury Lane.
On 13th May he therefore wrote to Cowen as follows:

> ... I suppose you have heard of my new English Opera enter-
> prise at the New Theatre. Would you be disposed to enter into
> an arrangement to write a grand opera or a comedy piece for
> me. I mean a serious and important work . . .

Whether Cowen would or would not be so disposed was to become
an academic question (Cowen's *Signa*, his next opera, was given its
première in Milan in 1894); but it is not true to say—as it was said
—that Carte took no steps to provide a follow-up for *Ivanhoe*.[1] But
by now Carte was having to build up his bastions of defence against
the litigious Gilbert in an atmosphere in which everybody involved
was beginning to look ridiculous. 'What a niggard Nature was,'
commented the *New York World*, 'in not making Gilbert and Sullivan
one person—a sort of "Lord High Everything Else" of comic opera!
Then they might have quarrelled as much as they pleased without
eclipsing the gaiety of nations.'[2] Carte was not feeling that humour
was in place. He was, indeed, far from his urbane self and, faced
with a writ from Gilbert, felt that Sullivan ought to prove himself
a more tenacious ally. So on 13th August he wrote a pained note:

> ... but if *you* my friend of so long standing with whom I have
> been working so long, who has advised me through this worry,
> for whose great work I have actually built my new theatre, if
> you—I say are not going to back me up thoroughly in the
> trouble—then it is hard and I feel disheartened for the first
> time and in a way that nothing else could make me. What you
> should have written to G. was that if *he* did not behave in this
> outrageous manner these troubles would not arise.

Bombarded also by Gilbert, Sullivan tried hard to pursue the
course of discretion. 'My object now,' he wrote to Gilbert on 16th
July, 'is to do nothing that will add fuel to the fire, and consequently
I hold entirely aloof from taking part in this unhappy dispute.'
Sullivan was trying to write an opera. He completed the Finale to the
first act in June, stopped for a while, and then wrote the duet between

Rebecca and the Templar, and—two weeks later—King Richard's
song in the second act.

On 20th August the case of Gilbert v. Carte, regarding the accounts
(or, rather, Carte's refusal to produce them) and the disposal of the
profits of *The Gondoliers*, came up. After a brief statement a week's
adjournment was ordered—to enable Gilbert to establish Sullivan
with Carte as joint defendant. Next day Carte wrote to his solicitor,
Frank Stanley (of Stanley, Woodhouse and Hederwick, 18 Essex
St, Strand), concerning any proof of malice that might be contained
in communications from Gilbert to Sullivan.

> . . . I understand [Gilbert's last letter to Sullivan] is very
> abusive as regards myself so much that Sir Arthur has refused
> to show it to me, but perhaps if you explained to Sir Arthur
> that it would be useful to you to see this letter as a means of
> assisting me defeating Mr. Gilbert's attempts I think he might
> let you see it even if he will not show it to me. . . .
> I have no doubt from what I have heard from Mr. Cellier
> who has seen the letter that it contains a libel, and as I presume
> it is not a privileged communication but is avowedly written
> with the intention of inducing Sir Arthur Sullivan to side
> against me, it may be important, first, that it should not be
> destroyed, and secondly that we should be able to get to see
> it. . . .

After the week's adjournment T. H. Fischer, Q.C., appearing for
Gilbert, asked for a further adjournment. His client, he explained,
had gone to Karlsbad for health reasons and it was not possible for
affidavits to be sworn there. Carte's counsel, A. G. Marten, Q.C.,
and E. C. Macnaghten who was acting for Sullivan, protested at
the delay, but Mr Justice Lawrence saw no reason to deny the
application. On 3rd September the parties met again, in the Vaca-
tion Court, and the main information to reach and to catch the
attention of the public was that over a period of eleven years each
of the partners had collected no less than £90,000. 'Human nature,'
remarked the *Musical Times*,[3] 'cannot stand such prosperity without
arriving at the point where it is prepared to make a *casus belli* out
of a carpet.' Gilbert complained that Carte had held back the
January and April accounts, and that he refused to present those due
from July. He demanded £3,000, two-thirds to be paid at once.
After discussion Carte agreed to pay £1,000 and to make up the

tardy accounts within three weeks. The judge approved, and the lawyers went home to prepare their own accounts—which took a fair slice out of the first profits of *The Gondoliers*.

On 6th September Gilbert wrote to Helen Carte (Helen Lenoir, his long-time secretary, had become Carte's second wife in 1888) regretting 'that relations which have continued on so friendly a basis for so many years should be terminated in such a manner'. But Carte, understandably, was full of resentment—as his wife pointed out in her reply. In a letter (undated) of the same period Sullivan pleaded for some sanity to be restored to the situation, which by now was virtually a national scandal:

> . . . My old personal regard for you as a friend pleads very strongly to let the past five months be blotted out of our years of friendship as if they had never been lived through,—as if the pain and suffering I (and I honestly believe you also) have endured had been only a nightmare. But I am only human and I confess frankly that I am still smarting under a sense of the unjust and ungenerous treatment that I have received at your hands . . . the scandal of last Wednesday's proceedings still vividly before me . . . Don't think me exaggerating when I tell you that I am physically and mentally ill over this wretched business.

He asked that Gilbert should put aside all thought of any further proceedings against Carte, but all he got for his pains were more abusive letters on 9th September and 14th October. The situation grew worse and worse. Sturgis came regularly to talk about the opera, to which Sullivan devoted himself more or less exclusively from the end of September. His programme until mid-December was rigorous in the extreme—he often worked twelve hours a day and at other times, according to his custom, through most of the night. On the last page of the autograph score Sullivan noted that the work was completed on 11th December.

On 1st January 1891, an amending agreement [4] was signed by which Sullivan was obliged to refund £3,000 to Carte in respect of expenses incurred by the latter in connection with the delayed delivery of the opera. The agreement went on to deal with the extinction of Sullivan's liability in the event of the opera running for a certain period, and the repayment of his indemnity if the receipts were above a stated figure. It is clear from the contractual documents that Sullivan was almost a year late in delivering his opera, a circumstance that must have borne heavily on Carte when he was wrestling with the apparently insoluble problem presented by Gilbert.

This problem continued also to beset Sullivan. On 28th January 1891, he wrote to Gilbert thanking him for 'Songs of a Savoyand' [sic] and for the 'graceful and flattering compliment' paid to him by Gilbert. 'I hope,' he added, 'you will come to the new Theatre next Saturday & hear "Ivanhoe"—I should take it much to heart if you were not present, so pray come.' But Gilbert reverted to his contentious ways in a letter written on 30th January. On the very day of the première Sullivan waved yet another olive branch and renewed his invitation. 'I decline your stalls,' replied Gilbert.

After the excitement of the production of Ivanhoe had subsided Sullivan was thrilled by a command performance of The Gondoliers in the Waterloo Chamber of Windsor Castle on 6th March. But then depression set in. The pity of Gilbert's estrangement from his partners, and theirs from him, urged Tom Chappell to offer himself as an honest broker. On 4th October Sullivan heard from him his proposal that the differences between him and Gilbert should be submitted to a third party, by whose adjudication both should abide. Sullivan wrote promptly to Gilbert urging a peace treaty, and on Wednesday 7th October he was gratified to hear from him (although he still harped back on the original casus belli) that he would call on Sullivan on the Monday following. Gilbert duly came. There was, according to Sullivan's too optimistic diary note, a 'full reconciliation'. On 14th October Sullivan wrote again to Gilbert from the Jockey Club Room, Newmarket, saying that he was 'sincerely anxious to work together again'.

But it was not immediately easy to restore the status quo. Indeed the status quo never was restored—through no fault of Sullivan's. In 1891 both men had looked to their independent interests. While Sullivan was busied with the first few glorious months of Ivanhoe Gilbert had been working on a skit on Hamlet. Entitled Rosencrantz and Guildenstern, this was produced at the Vaudeville Theatre on 3rd June. There were those who said that this was not the real Gilbert. But for the British people there was by now no 'real' Gilbert, and no 'real' Sullivan; only a bicorporate, or bicephalic, Gilbert-and-Sullivan. Sullivan next became committed to collaboration with Sydney Grundy (1848–1914), whose Haddon Hall lay somewhere in the middle region between *Ivanhoe* and the more familiar type of operetta. This was commissioned by Carte (whose father had died at the age of eighty-four on 26th November) for the Savoy.[5] For his part Gilbert was busy on pieces written in conjunction with Alfred Cellier and Grossmith. The one, *The Mountebanks* (which in the first place was attempted by Goring Thomas),[6] was produced at the Lyric Theatre on 4th January 1892—less than a week after Cellier's death; the other, *Haste to the wedding*, was played at the Criterion during the summer of that year.

At the end of 1891 Sullivan was drawn back into association with Tennyson, whose last attempt at poetic drama, *The Foresters*, was to be produced at Daly's Theatre in New York. Sullivan grumbled at Tennyson's title and undertook this task more out of regard for the aged poet than for the work, which was devoid of any kind of merit whatever. Apart from a near-Dorian tune for the opening ballad, 'The Warrior Earl of Allandale', which is sufficiently virtuous to have pleased folk-song neophytes of twenty years later, the score is one of Sullivan's lamest. Titania and her fairies for once found him resourceless in magic. In 'There is no land like England' the signature might be thought to have been that of Edward German (1862–1936). *The Foresters* was duly performed in New York and in 1893 it was given in Daly's new theatre in London.[7]

After he had finished work on *The Foresters* Sullivan went into retreat in a rented villa at Monte Carlo. He worked at *Haddon Hall*, looked through a draft script—*The Happy Valley*—from Gilbert, and then collapsed. His kidney trouble, as was predictable, recurred, and this time with greater severity. In England it was even rumoured that Sullivan was dying. But gradually he turned the corner into a slow recovery, and in the summer he was to be seen again in London. Among the pleasures of recuperation was cricket, and on sunny days he went to Lord's. In August [8] he wrote Gilbert a letter from Windsor to say

> . . . I am getting better & stronger every day, & hope to be in harness again soon—also to come down to see you at Grim's Dyke.

Gilbert now appeared at his most insensitive. Sullivan had been gravely ill and out of action for half a year, and all that seemed to concern Gilbert was the extraction of a new, and more favourable, contract from Carte. On 30th August Sullivan, who had pulled himself together so far as to concentrate all his available energy on the final sections of *Haddon Hall*, wrote:

> . . . But if you want me now to annul my agreement with Carte & consider the question of a new arrangement do please let the matter stand over for a few weeks (until after the [Leeds] Festival) as a fresh distraction in the midst of all the work I have in hand now is more than I am equal to.
>
> Pray don't think I write this in an ungracious spirit, but I am at work day & night, writing & rehearsing both for the theatre & the [Leeds] Festival, & cannot turn my thoughts to anything else.

Sullivan completed the score of *Haddon Hall* on 11th September and the first performance took place thirteen days later. Many critics were less than enthusiastic, lamenting that Grundy was not Gilbert. Bernard Shaw was an exception and his account of this opera contains a shrewd appraisal of Sullivan's particular gifts and the generous manner in which Grundy had taken them into account in making his libretto.[9] Although in the long term a relative failure, *Haddon Hall* went off with an initial run of 200 performances.

The next event in the calendar was the Leeds Festival (see page 213), after which Sullivan patiently and courteously resumed contact with Gilbert. He wrote on 20th October, offering 'a chat'. The response was sour:

> If I want a chat with you? Certainly, if *you* want one with *me*. That is to say if we both want one with each other. . . .

It is small wonder that at the beginning of November Sullivan observed that a letter which Gilbert had written to Carte, and of which Sullivan had seen a copy, made 'fresh difficulties'. Naturally Gilbert took umbrage and next day, 4th November, expressed the following conclusion:

> Having regard to the tone and purport of your last letter [& the expressions therein contained] [10] I must assume that it was written with the definite object of putting an end to the possibility of a collaboration. . . .

Characteristically, Sullivan promptly apologized to Gilbert. At the end of the month a Miss Heath tried to meet Sullivan, but apparently did not succeed. Writing of her disappointment to

Grove, she received back this character reference. Grove was now seventy-two, and the air of autumn hangs about his words:

> . . . Why didn't you say to Sullivan that you are a friend of mine? He would have been awfully nice to you. To me he is always what he was in 1863, when I first knew him—the same simple, good, gay creature that he was then. That was the second youth of my life. Everything budded and blossomed to me, and for the first time, though then forty-three, I understood, poetry, music—all the world, and Sullivan is bound up with it . . .[11]

At this juncture Sullivan betook himself once more to the Riviera, where he had rented a villa for the winter at Cappé-Roquebrune. Before he left Gilbert had presented him with an outline plot for what was to be *Utopia Limited*, and between taking the waters he turned it over in his mind. There was, in fact, not much else to do. There was nothing congenial happening in Monte Carlo so he avoided the town, preferring vicariously to live in London through the *Daily Telegraph*. One day he noticed an eye-catching item, and on 12th December he wrote to Gilbert in the spirit of renewed friendship:

> . . . I see a letter from you in the 'Telegraph' in re an old musician named Martin. What is his case, and is five pounds too much or too little for me to send you for him? In any case the fact that you are interested in him is a sufficient reason for the enclosed, so employ it as you think right. . . .
> . . . I feel better than I have felt for months—sleep well at night, and am rapidly losing that horrible nervous depression I suffered from . . .

Sullivan also wrote to Grove inviting the old man to come to Cappé-Roquebrune for Christmas, and offering to pay his first-class fare.[12]

In the middle of January it became clear that if *Utopia Limited* was to get anywhere a meeting was necessary, and Sullivan accordingly invited Gilbert to Roquebrune—giving him a full schedule of train times. The winter passed and in the spring Sullivan was required to write and direct the performance of an *Imperial March* for the opening of the Imperial Institute by the Queen. On 6th May, in response to a message from the Queen, Sullivan wrote to Edward Lloyd telling him that Her Majesty wished him to sing at a State

Concert on 18th May. In June he set about the composition of the new opera, and after completing the first act had serious misgivings about what he read in the second. He wrote to Gilbert on 1st July 1893 from Weybridge:

> . . . The part of Lady Sophy, as it is to be treated in the 2nd Act is in my opinion a blot on an otherwise brilliant picture, and to me personally, unsympathetic and distasteful. If there is to be an old or middle aged woman at all in the piece, is it necessary that she should be very old, ugly, raddled, and perhaps grotesque, and still more is it necessary that she should be seething with love and passion (requited or unrequited) and other feelings not usually associated with old age. I thought that 'Katisha' was to be the last example of that type—(a type which however cleverly drawn can never be popular with the public, as experience has taught me)—because the same point was raised then and you even modified a good many of the lines at my request. . . .
>
> I am only giving you my own personal feeling in the matter— telling you what I like and what I don't like. I like every word you have given me hitherto of the new piece, and I don't like the prospect of Lady Sophy in the 2nd Act. Furthermore, I am sure you won't take offence at my plain & outspoken opinion for I count on equally frank opinion from you on anything in my share of the work which you don't like or which doesn't fit in with your intention.
>
> Yours ever sincerely,
A.S.

This communication underlines the great difference between Gilbert and Sullivan. However bizarre his plots, Gilbert was aware of the realities of life. He was, as Sullivan suggests, ruthless in analysis; but if this is a demerit in personal relationships it is an indispensable attribute of dramatic exposition. Gilbert saw life as it was and expressed himself accordingly, whereas Sullivan preferred to see reflections in a mirror. It is to be noted as a credit mark to Gilbert at this time that he took little or no umbrage at Sullivan's criticism. He defended his conception and cleared up what he took as a misconception on Sullivan's part, but nevertheless modified his lines for Lady Sophy.

During the summer Sullivan was in excellent form and spirits. He spent the summer months at Weybridge, where from time to time he was disconcerted by the vagaries of climate. Some days it was too hot to do anything, on others it rained ceaselessly. In the temperate interludes he played tennis, tricycled, rowed on the river or went to race-meetings at Kempton Park. It was a summer made otherwise memorable by the marriage of the Duke of York (the future King George V) to Princess Mary of Teck (it had been intended to marry her to the Duke of Clarence, who had died, however, during the previous year). On the night of the wedding, July 6th, forty-eight royal personages dined at Marlborough House, and after dinner they mounted a specially erected stand in the garden which enabled them to watch the crowds in Pall Mall who were entertained by the illuminations. Sullivan's particular friend among the royals had this year relinquished his British title in order to succeed to the Duchy of Saxe-Coburg—the Order of which Duchy was in due course bestowed on Sullivan. When *Utopia Limited* burst on the public on 7th October the fact that a royal 'Drawing Room' was held up for ridicule by Gilbert did not go down well either with some of those who had looked out on the world from behind the wall of Marlborough House in July, or with some critics. Nevertheless *Utopia Limited* enjoyed a run of 245 performances, and the music was highly praised by Bernard Shaw.

Carte was a shrewd man and recognized that the post-quarrel Gilbert-and-Sullivan partnership was not the power that it had formerly been. The old pieces, up to *The Gondoliers*, were classics; but the new pieces did not look like being admitted to the same rank. The public, Carte correctly opined, wanted something new. He indicated that cheaper productions (*Utopia Limited* had cost a fortune to produce) of slighter subjects could very well be reasonably profitable.

Gilbert and Sullivan discussed the possibility of a new piece, but neither was enthusiastic. Enjoying an income of £20,000 a year, Sullivan was inclined to take life more easily. He had his many interests and friends, and in any case his health was far from robust. Gilbert was tired, and his output was in process of rapid decline both in quantity and quality. Sullivan went over to Belfast (where *Utopia* was being played) and on 1st April 1894 Gilbert wrote to him:

> . . . By the time you return April will be half through—to the first July will be [two months & a half] [13] about ten weeks. Now it will take *at least* six weeks to rehearse the piece *which*

will leave only four weeks in which to write the libretto & compose the music [I feel sure that I couldn't write the libretto in that time & I feel equally sure that, if I did you couldn't write & score the music in time for production before the season was quite over.] [13] However we can discuss this when we meet.

Convenu about the other author.[14] One librettist is as good as another, if not better moreover. This is the last libretto I shall ever write & it matters nothing to me who is to succeed me.

Yrs [illegible]

W. S. Gilbert.

The situation was an uneasy one and not improved by a statement issued by Gilbert on 19th April to the *Sheffield Daily Telegraph*, in rebuttal of a report that had been published in that paper to the effect that the dispute between Gilbert and Sullivan had been caused by a difference of opinion in respect of the casting in *The Mikado*. He insisted instead that the source of friction had been the 'unreasonable and inadequate' contractual conditions that Sullivan imposed before agreeing to compose the music for a new libretto.

In due course this matter was cleared up in so far as the new piece, *The Grand Duke*, was concerned, but it was clear that there was not much of a future for the uneasily reassembled partnership. However, life had its bright side. Among the dinner parties which Sullivan attended at that time one in particular stood out. This was given by Hermann Klein at his flat on 3rd May, and Barnby, Mackenzie, Garcia, Piatti and Sullivan were invited to meet Paderewski, who by now had firmly established himself in the affections of the English. Concerning this evening Paderewski expressed himself to Klein in these terms:

> . . . Inutile de vous dire que je serai absolument enchanté de passer une soirée chez vous, avec vous, et de rencontrer Sir Sullivan [*sic*], que j'admire beaucoup.[15]

At the end of that month the Curtis Publishing Company of Philadelphia paid £100 for the right to print *Bid me at least goodbye* in *The Ladies Home Journal* for a period of three months. Otherwise the main occupation of the season was horse-racing, and the profit on the sale of American serial rights in *Bid me at least goodbye* (an apt title to the situation) almost exactly balanced the loss incurred on the buying and selling of Blue Mark. This animal, which had performed well for Mr J. Lowe and also for Capt. J. Orr-Ewing at Salisbury and Newmarket at the beginning of the 1894 season, beat Sullivan's Cranmer into second place in a Selling Plate on 10th October. This convinced Sullivan that Blue Mark was the horse he had been looking for. But when ridden under his colours of pink, with violet belt and cap, the filly showed a disinclination to hurry and won no races for her owner. In November Blue Mark was representing Sir John Blundell Maple, the shop-keeper—but no more successfully than she had represented Sullivan.[16]

In the course of the summer, during which Carte put on Messager's *Mirette*, Sullivan discussed the possibility of a renovated *Contrabandista*. Revised, and with some additional numbers, and entitled *The Chieftain*, this had a brief run at the end of the year, when Sullivan became involved in another commission for incidental music. This was for Comyns Carr's *King Arthur*, written for Irving to produce at the Lyceum Theatre, and for which the scenery and costumes were being designed by Burne-Jones. Comyns Carr, a half-Irish barrister turned free-lance writer, and currently art critic of the *Pall Mall Gazette*, was a friend of most people, including Burne-Jones, Rossetti, Millais and Sullivan.

King Arthur was produced on 12th January with Irving in the title part, Lena Ashwell as Elaine and Ellen Terry as Guinevere, and with Burne-Jones's 'exquisite design for armour and dresses, as well as the scenery'.[17] Meanwhile Sullivan discovered that despite his additions and alterations *The Chieftain* was being increasingly regarded as an error of judgment. Always anxious to preserve what he could from disaster, Sullivan turned his attention to *Ivanhoe* and gave the rights of stage performance in Britain to the Carl Rosa Company—but to no avail.[18] On 28th June 1895 he signed up with the Alhambra Company to 'supply' ballet music for the Diamond Jubilee planned for 1897, and a few weeks later he responded to the new libretto which Gilbert had sent to him. This letter was sent from Walton-on-Thames on 11th August.

> . . . How would it do to make Lisa the *principal* Soprano part, and make Elsa the contralto. She might be the leading tragedy lady of Ludwig's troupe, and contralto of the Operatic company—not necessarily old, but (if played by Brandram), staid and earnest, a suitable wife for the manager, and from whose mouth the theatrically high flown sentiments from romantic plays would come very forcibly, especially as they would be uttered in rich contralto register. Then see what an advantage

this will be to me. In all the concerted music there would be a soprano and contralto, instead of two sopranos, and where Countess Krakenfeld is the only female in concerted pieces we shall have the immense advantage of having a soprano and not a contralto at the top, getting plenty of brightness . . .

The Grand Duke was produced for the first time on 7th March 1896, five days after the première of Stanford's Shamus O'Brien. This comedy piece went down well and, coming when it did, helped to queer the pitch of the Savoy team. The Grand Duke, which had 123 performances only, was the last collaboration of Gilbert and Sullivan. So far as the public was concerned the old magic had gone. The partners were unbeatable on their native ground, but were entitled to no propriet-ary rights in Ruritania. During the summer the opera was given a performance at the Unter den Linden theatre in Berlin, after which it was shelved. The world in general turned back with relief to works of the old, pre-carpet-quarrel dispensation. On the last day of October The Mikado was performed in London for the thousandth time, and D'Oyly Carte presented each member of the audience with a fan-shaped programme.

NOTES TO CHAPTER NINE

1. See, for example, Hermann Klein, The Golden Age of Opera, London, 1933, pp. 167–8. Regarding Carte's efforts in general to provide a repertoire for his new theatre, see pp. 236–70.
2. Quoted in Musical Times, 31st July 1890, p. 605.
3. Musical Times, 31st October 1890, p. 594.
4. In the Agreement of 'even date' Sullivan agreed 'to deliver the said Opera complete . . . in such time as to enable the said Richard D'Oyly Carte to produce it at his new Theatre not later than tenth January 1891 . . .'
5. Carte anticipated another Grundy-Sullivan piece, and on 15th February 1892 Sullivan agreed to compose another comic opera to be put on after The Vicar of Bray (Grundy and Edward Solomon).
6. BM. Add. MS. 36739, ff. 172–180.
7. See Musical Times, 34, November 1893, p. 663.
8. Undated.
9. The World, 28th September 1892.
10. Deleted in MS.
11. Graves, Life of Grove, pp. 391–2.

12. *Ibid.*
13. Deleted in MS.
14. Probably Sydney Grundy, with whom a work (*The Vicar of Bray*) had been tentatively discussed.
15. Klein, *Golden Age of Opera*, p. 300.
16. For full details of Sullivan's career as race-horse owner, *see* Appendix 2.
17. Alice Comyns Carr, *J. Comyns Carr, Stray Memories, by his Wife*, London 1920, p. 87.
18. The contract was signed on 1st January. In the first place the arrangement was to be operative for one year, which, however, could be extended. For each performance £15 was due to the composer, but if there were three performances in any one town, then only £5 should be due on the third performance. By all his accustomed standards this, of course, was chicken-feed to Sullivan. This is where he might have ended had he virtuously followed the path of 'serious music' throughout his life.

10

Festival Director at Leeds

Sullivan's connection with Leeds began on 12th December 1877, when the Festival Committee resolved that he should be invited to compose an oratorio for the 1880 Festival. The fee was to be 100 guineas, inclusive of the composer's expenses for travelling and for the supplying of choral and orchestral parts. On 2nd January 1878, Frederick Spark wrote to Sullivan informing him of the committee's resolution. An acknowledgment of the receipt of this letter, on Sullivan's behalf, by Markham Law, his assistant, together with the information that Sullivan was abroad, was not satisfactory to Spark, who sent further letters in pursuit of the composer. On 12th March Sullivan replied, showing signs of the hypochondriac tendencies that were to increase as the years went by:

> . . . When I first received your letter at Nice, I was so ill & worn out that I at once wrote declining the offer of the Leeds Festival. But upon consideration, I thought it would be wise to keep it back a short time, in case I might get better & stronger.
>
> I was constantly ill at Nice, consequently the letter was never sent. . . .
>
> I should not be unwilling to write a work of the same length & character as the 'Prodigal Son'.

The work, he said, would be long enough for half a concert. A month later he was firmly commissioned to write an oratorio on the subject of *David and Jonathan*. In Leeds they liked to know exactly what they were going to get for their money.

A Music Festival in England in the nineteenth century, as it had been in the eighteenth, was undertaken primarily to finance the health services. The Home of Recovery—or Fever Hospital—in Leeds, founded in 1802, moved into a new building in 1846. Seven years later a Hospital for Women and Children was founded in the city. In 1867 the Public Dispensary (1824) moved into new premises, and

203

a year later those of the century-old General Infirmary were replaced by a vast building designed by Sir Giles Gilbert Scott. When the General Infirmary had been founded its first costs were recovered by means of Handelian oratorio. Nineteenth-century expansion of hospital amenities, and a consideration of the requirements of the dignity of a rapidly growing town, encouraged the institution of a Triennial Musical Festival.

The power behind this enterprise was Frederick Robert Spark (1831–1919), the very embodiment of Victorian man. The third son of a lay-vicar at Exeter Cathedral and himself a chorister in the cathedral under S. S. Wesley, Spark moved to Leeds in the wake of his eldest brother William. William Spark (1823–97), an articled pupil of Wesley, accompanied his master north when Wesley was appointed organist of Leeds Parish Church. William became a leading professional in the field of music in Yorkshire; Frederick on the other hand, having served his time in another trade, remained an amateur. He became editor and manager of the *Leeds Express*, and in 1875 was elected to the Town Council as a Liberal. Nine years later he became an alderman, and in 1886 served as Mayor. There was very little that happened in Leeds without Fred Spark's being involved, and as a man of substance—he was President of the Building Society among other offices—his influence was irresistible. Spark was tough, and blunt. And, in the way of so many northern Englishmen of his time, he was cultured. He belonged to a musical family (his sister, Mrs Fanny Frazer Foster, was a well-known singing-teacher in Boston, U.S.A.) [1] and his own interest in the art was profound. His musical 'at homes' at 29 Hyde Terrace were a feature of the social and musical life of Leeds,[2] and he was Honorary Secretary of the Musical Festival from its inception for fifty years.

The first Festival was directed by Sterndale Bennett, himself a Yorkshireman. Because of local in-fighting among the musicians there was no further festival until 1874, when Costa was appointed conductor. Costa was re-engaged for 1877, but his request that the dates should be adjusted to suit his annual thermal-bath-taking brought him into the early stages of disfavour with the Committee. He also annoyed the progressives by refusing to perform Beethoven's Choral Symphony and Bach's Mass in B Minor. The Festival, however, was a financial success. At the 'People's Festival Concert' on the Saturday night, the most popular items were by Sullivan: *The lost chord*, sung by Mrs Mudie-Bolingbroke, with organ obbligato by Dr W. Spark; *Thou'rt passing hence, my brother*, sung by Santley; and *Sweethearts*, sung by Edward Lloyd.

The works of Sullivan were, indeed, familiar all over Yorkshire. An interesting sidelight on English music is provided by the programme of a concert given in Filey on 17th August 1879 (see illustration between pages 146 and 147) in which Sullivan was represented by selections from *H.M.S. Pinafore*, and in which Mr Fritz Delius and his sister, of Bradford, took part. Mr Delius was an amateur, just out of school, and about to commence a short-lived career in the wool trade.

Meanwhile Sullivan was busy with his 'sacred drama'. Uneasy at the thought of the probable comparison with Handel if he stayed with his original subject of *David and Jonathan*, he had switched to that of *The Martyr of Antioch*. Gilbert had doctored a poem by Dean Milman to provide a by-no-means unpromising libretto. As 1879 wore on the Leeds Committee were concerned that the 1880 Festival might never take place. There was something of a trade recession and there was a General Election [3] in the offing. When Sullivan was consulted he observed that since he was going to be in the United States, the extra time afforded by a postponement would be convenient to him in so far as completion of *The Martyr* was concerned. In the end, however, it was decided to go ahead. But the Committee had other worries. When the matter of conductor for the Festival was raised the anti-Costa lobby was loud in denunciation of Costa's most recent evidence of arrogance. He insisted that he should have the decisive voice in the selection of music, singers and players, which the Committee considered its prerogative. The consequence was that when Costa was proposed, another faction nominated Charles Hallé, and a third group put forward the name of Sullivan.

Discussions concerning the conductor for the 1880 Festival came to their critical point when Sullivan was being lionized in the United States. Hallé took reasonable offence during the negotiations with him when Spark wrote on 12th December 1879 saying: 'The opinion is also held that your usual Manchester band is not sufficiently good for a Leeds Festival.' Costa—who had received eight votes to Sullivan's six in a second ballot—peremptorily refused to have any more to do with Leeds when he was further contacted. That left Sullivan who, in the eyes of some, was somewhat young for the responsibilities of the Leeds Festival. However, he was alerted to an invitation in transit by a telegram sent on 8th January

1880, to 'Arthur Sullivan, musician, New York'. A letter followed two days later, and on 13th January Sullivan responded with a conditional acceptance. On 28th January, back from Baltimore, he sent a longer letter written from the New York Club. Sullivan wanted what Costa wanted—artistic control of the Festival. He was, however, more tactful in his approaches.

On 5th June 1880, Sullivan was introduced to the choristers before his first rehearsal. There were new works by Barnett and Macfarren (which their composers would conduct), Handel's *Samson* (for which Ebenezer Prout had specially written additional accompaniments), and Beethoven's Mass in C and Choral Symphony to rehearse. But what was particularly looked forward to was Sullivan's new work. On 31st August Sullivan returned to Leeds to take his second rehearsal, the chorus in the meantime having been prepared by their regular chorus-master, James Broughton. On this occasion he took 'his talented pupil' Eugene D'Albert to play the accompaniments on the piano.[4] The first thing Sullivan did was to ensure the interest of his singers by giving them an outline of the narrative of his work. Costa had never done this, and the choristers were delighted. The choristers otherwise approved his practical sense. Where the sopranos were faced with sustained high notes in the Choral Symphony, Sullivan rested them alternately in groups to ensure continued freshness of tone and steady intonation. The authorities of Leeds most of all congratulated themselves on their selection of conductor because Sullivan, without much difficulty, had persuaded the Duke of Edinburgh to undertake the Presidency of the Festival.

At the morning concert on 15th October *The Martyr* went splendidly, and '. . . the Duke of Edinburgh sent for Mr. Sullivan at the conclusion and congratulated him upon the success the piece had attained at the hands, perhaps, of one of the most critical audiences to be found'.[5]

At the evening concert on the same day as the première Sullivan conducted the 'Dance of nymphs and reapers' from *The Tempest*. Other works performed during the Festival included Weelkes's *As Vesta was from Latmos Hill descending*, Schubert's *Song of Miriam* and Bach's *O light everlasting*.

On 20th October Sullivan wrote to Frederick Spark from Albert Mansions '. . . to thank you personally for your unvarying kindness to me & your unceasing efforts to make my somewhat difficult path a smooth one . . .'[6] Five days later he sent a donation of £25 to the charities.

Being Conductor of the Leeds Festival was no sinecure. Although there was no security of tenure, the conductor being chosen for one Festival only, it was expected that he should be available for consultation for the period following his appointment and until his re-election or dismissal. At the beginning of 1881 Sullivan's advice was sought about the commissioning of a new oratorio. On 10th March he gave it as his opinion that 'Macfarren was the only Englishman whom it would be "safe" to ask', but he suggested that approaches should be made to Verdi. At the end of the year, therefore, Sullivan wrote to Verdi enclosing an official letter from Spark. No reply being received, a second communication was sent. On 22nd February Verdi, noting that the first letter seemed to have miscarried, replied. Writing in French he excused himself from undertaking the commission on the grounds that he had now given up composition. This, indeed, he thought he had done, and had announced his intention of resignation to his friends. Disappointed at not managing to obtain a work from Verdi, the Leeds Committee put it to Sullivan that he should write a symphony. Sullivan did not immediately give an answer; but when he was pressed for one during 1882 said that as he had had his chance he hoped the Committee would secure another Englishman. He proposed Fred Clay, who for months blew hot and cold over a projected setting of Byron's *Sardanapalus* and then decided that he could not produce it as he required more resources in the way of soloists than would be available at Leeds. On Sullivan's recommendation Arthur Cellier's setting of Gray's *Elegy* took the place reserved for a principal secular work.

Before the 1880 Festival Sullivan had asked that the orchestra should be increased from 121 to 133 players, but the Committee had turned down this request. At the beginning of 1883 he suggested that the pitch of the organ—built by Gray and Davidson—should be raised to accommodate the wood-wind players who had difficulty in tuning down. The Committee sent a deputation to the 'Corporate Property Committee', which decided that if the organ were merely cleaned the desired result might be achieved at minimal cost. It was a matter of priorities; and this year, for the first time, the Victoria Hall was to be lit by electricity.

This was altogether a remarkable Festival. On 6th October the Mayor, Edwin Woodhouse, gave a dinner in the Town Hall for the

Committee of the Festival and for other notabilities to meet Sir Arthur—as he now was. Those who met at the Town Hall that evening spoke of little else than the latest wonders of the scientific age and the enterprise of the National Telephone Company, which had offered its subscribers a unique opportunity, so that

> . . . by means of that most wonderful of modern inventions, the telephone, the magnificent chorus of the Victoria Hall will be listened to this morning by auditors who are removed by many miles from the building. . . . Who would have dreamt nine years ago that any one stationed in Bradford or Wakefield would be able in 1883 to hear the actual singing of the chorus in the Leeds Town Hall? [7]

Once again the Festival enjoyed royal patronage, Sullivan on behalf of the Committee having spoken with the Duke and Duchess of Albany, whose consideration in travelling through the town in an open carriage in inclement weather was much commended.

The chief modern work of the Festival was Joachim Raff's *The End of the World*, to which there was added the melancholy interest of the composer's having died between fulfilment of the commission and performance. The audience were pleased to see Joseph Barnby —a local boy who had done well for himself in the south—on the rostrum. His original contribution was no more than a brief anthem, but his vigour in conducting was approved by some who thought Sir Arthur a deal too restrained. Having heard of such unfavourable comparisons, Sullivan demonstrated his awareness by briefly 'beating time like a windmill'. 'By gow,' someone said, 'Sullivan *has* improved.'

With no new work of his own written for the Festival, Sullivan put 'How sweet the moonlight sleeps', from *Kenilworth*, 'King Henry's Song', from *Henry VIII*, and *In Memoriam* into the programme. The renascence of interest in the English madrigal school was recognized in the performance of Wilbye's *The Lady Oriana*, while the force of the Bach movement was responsible for the first English performance of *Thou guide of Israel*. The most notable achievement, however, was the *Missa Solemnis*, which was described as the best performance of this work ever to have taken place in England. In writing to Spark on 18th October Sullivan said of the Festival that, even if the receipts were down,[8] 'taking it all round, it is the greatest and most sublime music meeting that has ever been held'.[9]

Hardly was the Festival over before preparations for the next began, and on 25th March 1884 it was agreed that Antonin Dvořák would compose a major work for 1886. It was also hoped that Sullivan would provide a work, preferably for orchestra. Once again he showed a reluctance that is, perhaps, surprising in view of his ever-present desire to compose serious music. He was, however, prepared to 'do a short choral work', and at the end of December accepted the commission for a cantata which was to last for approximately an hour. This work cost him much trouble and as in the case of *The Martyr of Antioch* he displayed an uncertainty that was in marked contrast to his Savoy undertakings. A year after he had agreed to write a work he had to write to Spark:

> I wish I *could* tell you the name of my new work. I have three subjects now under consideration, but have settled nothing.

Two months later, however, at the beginning of February 1886, a newspaper published the news that Sullivan's new Leeds piece was to be *The Golden Legend*. The Leeds Committee was angry with Sullivan, and he with whomever in his retinue had leaked the information. He sent a telegram to Leeds:

> Have been working at 'Golden Legend' some time. Just got it satisfactory, I think, but cannot yet give authority to announce it. Some injudicious friend has been chattering. Will write.

On 3rd February he did write to Spark, apologizing for the apparent breach of protocol. He also added a note concerning a curious coincidence:

> Today I have received a letter from Dr. [William] Creser [organist of Leeds Parish Church], who, it seems, has written a work on the same subject. Of course I cannot give mine up, as my musical ideas are already on the road; but I am very sorry to clash with any fellow musician.[10]

In July Sullivan reported from Godolphin House, Newmarket, that he was working hard, but he added: 'I am very tired and seedy, & feel really over-worked for the first time for some years.' [11] On 24th August, however, he was able to say that the work was finished.

Earlier in the year Sullivan had been much exercised in mind over the Festival programme as a whole. The Committee had at first intended to include a symphony by Brahms, Mendelssohn's *A Midsummer Night's Dream* music, the 'Jupiter' Symphony, and a 'selection' from *Die Walküre* in place of the previously intended Choral Symphony. On 27th February Sullivan suggested excising the symphony and substituting a suite or overture by Brahms, and exchanging *A Midsummer Night's Dream* for, say, the 'Scotch' Symphony. '. . . I yield to no one in my admiration of the Jupiter Symphony,' he added, '[but] it is hardly of the character to suit an orchestra of such grandeur as that of the Leeds Festival.'

In March a revised draft was submitted to Sullivan by the Honorary Secretary in person. Finding the 'Jupiter' still down for performance, he spoke again on the inadvisability of playing the work with an orchestra as massive as that used at Leeds, asking whether a 'selection from one of Mozart's operas' could not be put in its place. The Committee agreed with his suggestions and approved his choice of *Idomeneo*. At the final programme-conference Sullivan quietly got his own back for the Committee's refusal to allow him extra players six years before. 'I presume,' he said, 'the committee have not lost sight of the fact that the performance of any part of "Die Walküre" will entail an additional cost of about 100 guineas for extra instruments.' The Committee had lost sight of the fact, and took grateful note of their conductor's advice.

During the preparation for this Festival James Broughton gave up being chorus-master, feeling that his health would not stand the strain. He was succeeded by his brother, Alfred, hitherto the rehearsal pianist. It was, indeed, a testing time for the chorus. In addition to Sullivan's new work there were Dvořák's *St Ludmilla*, Stanford's *Revenge*, Mackenzie's *Story of Sayid*, *Israel in Egypt*, and the Mass in B Minor, not to mention *Elijah*. Stanford's work had not been ordered but submitted on the composer's behalf by a friend. So far as the Bach Mass was concerned its inclusion had been determined at a Committee Meeting in these terms: '. . . the claims of Bach's Mass in B Minor were held superior to those of Cherubini's in D, which was accordingly struck out.' Sullivan was not particularly pleased at being presented with a *fait accompli*, and on 18th June he wrote to Otto Goldschmidt from Yorktown, Farnborough:

> . . . the Leeds Committee brought their choral parts & scores & began to rehearse [the Mass] before I knew anything of the matter. I learnt it only when I sent to Novellos to enquire about your edition—then they told me that they had already sent the

German Edition to Leeds. This means of course that I must now produce the work on my own responsibility. . . .

On 19th July he wrote again to Goldschmidt:

. . . I have now resolved to do the Mass in its *natural state*, with the three trumpets & extra oboes & flutes, & *No cuts*. The only thing I shall do is to put in a few p's & f's according to the character of the words . . . They [the Leeds choir] sing it with the precision of keyed instruments & the body of the tone is superb. I hope you will come and hear it.

The programme for the 1886 Festival, referring to the Mass, noted that 'the organ part [was] arranged by Mr. Frederic Cliffe [12] under Sir Arthur Sullivan's personal supervision', and that the 'trumpets [were] made for this Festival on the old German model'. This recourse to musicology in order to re-create an authentic tone-colour led Sullivan a few years later to have special trumpets constructed for the Heralds in *Ivanhoe*. Such details in the consideration of referential effect were, *mutatis mutandis*, also endemic in the painterly methods of the Pre-Raphaelites.

During the time of the 1886 Festival Sullivan, treated now less as a friend of royalty than as a royal personage in his own right, was granted the use of the Judge's Lodgings. Here he held court, and among his house-guests were the Earl and Countess Lathom, Lady Bertha Wilbraham, Lady Fedora Sturt, Sir George Grove, Signor Tosti and Mrs Ronalds. The two main causes of enthusiasm during the four days were the works by Dvořák and Sullivan. Dvořák was greatly indebted to Sullivan for the help he was able to give, for

The composer, understanding English but very little, had frequently to appeal for assistance in conveying his wishes respecting the correctness and style of the performance to the orchestra to Sir Arthur Sullivan, who rendered invaluable aid in this respect. At the conclusion of the rehearsal the composer was greeted by the combined orchestra of band and chorus with a right hearty English cheer, which he acknowledged with evident surprise and satisfaction.[13]

After the performance of *St Ludmilla* there was shouting and cheering, and 'such a Babel of rejoicing has rarely been witnessed anywhere'. Nevertheless,

. . . At the end of Sullivan's queen of cantatas [*The Golden Legend*] this scene was enacted with even more boisterous surroundings; cheer after cheer rang through the hall; the audience were excited and the choristers simply crazy. The girls pelted the composer with flowers. The men fairly roared their plaudits, and such a frenzy of congratulations has surely never before rung in the ears of any living man as that amid which Sir Arthur left the platform.[14]

As was the case at Birmingham Dvořák left Leeds full of appreciation of the quality of English choral performance. He wrote to Spark of how he wished that he could kiss the hands of the ladies and shake those of the gentlemen.

The Committee was soon looking forward to 1889. On 7th November 1887 Sullivan dropped a hint to Cowen by thinking that 'the Leeds people would be favourably disposed towards a new work' from him. But the Leeds people were setting their sights a good deal higher, and before the year was out an invitation to write a work had been sent to Brahms. When he declined the invitation the help of Gustav Nathan—the British Consul in Vienna—was enlisted. Nathan had once lived in Leeds and could, therefore, speak to the master from the heart. But his efforts were unavailing. Although Brahms would not write a work the Committee nevertheless insisted on acknowledging his eminence by including the *German Requiem* in the programme.

Sullivan was no great admirer of Brahms's music and it is not, perhaps, surprising that when, after Brahms's first refusal, he was asked to contribute a symphony—even a 'Leeds symphony' it was suggested—he temporized. He did not know, he said, who would be the conductor of the 1889 Festival, and not knowing who would conduct it could not be expected to compose such a work. Moreover he was busy writing an opera and music for *Macbeth*. In October 1888 he positively refused to write a symphony.[15]

The 1889 programme was exhausting for all concerned, not least for the singers. In addition to Brahms's Requiem the main works were Berlioz's *Faust*, Parry's commissioned *Ode on St Cecilia's Day*, Stanford's *Voyage of Maeldune* (also a first performance), *The Golden Legend*, and the Choral Symphony. At the final, Saturday night concert Sullivan conducted his *Macbeth* music—the Overture, the Preludes to the 3rd, 5th, and 6th acts (Irving had divided Act V into two parts, hence an unexpected 6th act), and the choruses of 'Spirits in the Air' and 'Over hills and over mountains'. Handel was represented by *Acis and Galatea*, and Schubert by the Mass in E flat. From Bach, now laying claim to a permanent place in the Festival, there was *God's time is the best* (in John Troutbeck's translation), and Weelkes's *Sweet honey-sucking bees* acknowledged the strength of a growing belief in the virtues of older English music. As Mendelssohn had done when reintroducing Bach to a sceptical audience in Berlin sixty years earlier, so Sullivan felt obliged to make concessions to local feeling. The (bass) aria 'Set in order thine house' was sung by a collective force of eighty basses, and the speed was practically halved to suit the sixteenth-note (semiquaver) runs.

Otto Lessmann attended this Festival and wrote his impressions in the *Allgemeine Musik-Zeitung*. He said that he 'had heard choral performances of greater beauty in Leeds than in any town on the Continent'. The Festival was 'a warning to the German public and the German world of art not to underrate, as formerly, the pains bestowed upon the cultivation of music in England'.[16] While the chorus at Leeds was thus praised by Lessmann, others were less happy. There had, it was felt, been a 'manifest diminution of the power and deterioration of the tone owing to the strain involved on the voices of the chorus in the great works of Beethoven, Bach, etc.' On the Monday preceding the opening of the Festival on Wednesday, the chorus had been rehearsed for twelve hours.

Criticism of the Leeds singers,[17] whether merited or not, hurt Sullivan, who wrote to Spark of 'my splendid Yorkshire chorus, for whom I have a real personal affection'; but it was used by the Leeds Committee as a reason for introducing a new system and a stricter discipline. In accordance with a long-standing tradition most of the chorus singers, who came from various parts of the West Riding, were professional—that is, they were paid for 'broken time'. They were also severely auditioned (it would be a good musician today who could sing at sight the tests that were then set).[18] For 1892 it was decided that 120 members of the chorus should come from Leeds, and contingents of 56 from Bradford, Huddersfield, Halifax, Dewsbury and Batley. Each contingent was rehearsed by its own chorus-master and all were brought together in Leeds, eight or ten times, to rehearse with Sullivan prior to the final rehearsals.

In 1892 it appeared at one time unlikely that Sullivan would be able to take charge at Leeds. He was very ill during that year, his relationship with Gilbert had once again sunk below the mark of

toleration, and he was involved with *Haddon Hall*. When he was at
the lowest ebb William Spark—Frederick's brother—who had been
organist of the Town Hall since its opening, Festival organist, and a
powerful influence in Leeds musical affairs for more than forty
years, exploded into acrimony. On 5th May he wrote a letter to the
Leeds Mercury, in which he compared the new with the old, to the
disadvantage of the former:

> . . . During the reign of the incomparable conductor, Sir
> Michael Costa, all went smoothly with the organ, and its
> proper use was established in conjunction with the functions
> of the orchestra, chorus, and principal artists.
> He knew what grand effects could be produced from our
> magnificent instrument, whose tones, he always affirmed,
> mixed better with a band than any other instrument he had
> ever known. Those who remember the performance of 'The
> Mount of Olives', 'Solomon', etc., under Costa, will never
> forget the thrilling, overwhelming effects produced in the
> 'ensembles' and finales, by the quickening powers of the com-
> bined and unstinted employment of the organ, orchestra and
> chorus. 'Tout cela change!'
> Under the new conductorship, the organ was relegated, to
> the back stairs or the kitchen, degraded from the high distinctive
> position Costa gave to it, and made to sing small. No wonder,
> then, that with my long experience I should feel chagrined and
> disappointed, and become almost indifferent to, and perhaps
> careless, in the discharge of some of my duties.

Sullivan had never given the impression that he thought the organ
the king of instruments, even when he was a church organist. His
reduction of its importance in the Festival, although disagreeable
to old Spark, was in keeping with his general preference for restraint
in dynamic power and his acute appreciation of relationships of
sonorities. William Spark having thus retired, his place in the
Festival was taken by Alfred Benton, organist of the Parish Church.
Another change was necessitated by the death on 13th July of John
Carrodus (Carruthers) (1836–95), the famous orchestral leader who,
as a native of the county, held a special place in the affections of
Yorkshire audiences. His place was taken by W. Frye Parker.
So far as the early combined rehearsals of the choristers were
concerned, in 1892 Sullivan asked his old friend Barnby to help him,
and in token of his assistance gave him an 'express invitation' to

conduct Dvořák's *Stabat Mater* at the Festival. From his own works Sullivan gave a selection of the music for *The Tempest*. He included a *Suite de ballet* by Goring Thomas, who had recently died; works by Alan Gray and Frederick Cliffe, both Yorkshiremen; and by Edward German. The Mass in B Minor was repeated; Mozart's Requiem was performed for the first time at Leeds; and knowledge of Brahms was extended through *The Song of Destiny*.

Three years later the bicentenary of the death of Purcell was celebrated by Parry's *Invocation to Music*, specially written for the occasion. There were also composed for this Festival a symphonic poem, *Visions*, by Massenet (a composer whose merits Sullivan had brought to the attention of the Committee in 1886) and an orchestral suite by Edward German. *Messiah*, which surprisingly had not been included in a Leeds programme since 1874, was restored to a place of honour, while *Elijah* was dropped in favour of *The First Walpurgis Night*. *The Golden Legend* was performed yet again.

The more advanced among the critics were particularly interested in Sullivan's treatment of the baroque masterpieces performed: *Messiah* and the first two parts of Bach's *Christmas Oratorio*. *The Guardian* (London) of 9th October found 'his readings . . . often open to criticism in the matter of *tempo*, and his editing of Handel and Bach could not always be commended'. *The Birmingham Post* of 4th October once again chose to carp at the Leeds chorus who seemed less at ease with Bach than with Handel, but conceded that: 'Bach must soon make his way in this country, and when these Yorkshire singers know Bach as well as they do Handel we may expect great things.' There were, as in the case of the Bach cantata in 1889, some liberties taken,

> . . . the recitatives for soprano voice being allotted to that section of the chorus, and in the solo numbers the 'repeats' were shortened. I suppose it is of little use to point out that these great festivals are not the place for such petty tinkering.[19]

The same writer complained of the falsification caused in the 'Pastoral Symphony' by the shortening of *appoggiature*. On the other hand this movement had one virtue appreciated by the *Sunday Times* of 6th October: '. . . a new experience was yielded by the restoration of the original Bach scoring . . .' What is interesting in this early exposition of musicological opinion is Sullivan's concern for baroque instrumental sonorities. He had in his time taken a part in the supply of 'additional accompaniments' (see page 61), but here, towards the end of the century, he was moving well towards redemption.

The 1895 Festival was distinguished by the patronage of the Prince of Wales, who was the guest of E. W. Beckett at Kirkstall Grange, and of the Marquis of Lorne and Princess Louise, who stayed with Sullivan at the Judge's Lodging.

Sullivan's last Festival was that of 1898. The programme contained new works by Engelbert Humperdinck, who came to conduct his, Cowen, Gray, Parry, Stanford and Elgar. It was, indeed, Elgar's *Caractacus* which made the headlines. Backed by *King Olaf*, the *Imperial March*, *Songs from the Bavarian Highlands* and a handful of other works, Elgar came to Leeds as the brightest rising star in the native sky. For him it was make or break, but the auguries were good. On 9th July the chorus rehearsed *Caractacus* for the first time at Leeds and Elgar was assured by telegram that all had gone well. At the beginning of August Sir Walter Parratt notified him of the Queen's gracious acceptance of the Dedication. After the Three Choirs Festival was over Elgar travelled to London to rehearse with the principals and orchestra in St James's Hall. There was, Alice Elgar observed in her diary, 'much excitement and applause'. Years afterwards Elgar commented on Sullivan's kindness during the London rehearsals:

> I urged him to rest while I went through *Caractacus*, but he remained and made notes of anything which struck him, in that most charming self-sacrificing way which was always his.[20]

At Leeds all went well—except that 'Mr. Spark interfered' in the rehearsal according to Alice Elgar—and Elgar, surrounded by his entourage, was considerably lionized. However this may have been, Elgar always remembered with gratitude that Sullivan had unreservedly encouraged him; he also held *The Golden Legend* in high respect, and after Sullivan's death vigorously denounced what he considered to be a vicious attack on his integrity by Fuller-Maitland.

Sullivan went through the 1898 Festival with great difficulty, and he showed remarkable courage in carrying out his obligations, both professional and social. Once again he had to cope with the B Minor Mass, and the Choral Symphony was repeated. Other major works were Brahms's *Alto Rhapsody*, *Elijah*, and Handel's *Alexander's Feast*. There was also a performance of Palestrina's

Stabat Mater, and Sullivan gave further evidence of his concern for a proper exposition of the values of music of earlier times and traditions.

> Sir Arthur Sullivan has ideas of his own concerning the [*Stabat Mater*], and all things considered they are such as commend themselves. Thus the soli parts and semi-chorus indicated by Wagner are intelligibly rejected, as are some of his marks of expression, including the fortissimo on 'crucifixi'. . . .[21]

Sullivan was not in any sense a virtuoso conductor (as we now understand the term, there were few such at that time). He was said by Hanslick, who heard a Philharmonic Concert under his direction in 1886, to have been 'drowsy', and by Plunket Greene to have been 'easy-going'.[22] Such manifestations, however, were misleading, and may in any case be ascribed to some extent to his physical condition. He often conducted performances when he was in considerable pain. On the other hand, he knew what he wanted (cf. pages 113 and 206), and he did at least take care in preparing his scores beforehand.

Costa quarrelled with the Leeds Committee, and so too did Sullivan's successor, Stanford, who indicated that everything was not always plain sailing for Sullivan.[23] This was evident in respect of the choice of the B Minor Mass. Nevertheless Sullivan managed the tough Yorkshiremen—whose most marked characteristic was a determination not to be told what to do from London—diplomatically. He remained in control for eighteen years, only terminating his engagement when it was physically impossible for him to continue in it.[24]

Had Sullivan not been leading a double life—as the great composer on the one hand, and the most prolific purveyor of popular hits on the other—it is likely that his tally of serious works would have been considerably increased through his connection with Leeds. There might have been one more symphony, one more oratorio, and one more cantata. The two works which do belong to Leeds, however, are of some significance, both in particular and in general. They stand away from the general run of oratorio as it was understood in the Victorian age, and on the edge of opera, and it is perhaps possible to conclude that here and there they even run across the borders of comic opera. *The Martyr of Antioch* was in fact leased to the Carl Rosa Opera Company, by whom it was staged in Liverpool in 1899. *The Golden Legend*, after the ancient and honourable Handel tradition, was performed concert-wise on 28th February 1891, as the third concert of an Oratorio Series organized by Augustus Harris at Covent Garden. It was sold out, and indeed the house could have been filled several times over. In the general context of choral music of that era both works represented a departure from the overriding convention of religiosity, and by so doing helped to emancipate such music from the shackles by which it was bound. There is no doubt that Elgar, in particular, was influenced by Sullivan's boldness of conception; not least in respect of the enhanced significance of orchestral and choral sonorities. Both works are uneven, and it is to be regretted that the most popular excerpt from *The Martyr* was the chorus 'Brother, thou art gone before us' (sung at Sullivan's funeral service), and that from *The Golden Legend* was also an *a cappella* piece with strong Church of England overtones, 'O gladsome light'.

The libretto of *The Martyr of Antioch* was prepared from Milman's dramatic poem by Sullivan himself, with some help in the matter of versification from Gilbert. Milman was a fine and original scholar and an enterprising dramatist with a genuine gift for the presentation of the conflict of ideas. *The Martyr* is a study of conflicting ideologies, the victim and heroine being Margarita, whose acceptance of Christianity was to lead her to the stake. The conflict, then, is between the reality of heathendom and the idealism of Christianity. Sullivan's delineation of the allurements of the former is beguiling; his representation of the latter unconvincing. In Scene IV, on the Road to the Temple of Apollo, the heathen women are heard singing outside the prison in which the Christians are kept. (See example on page 220.) The Christians too are heard to sing. The songs are heard separately and then together, quite in the manner of the Savoy Operas. The 'song of faith', however, would not have found a place in one of the operas and is so dull that one is inclined secretly to hope for the continued incarceration of the singers. Margarita's 'Hymn of victory at the stake' is also smug with respectability, and is not calculated to stir sympathy.

This 'hymn of victory' motiv is placed at the beginning of the introduction to the work, but Sullivan soon thankfully moves to the sun-worshippers, whose preliminary exercises provide a brilliant *danse profane*. The 'heathen maidens' of *The Martyr* came between

Major-General Stanley's daughters and the love-lorn girls of *Patience*
in the Sullivan time-scale and show characteristics of both. In the
first scene Julia's 'love-sick damsel' lies under the myrtle amid these
scented harmonies:

As so often, Sullivan garlanded his young ladies with Italianate
thirds, and the 'Evening Song of the Maidens' in the Palace of the
Prefect (Scene III) invites speculative dalliance. When called to her
customary duties by Olybius Margarita's doubts are somewhat
written into the command, which has its own sense of tenderness.

Ernest Walker did not much like Sullivan, and of Sullivan's works *The Martyr of Antioch* was not the one that he rated most highly. 'Apart from a certain amount of a sort of mildly pleasant picturesqueness,' he wrote, '[it] alternates between dullness and vulgarity, and sometimes attains both at once.' [25] This is not so. *The Martyr of Antioch* lacks the tension of true drama, but its evocation of atmosphere and its delineation of certain aspects of personality are splendidly accomplished. The heathen were not barbarian, but sophisticated and often charming. Sullivan was no primitivist and he took hints from the society in which he lived. His 'unbelievers' worshipped the sun—and an affluent society. And they were cynical:

As for the Christians, Sullivan drew the face of Anglicanism as he knew it. Perhaps the 'hymn of faith' after all was meant to be a parody.

The Golden Legend meant a great deal to Sullivan, for it was to be a 'great work'.[26]

Two other composers had treated 'The Golden Legend' (the second part of Longfellow's epic *Christus*) before Sullivan. Liszt's *Die Glocken des Strassburger Münsters*, which was dedicated to Longfellow and was composed in 1874, dealt only with the Prologue. It is difficult to believe that Sullivan was unaware of this score (from which Wagner borrowed thematic ideas for *Parsifal*). His own work is orchestrated with a fire and power that, as Klein observes, he had never shown before, while the harmonic colouring in its chromatic adventures was positively Lisztian.

Five years after Liszt composed *Die Glocken*, Dudley Buck—once a fellow-student with Sullivan in Leipzig and now an organist in New York—wrote a more extended cantata, *The Golden Legend*, which was among the twenty-five works submitted for the \$1000 prize offered for a new work by an American composer by the Cincinnati Musical Festival.[27] Buck's *Golden Legend*, like Liszt's work, was dedicated to Longfellow and its first performance was conducted by Theodore Thomas at Cincinnati on 20th May 1880.[28] During the period that Buck was composing his *Golden Legend* Sullivan was in the United States. It is by no means impossible that his later interest in the subject was to some extent stimulated by a conscious or unconscious recall of Buck's treatment of Longfellow's poem.

Buck's selection from the poem covers some two-thirds of Sullivan's, and more or less the whole of the text of Sullivan's Prologue and first four Scenes appears in Buck's cantata. The most important material incorporated by Buck but omitted by Sullivan was the 'Gaudiolum of Monks' in the Convent of Hirschau. In this episode (Scene VII) Buck shows a lively sense of parody in an hilarious drinking song, sung by a drunken, golliardish monk.

Within its context Buck's is no bad work. Realizing that Longfellow's poem was sometimes better expressed by omitting the words (Sullivan often gave priority to the orchestra) he wrote two long and purely orchestral episodes. These—the March to Salerno in Scene VI and the Barcarolle in Scene X—show sufficient traces of a common enthusiasm to justify the critics' comments that Buck was influenced by Berlioz and Wagner; but they are sturdy and purposeful. Buck was among those who, through choral festivals, were trying to establish a national tradition, and this is exemplified by the plain-spun texture of the choruses. In Scene IX ('The night is calm', cf. Sullivan, Scene III), the soprano solo rises above the Kyrie of the chorus in G major suggesting acquaintance with the fifth movement in Brahms's Requiem.

Trained in the same school, it is not surprising that Buck's score at times sounds like Sullivan (but the Sullivan of *The Prodigal Son* rather than *The Golden Legend*). The closest point of contact is in the following passage. These words were also treated *a cappella* by Sullivan:

In its transmutation from a medieval German tale *The Golden Legend* suffered a good deal at Longfellow's hands. There are, as has been suggested, occasions where music is more instructive than words. The Prologue is a particular case in point, as Lucifer uses these words to instruct his assistants to tear down the spire of Strassburg Cathedral:

Hasten! Hasten!
O ye spirits!
From its station drag the ponderous
Cross of iron, that to mock us
Is uplifted high in air.

Another case is at the beginning of the second scene when—the villagers having assembled in the evening outside her house—Ursula is required to sing:

> Slowly, slowly up the wall,
> Steals the sunshine, steals the shade.

On the other hand there are certain passages in which something of the 'larger' feelings associated with Longfellow are to be felt. Prince Henry, Elsie and their attendants, on the way to Salerno, pitch their camp on a hill overlooking the sea, and Prince Henry sings:

> It is the sea, it is the sea,
> In all its vague immensity
> Fading and darkening in the distance!
> Silent, majestical, and slow
> The white ships haunt it to and fro,
> With all their ghostly sails unfurled,
> As phantoms from another world
> Haunt the dim confines of existence.

Sullivan was as good as his poets and librettists allowed. He lacked the Schubertian gift for turning verbal dross into musical gold (not that Schubert was not, as in his operas, sometimes at a loss) and the limper stanzas of Longfellow led to musical debility. But the sea-scape quoted above (which belongs to an episode admirably varied in pace and tone) is finely done. Backed by a Schubertian security Sullivan sets a broad sweep of melody amid the shifting light of harmonically contrasted arpeggios. There is a suggestion here of the best of Stanford; and it is not surprising that Stanford found much to praise in the oratorio.

It may well be that if Lucifer is to be introduced in person into drama the most satisfactory way to handle him is through comedy. Longfellow and Sullivan played him as straight as possible. This devil, then, is a most amiable devil, already preparing himself for his role in *The Beauty Stone*. Whether in his guise as a peripatetic physician or as Friar Angelo, Lucifer rides on a motiv (Sullivan makes limited use of *Leitmotiv* in the work) that is completely English-country-gentleman. In its vigorous, diatonic, 3/4 pattern (into which Sullivan occasionally, a little wilfully, slips a patch of 2/4), it is rather more like Parry. In fact there was something of a miscarriage of effect here. The apparently athletic counterpoint of this Luciferous motiv was intended humorously to convey the idea that according to legend the devil (in human form) suffered from a limp. In the third scene Lucifer is represented as a Friar on the road to Salerno, and here Sullivan allows him expression in terms of comedy that are not quite out of keeping with Longfellow's portraiture at this point. 'I must,' says Lucifer, 'act to my heart's content/This mummery and this merriment.' Against a pointed rhythm marked out by brass (Sullivan used the brass economically and, with subdued dynamics, effectively), the voice alternates between 12/8 and 6/8, with occasional interjections of 2/4. And then when Lucifer has thus disported himself alone he repeats himself against the monk's hymn of 'Cujus faber auctor lucis . . .' The resultant conflict of patterns is less oratorio than comic opera; for the device was one which Sullivan used with unfailing regularity in that field.

Sullivan began *The Golden Legend* in the grand style, with an unaccustomed wealth of orchestral resources. (He could, of course, enjoy this plenty at Leeds but not at the Savoy.) The storm music calls not only for the normal double wood-wind but for two piccolos, bass clarinet, and contrafagotto as well. There are four horns and two trumpets in addition to two cornets. There are bells, harp and organ—enough of the last to have satisfied William Spark. Sullivan had reservations concerning Wagner (except that he considered *Die Meistersinger* the finest comic opera ever written), but in *The Golden Legend* there is a strong suspicion that for a lot of the time what matters belongs essentially and in the Wagnerian manner to the orchestra, the vocal parts providing commentary.

In the Prologue, trumpets, cornets and trombones 'clash and clang' to good effect against the bowed tremolo of the violins and the cellos. As the ashes of the dead are scattered a rush of chromatic strings tears through the score. A relationship with Liszt's *Die Glocken* is further strengthened in the opening scene by the fact that, like Liszt, Sullivan begins Lucifer's first recitative with a falling minor third (Buck opts for a falling fourth). There are also suggestions of the devils of Berlioz's *Faust*.

The Golden Legend contains some of Sullivan's best string writing. In the accompaniment to Ursula in the second scene the soft radiance of string tone is enough to indicate the setting sun, and to render the text superfluous. When Elsie speaks of her vision (cf. Berlioz's 'Apotheosis of Margaret') the first violins are *divisi à* 3, with second violins and violas also *divisi*, and the ascent of Christ is illuminated by single harp notes. In the same movement the angelic cries of 'Amen' are also accompanied by divided strings which are now muted. There is one more outstanding example of the effective use of *divisi*. At the beginning of the first scene Prince Henry cannot sleep. His 'fever'd brain calls up the vanished past, and throws its misty splendours deep':

As in his other works, however, Sullivan's originality showed most conspicuously in his use of the brighter colours of the orchestral palette. When Lucifer offers to the Prince his little flask containing the quintessence of 'all the knowledge man can ask', the instruments are disposed in a Bartókian manner. Sullivan's texture is luminous with the play of two piccolos, flute, two clarinets, and harp, and the pattern later merges into a wide spread of upward and downward moving triplets in the strings—representing 'golden vapours'.

The Golden Legend suffers because of the limitations which were set

on the expression of emotional conditions. The devil is not credible,
nor is the heroine, whose resolve to sacrifice her own life to save that
of Prince Henry is conveyed, alas, in terms more suitable for a governess. Sullivan was not the first composer who had to write a heroine
out of this world. Had he looked more closely at Handel's unfor-
tunates he would have noticed that that master did not deny them
life while they were living. Neither here nor in *The Martyr* did
Sullivan show much concern for women's rights.

This oratorio was intended to be a major work. Maybe Sullivan
tried too hard, for, as his friends testified, he devoted a great deal of
thought and energy to its creation. In the end it is not a consistent
drama, but a series of episodes. Nor is it in the conventional English
sense a 'choral work', for the chorus throughout is generally sub-
ordinate to the orchestral textures. The virtues of *The Golden Legend*
are those of *Ivanhoe*, and so too are the demerits. The oratorio was
indeed a trial run over the territory of 'grand opera'. In this respect
it illuminates the frustrations of the British composer of the period,
whose only sure opportunity was through Town Hall oratorio.
Nevertheless the organizers of the Leeds Festival—and of the other
major Festivals—deserve praise rather than censure. They were
stirred by a not ignoble idealism.

NOTES TO CHAPTER TEN

1. Spark's married sister emigrated to the United States and settled
   in Boston, where she died on 27th January 1876. '. . . She was well
   known as the Fanny Frazer of the Frazer Opera Company, which
   came to this country several years ago, and she had for several
   years been a prominent teacher of music in the city. The concerts
   of her pupils have been quite popular entertainments.' *Boston Globe*,
   28th January 1876.
2. In 1883 the first performance of a work entitled *The Prodigal Son*
   by Rev. Jas. F. Downes was given at one of these occasions.
3. A General Election took place in April 1880, as a result of which
   Gladstone came to office for the second time.
4. Regarding D'Albert's association with Sullivan at this time, *see*
   Bennett, *Forty Years of Music*, pp. 77–8.
5. *Bradford Chronicle and Mail*, 16th October 1880.
6. Autograph letter in the Spark Collection, Leeds Central Library.
7. *Leeds Mercury*, 6th October 1883.

8. The sum of £2,000 was divided between the charities, and £329 retained and invested in 1880. Three years later the disbursement amounted to £1,950.

9. Autograph letter in the Spark Collection, Leeds Central Library.

10. Creser's *The Sacrifice of Freia* was performed at the 1889 Festival and two years later he left Leeds to become Organist of the Chapel Royal.

11. Sullivan seems to have disguised his condition from Bennett, who wrote the libretto, and who also had something to say about Sullivan's composition of *The Golden Legend* in *Forty Years of Music*, p. 78 f.

12. Frederic Cliffe (1857–1931), pianist, organist and composer, was a native of Bradford. He was a pupil of Sullivan at the National Training School of Music and was appointed a professor at the Royal College of Music in 1883. Cliffe's First Symphony in C Minor created a favourable impression at the Crystal Palace on its first performance in 1889. It had been rejected by the Leeds Committee, who, however, gave a place to his Second Symphony in E minor in 1892.

13. *The Manchester Guardian*, 13th October 1886.

14. *Liverpool Mercury*, 18th October 1886. Stanford welcomed *The Golden Legend* in words which were almost as ill-judged as those with which he later condemned Elgar's *Gerontius*. Referring to the former he wrote: 'It is natural, nay more, it is right, that in the Paradise of Music, as in other Paradises, there should be more rejoicing over Sullivan's great and legitimate success, than over the works of the ninety and nine just composers who have remained uninfluenced (perhaps because untempted) by consideration of profit and popularity.' Stanford, *Studies and Memories*, London, 1908, pp. 168–9.

J. A. Fuller-Maitland (1856–1936), a pupil of Stanford, remarked that *The Golden Legend*, in which he noted the influence of Berlioz, had been a 'welcome surprise'; Obituary of Sullivan, in *Cornhill Magazine*, March 1901, pp. 300–9.

15. The Committee of the Leeds Festival was singularly unfortunate in its attempts to obtain symphonies. In 1904 Elgar produced the overture *In the South* instead of the symphony he should have provided.

16. Fred R. Spark and Joseph Bennett, *A Full History of the Leeds Musical Festival (1858–89)*, Leeds/London, 1892, p. 359.

17. Bennett suggests that some of it had been maliciously stirred up from Birmingham: *see* Bennett, *Forty Years of Music*, pp. 76–7.

18. Examples are given in Spark and Bennett, *A Full History*.

19. *The Birmingham Post*, 4th October 1892.

20. Letter to Herbert Sullivan, 29th December 1926.

21. *Leeds Mercury*, 7th October 1898.

22. H. Plunket Greene, *Charles Villiers Stanford*, London, 1935, p. 129.

23. Letter to W. S. Hannam, 15th December 1900, quoted in H. Plunket Greene, *Stanford*, p. 128.
24. *See* Greene's moving account: *ibid.* p. 129.
25. Ernest Walker, *A History of Music in England*, 2nd edn., London, 1924, p. 294.
26. *See* Klein, *Thirty Years of Musical Life*, pp. 195–6.
27. Leopold Damrosch and Asger Hamerik, two of the judges, voted for George E. Whiting's *The Tale of the Viking*; Carl Zerrahn and Otto Singer preferred Buck's work, which was awarded the first prize on the casting vote of Theodore Thomas.
28. Buck's *The Golden Legend* was published by John Church & Co., Cincinnati, who were also one of Sullivan's publishers.

11

'Grand Opera'

For the composer wishing to compose an opera in the nineteenth century there were two especial challenges: the one in Shakespeare, the other in Walter Scott. Sullivan's career as a composer started with *The Tempest*, and he returned to Shakespearian themes from time to time. He was also stimulated by Scott at an early stage, and one work at least—*Marmion*—even promised that, given the opportunity, he could match that master's narrative with music both vital and colourful. The essence of opera is dramatic probability, the presentation of heroic propositions with compelling musical force. To what extent Sullivan would be able to do this was the question which invaded the thoughts of sceptical critics, as the long-awaited day of his entry into what was taken to be the senior department of opera approached. Scepticism stemmed from the composer's success in the province of *opéra comique*, and from his inability properly to engage in the heroic in his oratorios and cantatas. In the end scepticism was justified. Sullivan failed adequately to rise to the occasion, and by proving himself unable to take full advantage of the opportunity offered set back the cause of English opera for another half-century. If *Ivanhoe* had succeeded, and if D'Oyly Carte had been able to maintain his English Opera House for the purpose intended, it is possible that the subsequent course of British music would have been considerably different.

That Sullivan would fail in his attempt to encompass the heroic might well have seemed predictable if the starting base were to be the Savoy tradition, where he was the master of the well-tuned epigram. If, however, the line leading from *The Tempest* to *Macbeth*, by way of *Marmion*, had been independently considered, a more cogent work than was produced should not have seemed outside the bounds of possibility. The overture to *Macbeth* particularly, if uneven in inspiration, has some passages with an austerity unusual in Sullivan, while the manner in which the musical argument is conducted in the development of thematic material has a tragic sense not

otherwise found in his works. So far as motiv material is concerned
there is enough here to furnish the framework of an opera. After
three bars of peremptory tonic chords *à la* Beethoven in C minor,
Sullivan introduces a 'tragic' motiv which in recapitulation is
shown in A minor against a pulsating viola figure. The most striking
motiv in the first subject group, however, is one which suggests a
northern landscape, and that for once Sullivan had allowed the
deep-seated pessimism evident in some of his letters to come to the
surface. This motiv is heard in dramatic guise at the beginning of the
development section, after the pageantry of the second subject
themes in the warmer climates of E flat major and B flat major has
passed. These themes represent 'martial' ardour (used again for
Act I, Scenes 3 and 4, and for battle scenes in the last act of Irving's
production), and 'gracious Duncan'. The exposition of the Overture
ends in the distance, and as the last chord dies away the grimmer
aspects of life are revealed in terms later used by Sibelius:

After this the tonality of E minor is established, in which there is a
'witches' dance'.

In one form or another the triplet figure exploited in the previous example is found throughout *Ivanhoe*—for example, in the Templar's song and the 'Goodnight' finale of Act I, Scene 1, in the march songs of the Crusaders and the Saxons, and, most telling, to accompany the Templar's determination to 'woo and win' Rebecca in Act II, Scene 2.

Macbeth shows the facets of Sullivan's music that are least generally known, and how, perhaps, he could have succeeded in the field of serious opera if he had lived in the right kind of climate. One other remarkable passage in the exposition is the appearance of a motiv to delineate the ghost of Banquo (this was introduced into the Prelude to Act II). The violas linger on the dominant of E flat, and there then supervenes this tremulous passage, the first violins and flute transmuting the first subject:

Henry Irving had neither required nor expected music of such complexity, and the more recondite parts of the score show an appreciation of nervous tension that was alien to any concept of production by Irving. Taking into account all Sullivan's incidental music to the plays, it is to be regretted that no one thought of encouraging him to undertake a Shakespearian libretto. But when *Macbeth* was composed the intention to move over to Scott was already forming.

Ivanhoe was a magnificent subject, provided that the librettist could do an efficient job, and it had not hitherto been turned into a

consistent repertory opera. Parry's *Ivanhoe* (1815) was of no significance (nor was it really an opera), and neither the pasticcio
arranged out of Rossini by Antonio Pacini [1] nor the *opera seria* of
Giovanni Pacini (1790–1867) [2] achieved any success. That left
Heinrich Marschner's *Der Templer und die Jüdin* (1829). This work,
tense and serious, by its music did not unduly idealize the Middle
Ages, and its success was limited. Certainly it was unfamiliar in
London, where it had been played back in 1840, and Sullivan therefore had a more or less clear field. *Ivanhoe* enjoyed a publicity-drive
the like of which had not previously been experienced in respect
of an English grand opera. If in the end it proved one of the biggest
non-events in the history of music it is for Carte that sympathy must
be chiefly reserved. He had built a great theatre, at enormous cost,
because of his belief in the genius of one composer. But Carte was
not Ludwig II of Bavaria; Sullivan was not Wagner; and Cambridge
Circus was not Bayreuth. The odds were much against the enterprise from the start—because nobody really believed in English
opera—not even Sullivan.

At the beginning of 1891 Carte looked with pride on the red
Ellistown brick and Doulton Terra Cotta façade of his New Opera
House; the electric lighting of its interior, which alone had cost
as much as would build an ordinary theatre; the cantilevered galleries; the stage machinery; and the 'Royal Room'. It was, he boasted,
'the most perfectly equipped building of its class seen in England,
before or since the Elizabethan Age'. It was also 'a thing of Beauty,
no less than of Use'. And it was to be consecrated by the masterpiece of the greatest living British composer. In a little over eighteen
months the castle in the air was brought crashing down, together
with the Castle of Torquilstone.

Ivanhoe was performed for the first time on 31st January 1891.
The audience was as brilliant as could ever be desired. The Prince
and Princess of Wales, Princess Victoria, Princess Maude and the
Duke and Duchess of Edinburgh were present. So, in a box of her
own, was Mrs Ronalds, accompanied by her daughter. She, the
gossip-writers noted, held her own court. At the arrival of the royal
family at eight o'clock the national anthem was played. Three
minutes later Sullivan entered, to a 'tremendous reception by a
brilliant and packed house', as he proudly noted. Every one of the
1,976 seats was occupied. Each could have been filled several times
over, for, as the *Boston Sunday Herald* reported: 'the rush for places

was unheard of. There were 10,000 applications, and sojourning Americans have been offering $50 to $100 for seats without avail.'

The opera began at eight-fifteen and was conducted by Cellier. Predictably, it was greeted rapturously. The nature of the first-night audience was a guarantee of immediate approval, and in that no expense had been spared there was much to commend. Everything was on the grand scale—this, after all, was grand opera. Sullivan used the largest orchestra he had so far employed. Nor was he to be left behind in respect of the introduction of new sonorities, which was one of the features of those days. *The Times* of 6th February noted:

> . . . two orchestral innovations . . . the 'G' flute, which has all the brightness of the piccolo without the harshness of its upper notes or the weakness of its lower; and the [4] bass trumpets, made expressly for the production, and consisting of a combination of the old-fashioned slide trumpet with the modern valve appliances.[3]

The scenery had been designed by a four-man team, J. Harker, J. E. Ryan, W. Telbin, and Irving's designer, Hawes Craven, and it was not only splendid but correct in every architectural detail. A double cast had been engaged, in which there were no fewer than five Americans—Eugene Oudin (Sir Brian de Bois-Guilbert), Avon Saxon (Friar Tuck) and Esther Palliser [4] (Rowena) in the first team, and Marie Groebl (Ulrice) and Lucille Hall (Rowena) in the second. The singers were subject to a stronger discipline than was then common—for Sullivan was not satisfied with anything short of the highest standards—and one of them, at least, had demurred about the contract.

Margaret Macintyre (1865–1943), a Scottish soprano, had come into prominence in 1888 when she made her début at Covent Garden as Micaela in *Carmen*. In 1889 she sang at the Leeds Festival [5] and Sullivan decided that she should be cast as Rebecca in *Ivanhoe*. Her reaction to her contract drew this letter from Sullivan. It was written on 31st December 1890.

Dear Miss Macintyre:

I have seen Mr. Vert [6] today, and, as he has doubtless told you, explained to him my feeling with regard to the clause in your contracts with Mr. Carte which you object to sign—viz that one which refers to non-attendance at rehearsals. With the artists' contracts I have nothing whatever to do, and do not know the contents of them—with the exception of this particular clause which is one I insist upon, for my own protection. It would be absolutely impossible for me to carry on the rehearsals with so many artists concerned, if there were no means of enforcing a regular and conscientious attendance beyond that of moral persuasion. And if every other artist concerned in the production of my opera has signed such an undertaking you will I am sure see how impossible it is for me to make an exception in your favour, and how unjust to the others.

I fear your experience of opera in London has been such as to make you somewhat mistrustful of everyone and everything connected with the theatre, and has made you feel you must be on the defensive. I assure you that you will on the contrary find nothing but courtesy, goodwill and consideration in this theatre from everyone, and equally am I sure that once there, you will loyally and earnestly work with all of us for the success of the undertaking.

Yours sincerely,
Arthur Sullivan.

P.S. I rehearse every day from 12.30 to 4, and again from 8 to 11 ! I am rather tired but can't take any rest.

If for no other reason, *Ivanhoe* represented a landmark in the history of English opera because it had been thoroughly and professionally prepared in every detail.

Most of the critics succumbed to the atmosphere of the first night, but not Bernard Shaw, whose strictures in *The World* on 4th February were severe on Sturgis's pallid libretto and Sullivan's 'gentlemanly' expressions, and should have brought *Ivanhoe* to a quick end. But there were more than enough complimentary notices to keep the opera alive for a little while at least. Also it was by no means forbidden to pass round the information that the Queen, having read the approving notices, not only praised them but also claimed at least a little of the credit for the opera.

Reviews of new works depend on the background and prejudices of the reviewer—as is shown by the early notices of *Ivanhoe*. The correspondent of the *Boston Sunday Herald* (1st February 1891) wrote:

Of the music opinions varied. It is clearly the highest and finest work Sir Arthur Sullivan has done. It far surpasses the 'Golden Legend' and, notably in the orchestration, was superb.

Nevertheless the popular taste may possibly find a sameness in its course which will fail to win for it great popularity. There is no single movement, no grand aria or grand march—nor is there any particularly melodic movement calculated to arouse enthusiasm. It is complete and finished rather than inspirational.

In contrast to this readers of *The World* (1st February), New York, were assured that:

Sullivan has not lost a single opportunity to introduce ear-tickling choruses.

On 5th February the *Spectator* complained that there were too few choruses and vocal ensembles in *Ivanhoe*. The *Neue Freie Presse* of Vienna, in a kind notice also with the date-line 5th February, averred:

The music is English throughout, and the lyrical element dominates all else. With consummate taste, Sullivan has woven into the work a number of fine songs. There are in contrast numerous choruses, which express the British character.

By far the most interesting notice was that carried by *The Jewish Chronicle* (6th February), not for its critical quality but for its support for the proposition that Sullivan was of Jewish extraction (see page 2). Once again, there is no evidence that this was denied. The notice stated:

. . . Most of the prominent musical people in England are foreigners, and three of the most popular musicians, including the musician who has been invited by Mr. D'Oyly Carte to create English opera, are Jews, or of Jewish origin—Cowen, Solomon,[7] and Sullivan . . . A large number of Jewish faces were to be seen both at the dress rehearsal and at the première last Saturday of 'Ivanhoe'. Jewish interest in the experiment is undoubtedly stimulated by the accident of the first English opera [*sic*] being devoted to the story of the Jewish heroine whom the genius of Scott has made immortal. . . .

The same writer naturally picked up Rebecca's song, 'Lord of our chosen race', to remark how 'the oriental character of the air is intensified by the orchestral accompaniment in which harp and reed figure largely' (see page 241). Whether Sullivan considered the full implications that his subject might have before he started work on the opera is not to be discovered. If he had taken into account the cultural Jewish community in London which supported the arts in general and music in particular, he had an auspicious precedent in the case of Handel and *Judas Maccabaeus*. What is certain is that Sullivan was not unaware of the particular significance of one part of the opera at least as he worked on it (see page 240).

Within days of the first performance of *Ivanhoe* the newspapers reported that Count von Hochberg, Intendant of the Royal Prussian Opera House, had practically concluded arrangements for production in Berlin, and that negotiations were taking place in respect of the opera houses in Hamburg and München. The managements of the last two soon backed out—if indeed they were ever interested—and the production in Berlin did not take place until 1895. However, the publicity accorded by rumour was as valuable as that supported by fact. *Ivanhoe* continued to draw excellent houses and in May it reached its hundredth performance, which Sullivan himself conducted. The occasion was also marked by the issue of a Souvenir book.[8] In all, the opera ran consecutively for 160 performances, thus establishing a world record so far as 'grand' opera is concerned.

Carte's problem was what to do when *Ivanhoe* ended its run, and speculation was rife. As has already been shown, Carte had tried to interest Cowen in a commission. Cowen, indeed, was busy on a new opera, *Signa*, the libretto of which was based by Gilbert à Beckett on Ouida's novel of that name. It was not his but Goring Thomas's name, however, which was first floated by the press in connection with Carte's scheme. The *Daily Graphic* of 7th February, saying that Goring Thomas was already engaged on a work, suggested that Hubert Parry should be the obvious choice for an English opera. Carte, however, was not taking any more risks than he needed to. At the beginning of March he was reported as having paid Messager as much for *La Basoche* as had been paid for Gounod's *The Redemption* for Birmingham. He was also said to be negotiating for Herman Bemberg's *Elaine*, which, however, was taken over by Covent Garden and given its première there on 5th July 1892. Until *Elaine* was ready it was proposed to run *The Flying Dutchman* in double harness with *Ivanhoe*. But there were still other British composers in the queue. The *Pall Mall Gazette* of 24th March 1891 promoted the claims of the Scotsman Hamish McCunn, who was reported as considering the possibility of writing an opera on a story taken from a novel by Rider Haggard, of which the libretto would be prepared by Andrew

Lang and James Hatton. Carte also tried to persuade Sullivan to undertake a comic opera, *Jane Annie*, with a libretto written by Conan Doyle on a story by J. M. Barrie. Sullivan was not interested, and the commission passed to Ernest Ford [9]—associate conductor, with Cellier, of *Ivanhoe*—whose setting was played at the Savoy in 1893. It was an embarrassing flop.

When *Ivanhoe* came off *La Basoche* went on: an admirable comedy opera and admirably produced. Bernard Shaw commended the production and paid a handsome tribute to Carte:

> As the work has been thoroughly rehearsed, and the band is up to the best standard of delicacy and steadiness, I think it must be admitted that, incredible as it may sound, we have at last got an opera-house where musical works are treated as seriously and handsomely as dramatic works are at the Lyceum. [10]

After *La Basoche* Carte tried to keep the Opera House going by presenting Sarah Bernhardt in Sardou's *Cléopâtre*. A month later he gave up the attempt in despair, and amid a thunder of ridicule. What was described by the *City Leader* of 9th July 1892 as 'D'Oyly Carte's Folly' was sold to a syndicate, of which Sir Augustus Harris was the managing director, for use as a music-hall. 'Mammon rules,' wrote one of the editorial staff of the *East Anglia Daily Times*, 'and Mr. Carte may thank his American stars to be thus profitably relieved of a costly mistake. Since the general election has been in full blast the theatres have had a very hard time . . .' [11]

In England the times were normally unpropitious for 'grand opera', simply because it had never been built into the general social tradition. Between them Gilbert, Sullivan and Carte reactivated another tradition and, by an audacious union of flattery of, and contempt for, philistine values, established a fresh convention. This, symbolized as 'Gilbert and Sullivan', made the auspices for 'grand opera' even less favourable. In more senses than one Sullivan was *Ivanhoe*'s principal enemy, and when an attempt was made to promote it in Germany it failed ignominiously.

That *Ivanhoe* was performed at all at the Royal Opera House in Berlin was in some measure due to the 'special relationship' between England and Germany which had been encouraged by Queen Victoria and agreeable to the Germans, but which was now on the point of dissolution. (The Emperor was not to set foot in England again for five years.) The Opera House in Berlin was a department of propaganda and William II saw to it that the Intendant fulfilled his first function—to express political sentiments through productions where it was possible discreetly to do so. The then Intendant, Count Bolko von Hochberg, a wealthy Silesian aristocrat who ruled the Royal Opera from 1886 until 1902, found this a by-no-means uncongenial duty. So it was that *Ivanhoe*, *The Golden Legend* and *The Mikado* (Royal Command Performance, Berlin, 10th June 1900) was seen as testimony to Anglo-German understanding. Not everybody appreciated the point. Certainly not Sullivan. He had not been pleased with the reaction of the German press to *The Golden Legend*. When he read what was written about *Ivanhoe* after its production in Berlin he felt a deepening sense of disillusionment with the Germans.

Ivanhoe should have opened on 19th November, but the illness of two of the women principals necessitated a week's postponement. When it was put on—Karl Muck (1859–1940) [12] being the conductor —it was seen without remarkable enthusiasm.

> Arthur Sullivan's opera, *Ivanhoe*, had a very cool reception. Musically, the work is unremarkable, but the sumptuous decor makes it worth seeing. We cannot see this opera having a long life-span.[13]

A week later O[tto]. L[essmann]. followed this with a longer notice, of which the main points are contained in this excerpt:

> To this deplorable concoction the talented composer of *The Mikado* has written music that is so negative and dreary in invention, so conventional in its make-up, so destitute of any sort of originality, that it can worthily stand beside the libretto. A great deal of industry, a great deal of care and attention, and—above all—a great deal of money vanished in the performance; but, in spite of the marvellous staging (and the useless dedication of the conductor), the opera was irredeemable . . .
> . . . *Ivanhoe* was seen by the audience to be a flop, so it quickly disappeared from the repertory. The splendid sets could, perhaps, be used in Marschner's *Templer und Jüdin*, in which the same subject is treated. That would be no bad exchange.

Ivanhoe was composed for a number of reasons, all of which affected the kind of work it turned out to be. Sullivan wanted to write an opera, and as he entertained large ambitions in this respect it necessarily had to be on a large scale. This was in order with Carte, who was anxious to exploit what he enthusiastically described as 'the highest and deepest stage in any London Theatre, and, without doubt, the most perfectly equipped in the world'. With castle interior and exterior, jousting-ground and forest, and a plenitude of activity (if not action) on every set, *Ivanhoe* gave full opportunity to the technicians of the theatre to show their capabilities. Sullivan had two other duties to fulfil. He had to provide the foundation opera for a distinctively English national opera—always assuming that this had not already been done—and to embellish the theme of national greatness. The story of *Ivanhoe* is the triumph of good over bad—of Saxon over Norman, of virtue over vice—of Rebecca over the Templar. The intention of Sturgis and Sullivan was to present Scott's romance in terms of an allegorical pageant. Sullivan was from the start limited as to what he could do, and was obliged to emphasize the picturesque. This left him writing a good deal about summer greenery, simple myths of patriotic faith—from which emerged the impeccably suave heroics of Ivanhoe and King Richard—and some knock-about in the jousting-ground of which the end-result was only too predictable. The dramatic conflicts within Scott's story made no sense in the circles in which Sullivan moved: there was (had been, and would be) one nation in the world that counted. Sullivan lived at the wrong time to understand the horrors of overt racial conflict in one land. It is significant that the great combative operas of the nineteenth century were composed by those who knew something of the actuality of fighting for freedom and (as it was then understood) nationhood. Marschner's Norman and Saxon motivs are within reach of probability:

Those of Sullivan, 'eminently gentlemanly' as Shaw remarked, are not:

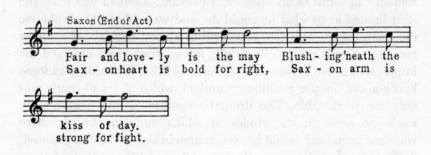

In one respect, however, Sullivan outdistances Marschner—in the characterization of Rebecca. In the context of Sullivan's putative origins this is not without interest, nor is a relevant passage in Klein's *Thirty Years of Musical Life in London* (page 336):

> I was particularly struck by the oriental character of the harmonies and 'intervals' in Rebecca's song, 'Lord of our chosen race', and told Sullivan that I thought nothing could be more distinctively Eastern or even Hebraic in type.
>
> 'That may well be so', he rejoined. 'The phrase on the words "guard me" you especially refer to is not strictly mine. Let me tell you where I heard it. When I was the "Mendelssohn scholar" and living at Leipsic [*sic*], I went once or twice to the old Jewish synagogue, and among the many Eastern melodies chanted by the minister, this quaint progression in the minor occurred so frequently that I have never forgotten it. It certainly comes in appropriately here' . . .

Guard_____ me, guard me, Guard_____

_____ me, Je - ho - vah, guard_____ me

Rebecca's prayer is one of Sullivan's most eloquent movements, and the plangent simplicity of the opening is deeply moving:

Lord of our cho-sen race, in hour of deep dis-

Rebecca

Vln. I & II
Harp

Cor anglais

Viola

String bass,
Harp

- tress, and oft - en lone - li - ness.

The comparable prayer in the third act of Marschner's opera sounds the more likely to have come from Sullivan's workshop:

Ivanhoe is a lyrical rather than a dramatic work, and the terrain in which Sullivan conducted his main musical operations is familiar. The popular numbers from the work were those sung respectively by King Richard and Friar Tuck at the beginning of the second act—when the King, in disguise, rests in the Forest. 'I ask nor wealth nor courtier's praise'—an easy, ambling tune, sails over divided violas and harps, until a Viennese switch of tonality around the dominant of one key which becomes the mediant of the next introduces the oboe. This is a strophic song, and in the last stanza Sullivan weaves Dvořák patterns in the strings and wood-wind. Friar Tuck—a Falstaff in Holy Orders—comes off well at Sullivan's

hands. He may be seen to emerge as a progressive, incantating pseudo-folk-song in his most popular song (see page 242), as though a candidate for inclusion in Vaughan Williams's *Hugh the Drover*.

Marschner's Friar would appear to have had a military training and speaks with an un-English brusqueness, albeit in the same key.

Brü-der wacht, Ha - bet Acht! Hör - ner-klang er - schallt,

Sullivan's strength in *Ivanhoe* lies where it might be expected to be found, in spontaneity of melody, in felicity of instrumentation, in scenic evocation. As in the case of *The Golden Legend* the distinctive feature of the orchestration is that it is 'not loud', and the best movements are to be found in the beautiful scoring at the end of the first and the beginning of the second scene of Act I. The former is the 'Goodnight' scene of Cedric and Rowena; the latter Rowena's soliloquy to the moon.

The Irish strain in Sullivan often sent him in search of a *Tír na n-Óc*—the mythical fairy land, the land of youth, of the ancient Celts. In his last years he travelled without the companionship of Gilbert, and from the musico-dramatic point of view this was unfortunate. Whether Gilbert would have put sharper edges on the libretto of *Ivanhoe* is open to question, but he would have stimulated Sullivan to consider its dramatic properties more than did the amiable Sturgis. *Ivanhoe*, however, was not the true end of Sullivan's operatic ambitions. He had thought of the subject of King Arthur at the beginning of his career. Towards the end of his life he was brought back to the theme by Comyns Carr.

Having written incidental music for *King Arthur*, Sullivan hoped that at some time he might come round to using it up in a more ambitious setting. Of the opera that might have been, there is a 'Grail' motiv which, used as an ostinato, builds into a brief, effective chorus, tinged with grief as the voices—mostly in octaves—move from A flat towards G major. The 'May Song' is one of Sullivan's happiest inventions—a *faux-bourdon* pattern for women's voices, floated above a tonic pedal with a fluttering background figure for the upper strings.

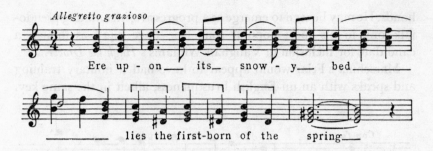

The poise of this choral writing anticipates the cool elegance of the voices in Arthur Bliss's *Pastoral*.

The final music of *King Arthur* is for the Funeral Procession of the King—surely to be marked, Elgarianly, *nobilmente*.

NOTES TO CHAPTER ELEVEN

1. *Ivanhoe*, libretto by Emile Deschamps and Gustave de Wailly, Odéon, Paris, 15th September 1826. As *The Maid of Judah, or The Knight Templar*, Covent Garden, 7th March 1829.
2. *Ivanhoe*, Venice, 1832; in German, Vienna, 14th February 1837.

3. cf. the use of 'old German trumpets' for the Mass in B Minor at Leeds in 1886.

4. Esther Palliser became a notable figure in English music, not least because of her prima donna behaviour. On 4th October 1898 the *London Daily News*, reporting the Leeds Festival, observed how '. . . On Saturday [she] caused much amusement by bringing to rehearsal—and, indeed, on to the platform—a pet dog. The dog is said to mark one of the stages in the rise in professional life of an American prima donna—Having, however, thus asserted herself on Saturday, Miss Palliser tonight was merciful, and on coming to sing in M. Fauré's "Ode", she left the interesting quadruped at home.'

5. The following letter, like that of 31st December 1890, is now preserved in the Library of the Royal College of Music:

1 Queen's Mansions
18 Sept. 1889.

Dear Miss Macintyre:

Many thanks for your note. I have selected the aria 'L'altra notte' [*Mefistofele*, Boito] as I think it will be far more interesting both for yourself and the public. I return home to the above address tomorrow in case you wish to communicate with me again.

Yours sincerely,
Arthur Sullivan.

Boito's aria was included in the second part of the evening concert on 10th October 1889.

6. Nathaniel Vert, concert agent.

7. Edward Solomon composed the music for *The Nautch Girl* which Carte put on at the Savoy in the summer of 1891.

8. '. . . with a full description of the libretto and twenty-one well executed drawings of Maurice Greiffenhagen, Herbert Railton, John Jellicoe, and others . . .' *Referee*, 31st May 1891.

9. Ernest Ford (1858–1919) entered the Royal Academy of Music as the first Goss Scholar in 1875. Sullivan was one of his teachers. He also studied in Paris with Lalo. He spent some time in the U.S.A. and his *Domine Deus* was sung at the 250th anniversary celebrations at Harvard University. Ford was official accompanist at the Saturday Popular Concerts in London for a time, and a busy composer.

10. *The World*, 27th April 1892.

11. Lord Salisbury had been defeated at the General Election and Gladstone became Prime Minister for the fourth time.

12. At that time there were two chief conductors at the Royal Opera, Karl Muck (from 1891 to 1912) and Felix Weingartner (from 1891 to 1898).

13. *Allgemeine Musik-Zeitung*, 24th November 1895, p. 615.

12

Last phase

Sullivan's creative sensitivity sharpened two normal phobias; of poverty and of death. The composer for the common man *par excellence*, Sullivan shared the ambitions and aversions of the average member of society of his time. At the back of his progress to affluence was the history of the hard times of his parents. Filled with morbid foreboding at the death of any member of his family, or friend, he dreaded every incidence of ill-health. He was never robust. His mode of life gave him little chance of building up adequate reserves of stamina, nor were there then adequate means of combating the infections to which he so frequently succumbed. In seeking recuperation he followed the normal practice of the time and loitered extravagantly, and often pointlessly, in fashionable health-resorts. In the summer of 1896 it was again time to take a cure, so he announced to Helen Carte his intention of going to the Hotel Victoria, St Moritz, Engadine, Switzerland:

> There I hope to pick up strength & return D.V. well & robust. I don't want to worry you, but I am overdrawn at Goslings; & *must* buy some things from their bank—So will you like a dear, pay my Grand Duke money to my account *there*, as soon as you can, & also my Rome money, when it is ready for distribution . . .

After the exertions of a wedding—that of Princess Maude to her cousin Prince Charles of Norway—various members of the royal family also felt in need of recuperation and they too made for St Moritz. Sullivan was delighted. He entertained the Duchess of York, her mother the Duchess of Teck, and Prince Francis of Battenberg to dinner at his hotel one evening. Next day after lunching with the Duchesses he went out walking with them. He gave gifts to the royal ladies and in return received a signed photograph of the Duchess of York and her children. After leaving St Moritz he went to München and Vienna. His next call was Kronberg, where he was invited to stay with the Dowager Queen of Prussia at Friedrichshof. The eldest daughter of Queen Victoria, and herself christened Victoria, she had been betrothed to Frederic William of Prussia when she was fifteen and married two years later. During the long years in which her husband was Crown Prince, she had done her best to exert a liberal influence in Prussian affairs, at every opportunity opposing the policies of Bismarck. Her husband became King-Emperor in March 1888, but, mortally ill with cancer, died only two months later. In her lonely retirement Victoria occupied herself with art, literature and philanthropy, maintaining her English connections and interests as she had always tried to do. Sullivan was a charming guest and his visit gave much pleasure to his hostess, and also to her daughters, Princess Adolph of Schaumburg-Lippe and Princess Louise of Hesse. The royal ladies were particularly delighted to receive a distinguished, and non-political, British subject at a time when the Emperor himself—not now on speaking terms with Queen Victoria—was showing marked signs of Anglophobia.

Back home, having travelled by way of Paris, Sullivan thought of the ballet commissioned for the Alhambra, but, with time in hand, postponed starting work on the score. Grove, who had resigned the Directorship of the Royal College of Music in 1894, saw him twice and reported to Mrs Lehmann:

> He was thin, but I thought his face very much improved, and very nice to look at. . . . I am sorry about the small houses in Edinburgh but on the other hand the *Mikado* is doing well here. The fact is that in music now (as there was in painting in pre-Raphaelite times) composers and hearers worship ugliness . . . There has come a turn or *kink* in the brains and heart-strings of composers: they have no affection, no love for their music. . . .[1]

There is no doubt that Grove was here interpreting the thoughts of Sullivan. The new masters of European music included Strauss and Mahler. The name of Debussy was often heard and as often disparaged. An expatriate Englishman, Frederick Delius, was also composing music that bore no relation to any hitherto known. The Diamond Jubilee was approaching, to celebrate an age that had already ended. If the state of music was uncertain, it was because life itself was increasingly uncertain. The trial of Oscar Wilde in 1895 signalized the beginning of the end of the old order. Sullivan's friend and solicitor Charles Russell—son of an older friend, Lord Chief Justice Russell—had acted for the Marquis of Queensberry in his defence of the libel action brought against him by Wilde, which precipitated the whole calamity. Sullivan was an Irishman; so was

Wilde, so was Russell, and so was Edward Carson whom Russell engaged as counsel for Queensberry. There had been a time when light-hearted satire had been in place. Now no longer was it so. Sullivan packed up and went to France, where he worked at the anachronisms of *Victoria and Merrie England*.[2] This score was completed at the end of March 1897.

In April Sullivan went to Cimiez—where the Queen was resting —to consult with the Queen's Private Secretary about a hymn to be composed for the Jubilee. On Sullivan's suggestion the Bishop of Wakefield was commanded to compose appropriate words— which Sullivan duly set. At his own request he was permitted to play the harmonium for the Queen's Easter Day service at Cimiez. On 24th May the Queen celebrated her seventy-eighth birthday and the Duke of Cambridge opened the Victorian Era Exhibition at Earl's Court. Next day the Duke, with other members of the royal family and, as Sullivan observed with satisfaction, 'all the *élite* of London' attended the Alhambra for the first performance of Sullivan's ballet, which he himself conducted. The *Neue Musik-Zeitung* (18 Jahrgang, page 166) did the work the honour of a serious notice. The production was lavish and Sullivan's music was 'often comic'. Nor did the com- poser fail to make use of 'old English folk-songs'. The comedy is reflected in a 'Comic Dance' which is, in fact, a fugue.[3] There are episodes in the fugue which draw the attention of the listener once again to the composer's sound Leipzig upbringing—as here.

Subject

Contrapuntal *jeux d'esprit*—Elgar often behaved in this way too—
appear also in a gigue *à la* Handel, and in the Finale. Here, however,
ingenuity was not equal to accommodating the Welsh nation, and
the not very effective quodlibet of English, Scottish and Irish folk-
songs is made doctrinally insecure by provocative citations from the
repertoire of the Orangemen. In the opening scene of the ballet,
showing a sleeping Britannia in a Druidic setting, Sullivan slyly
quotes Arne's most patriotic tune, also in soporific mood.[4] In a
Restoration scene (Scene VI) the 'Boar's Head Carol' is quoted.
Otherwise Sullivan invokes Schumann in a 'hobby-horse' piece and
Tchaikovsky in the solo dance that follows the fugue quoted above.

The summer passed in glorious pageantry. In June there was a
Thanksgiving Service at St Paul's Cathedral, and a Great Naval
Review off Portsmouth. At the beginning of July there was a review
of the military at Aldershot, and an Inspection of Colonial Troops
in the gardens of Buckingham Palace. The Colonial Troops were
reviewed to the strains of Hérold, Offenbach and Gung'l. Sullivan
—who had done his best to boost native martial music in the quodlibet of the last scene of his recent ballet—was not pleased. He wrote a
letter to *The Times* on 19th July pointing out the insult paid to British
music and musicians. Next month he left England and travelled
to Bayreuth, where he moved in elegant and distinguished company
and listened to Wagner with alternate boredom and distaste. Sullivan's comments on the performances betrayed, perhaps, his disillusionment over his own worldly success, his inner frustrations as a
serious composer, a feeling of inability to keep up with musical
developments in the broader fields, and a misguided patriotism.[5]

In July Sullivan had been a guest at Windsor Castle. On 14th
December he wrote to Carte

> . . . I have spent most of my time lately at Windsor, & have
> had *three* long and pleasant chats with the Queen (bless her,
> she is so kind & gracious). We are beginning to be talked about!

For some months Sullivan had been considering a new work, in
a rather dilatory manner. This was *The Beauty Stone*, of which the
libretto was by Pinero and Comyns Carr. Sullivan's interest in this
project was minimal, but he enjoyed Carr's company and, indeed,
was still hoping that he might produce a grand opera libretto for
him out of the King Arthur scheme of 1894.[6] Sullivan was not altogether satisfied with the text of *The Beauty Stone* and found it difficult

to persuade his collaborator to modify his style in the interests of musical setting. However, Comyns Carr was good company, and a good raconteur, and Sullivan was glad to invite him to Beaulieu to discuss the libretto. Life was boring without congenial companionship. Carr liked Sullivan and was by no means averse to a six-week holiday (as it turned out) on the Riviera.

He was impressed with two things in particular about Sullivan: his fortitude, and his extraordinary compulsion to gamble. Sullivan was in great pain almost daily '. . . yet even then the brightness of his disposition constantly asserted itself, and he rarely allowed others to be conscious of what he himself endured.' [7] As regards Sullivan at the tables, Carr noted his superstitious behaviour, and his feverish exhilaration. [8]

The Second Spring Meeting at Newmarket began on 10th May, and Sullivan was there. Reminding Helen Carte that he could be reached at the Jockey Club Rooms he gave evidence of the immediate effects of gambling on his fortunes.

> I have been staggered by receiving two accounts which for the moment I am unable to pay. A short time ago I was to the good, & in the last few days the slump has been so rapid and unexpected, that I am much to the bad. Can you (I know you *will* if you can) lend me the money (£1700) for three weeks?
>
> You shall have it then without fail. It will give me time to see how I stand at Rothschilds & Herries, & get the money. . . .

On 28th May *The Beauty Stone* opened at the Savoy, where it lasted for seven weeks. This work turns out as a medieval mishmash. The main theme of the story had its possibilities—that beauty is an inner quality and that love is a mutual recognition of this quality. [9] However, this is so wrapped up in travel-agents' Gothic that it disappears from view. In any case Sullivan was in no mood for working out what Pinero had at least in mind. The Beauty Stone itself is the means whereby Laine, the cripple girl of Mirlemont, in Flanders, casts away her disabilities to become radiant and beautiful and the winner of a beauty competition organized by Philip, Lord of Mirlemont. The Lord of Mirlemont, lately returned from captivity in Cephalonia, had brought home 'the Lady Saida', whose presence makes his pursuit of Laine more difficult than it otherwise would have been. The odds are further weighted against him by the activities of the *diabolus ex machina*—who brought some of his wardrobe and some of his music from *The Golden Legend*. The same work supplied Laine with the character of her 'Prayer before the Virgin' in Act I. The best of the music of *The Beauty Stone* is in Saida's dance, as she remembers her life in Cephalonia, and Sullivan his early oriental exercises (see page 73). In the end Laine loses the Beauty Stone and is as she was, while Philip returns blind from the wars. They then live happily ever afterwards.

The public were glad when *The Beauty Stone* was removed to make way for a revival of *The Gondoliers*, which was followed by a revival of *The Sorcerer*. Sullivan conducted the twenty-first anniversary performance of this work, at the end of which he and Gilbert took calls together for the last time. They had, indeed, on this occasion met each other only on the stage for this one purpose. Afterwards they went their separate ways and—although this was no fault of Sullivan's—they were never to meet again.

Sullivan had reserved all his energies that autumn for the Leeds Festival, and after the drain on the emotions that that imposed, was not disposed to do other than lead a fairly quiet life. He did begin to discuss the possibility of collaboration with Basil Hood, but otherwise devoted himself to tidying his business affairs.

On 14th October, no doubt remembering his early association with the instrument, Sullivan put some money into the James Clinton Combination Clarionet Co. Ltd.[10] On 12th December he wrote to J. N. Barry concerning a quite different kind of commercial undertaking:

> Dear Mr. Barry,
>
> In consideration of the valuable suggestions & assistance you have given me in the development & practical working of my invention (provisionally) called the Sullivan Safety Shaft & also for the benefit I expect to derive from your continued assistance & advice, I hereby undertake to pay you *one third* of the net profits which may accrue to me from the same invention.
>
> It is understood that you are to bear no pecuniary liability whatever, & that all money required for the working of the said invention cost of patents & other incidental expenses, is to be found by me.
>
> Yours truly
> Arthur Sullivan.

The Sullivan Safety Shaft was designed to prevent catastrophe to any passenger in a carriage of which the horse decided to run out of control. By pressing a lever the carriage became detached. The prototype was demonstrated to the Prince of Wales, whose carriage was duly fitted with the invention.

In respect of his music Sullivan signed an agreement with Bosworth of Leipzig for *The Merchant of Venice* [11] and he wrote to Booseys concerning his old contracts with them. The implications of this letter which was marked 'July' are melancholy. It was addressed by Sullivan to 'Arthur Sullivan Esq.' instead of 'Arthur Boosey' and on 28th October Boosey noted: 'Will go into it.'

> Dear Mr. Boosey:
>
> In looking over my Publishing Agreements I find I have had none with your firm respecting my various songs.
>
> At the urgent request of my legal adviser I am now settling all my papers in order, & am having prepared the necessary agreements with you which I will send for signature shortly.
>
> On examining the last royalty a/c I note, that only 4d is allowed on several songs which never bore a singers [*sic*] royalty.
>
> Of course I have no legal claims to 6d on them, still I think morally I am entitled to 6d on all those songs which are not otherwise burdened with royalty.
>
> Will you consider this matter & let me know your decision.
>
> > Yours very truly,
> > Arthur Sullivan.

During 1898 Sullivan alternated between a desire to compose and a growing doubt as to his capabilities. He assured them at Leeds that he would be ready with a cantata for 1901—though everyone who saw him there was certain that he would not see another festival through—but he told Rudyard Kipling that he could not manage a setting of the *Recessional*. He refused this but could not similarly refuse a royal command, so in December an anthem he had been asked to compose for funerals at the Royal Mausoleum at Frogmore was duly sung for the first time. Through the closing months of 1898 Sullivan discussed a new opera scheme with Basil Hood. Based on an oriental theme, *Hassan* (this was the working title) intrigued Sullivan, and if he did not pursue his setting at more than moderate pace he enjoyed Hood's company. By a coincidence

Carte put on a piece with an Eastern setting at the beginning of 1899, which made it imprudent to follow it with another of that kind. Sullivan went down with influenza and, according to custom, escaped from the English winter to the clearer air of Switzerland. At his request Hood came to see him, and a substitute for *Hassan* was discussed and even commenced. But it was determined after all to persist with the first idea. Sullivan stayed in Switzerland until the middle of August and when he came back to England it was to a house he had taken at Wokingham.

Meanwhile the Queen had celebrated her eightieth birthday; Prince Alfred of Coburg had died and the Duke of Connaught had renounced his right of succession to the Duchy in favour of the young Duke of Albany; there had been a March Past of 27,000 Volunteers. London life appeared to be as firmly based as ever. But in the autumn the might of Empire was challenged by the rebellious Boer farmers of South Africa. From the beginning of October troops were dispatched to South Africa where they were to serve under the command of Sir Redvers Buller. Rudyard Kipling, at the instigation of the *Daily Mail*, wrote *The absent-minded beggar*. On 5th November Sullivan completed its musical setting.[12] Eight days later it was performed at the Alhambra and the effect was as stirring as that of the first performance of *God Save the King* in 1745. *The absent-minded beggar* was one of Sullivan's greatest successes; but it did not prevent the repulse of Buller at the Tugela River on 16th December, in circumstances that left the nation aghast. Nonetheless there were soothing distractions at home. Among them was *The Rose of Persia*, under which name *Hassan* had finally been launched on 29th November. No doubt a Persian subject (however fantastic) was a convenient means of persuading the Persians—in London at least—that the British entertained nothing but the kindest feelings and warmest interest in their country. By coincidence *The Rose of Persia* was introduced to the public at a time when the Grand Vizier was being awkward, and the merchant bankers of London were considering how they could most profitably underpin the Persian economy.

This work (which ran for more than 200 performances) illustrates not so much decline in inspiration or talent, as a failure of judgment. *The Rose of Persia* is a sad parody of Gilbert by Hood, and of Sullivan by Sullivan. One or two moments of musical charm do not redeem a score that by Sullivan's best standards is merely dull. One particular section catches more than passing interest. The dance belonging to the trio of Persian ladies (see below) ties up with the piece in oriental style shown in the example on page 73. It too is almost a candidate for *Mikrokosmos*:

A new work by Sullivan was still noticed in the international press, but without much sympathy, as this extract from *Bühne und Welt* shows:

> The characters in the confused libretto are, *praeter propter*, the same as in *Mikado*, except that they are transferred from Japan to Persia. The Mikado in this work is the Sultan of Persia, Nanki Poo, the principal singer, is the ballad-singer Yussuf . . . , in place of the three little Japanese girls a trio of ladies from a Persian harem trip across the scene . . . an *a cappella* madrigal ['Joy and Sorrow alternate'] is included which also recalls the *Mikado* but not to the advantage of *The Rose of Persia* . . . I have scarcely ever heard so many wrong notes as from the female singers of the Savoy Theatre.[13]

Sullivan was pleased with *The Rose of Persia*, but the new year started badly for him. On 2nd January he went to the Crystal Palace for a horse show and on the way back to London slipped on the station platform and was almost caught between train and platform. He was also much troubled with his old complaint and, as usual, thought it expedient to go to the Riviera. Before going, however, he signed an agreement with the John Church Company of Cincinnati to compose three settings of poems from Tennyson's *The Princess*.[14]

On 20th March he wrote to Helen Carte from the Hotel de Paris, Monte Carlo, reporting on his state of health:

> . . . Monte Carlo always picks me up after I have been unwell. I passed portions of a 'quarry' before I left London, and suffered a good deal. So, I came down here to hang about in this sunshine, & the result was that the rest of the quarry came away with a good portion of it if not all. . . .

Sullivan, however, grew restless at Monte Carlo and after a month decided that he would be happier at home. The return journey was exhausting; so much so that he felt obliged to break it in Paris, where he spent a few days. In London again he felt somewhat better. The news from South Africa was encouraging. Bloemfontein had been captured and the relief of Mafeking appeared imminent. Indeed the end of the war seemed to be in sight, and in May, in preparation for the anticipated Service of Thanksgiving for Victory, Sullivan was prevailed on to begin the composition of a *Festival Te Deum*. At the end of May the spirits of the nation rose higher as a result of the racing achievements of the Prince of Wales. His horse, Diamond Jubilee, was a creature of uncertain temper, but in the Two Thousand Guineas, ridden by H. Jones, it behaved splendidly and ran home an easy winner, four lengths ahead of Sir Ernest Cassel's Bonarosa. On 30th May the same horse and rider performed with distinction at Epsom. Diamond Jubilee, the favourite, won the Derby, and Sullivan was there to join in the general rejoicing.

At this time Kitchener was engaged in the subjugation of the Sudan, and since this was placed under Anglo-Egyptian control (Egypt herself being under British protection) it was both courteous and tactful to invite the Khedive to London. Sullivan saw possibilities in such a visit, since the Khedive would be a guest at Windsor. On 28th June—a week after the Khedive's arrival in England—he wrote to Helen Carte from 'River Bank' at Shepperton, which he had taken as a country retreat for that summer. He also referred to Gilbert in such a way as to indicate that old animosities were still alive:

> . . . But it's a little strong on the part of Gilbert, to lay such stress on my coming and taking the call with him. I have no

doubt that it is in the highest degree amusing for him, and is a humorous situation such as he loves to go before the public in the most harmonious manner, and then turn his back deliberately upon me as we get on to the stage again.

He committed the outrage as I told you, of cutting me dead in the street. I survived it, but I am not going to, wittingly, indulge him in a similar pleasure if I can help it. Now for a business question—although the Rose of Persia is off the bill, would there be any difficulty in giving a performance of it at Windsor 'by command' if it were required?

. . . Of course it would be just the thing for the Khedive (if he dont think it was a joke on his religion).

It would mean either closing the theatre one night or getting up a country company for that occasion. But with all that, it would be worth it for the sake of the prestige. We were the first who gave the Queen an idea of what was going on in the way of light opera, and we oughtn't to let any similar thing step in— George Edwardes [15] for instance . . .

At the end of June Basil Hood brought the outline and some of the lyrics for a new opera. Possibly emboldened by Stanford's successful exploitation of Irish life in *Shamus O'Brien*,[16] and encouraged by the Queen's State Visit to Dublin, Hood and Sullivan were collaborating in *The Emerald Isle*. By July the *Te Deum* was virtually complete; all that was necessary for it to be performed was that the war—from which the troops were already coming back in considerable numbers —should end. To keep patriotism on the boil Sullivan conducted hundreds of sweating bandsmen from the provinces in a massed performance of *The absent-minded beggar* during the Brass Bands Contest at the Crystal Palace during July. But then again he suffered a grievous shock. On 31st July his old and valued friend the former Duke of Edinburgh, now ruler of Saxe-Coburg, died. Ten days later Charles Russell—Lord Chief Justice—also died. He too had been a close friend of Sullivan, who now packed up and departed for Switzerland.

At the beginning of September [17] he reported to Helen Carte that the first act of *The Emerald Isle* was done (so far as the vocal parts were concerned) but that he was

. . . stopped by violent neuralgia.

I have never had it before, & wish I had not had it at all. It takes the form of a violent headache with deadening pain all

down the side of my face, & renders me incapable of even
writing a letter when it comes on, which happens five or six
times a day. It has almost entirely stopped my work for five
days, for it invariably comes on when I begin to write.

In his diary Sullivan complained of a lack of ideas and at the end
of the month, when he was again in England, he found work impossible. He had, in fact, virtually written all that he was to write.
He went down to Tunbridge Wells where he suffered excruciating
pains from his kidney complaint. Quietened by injections of morphine
the spasms passed and, although very weak, he thought about working again. Stimulated by a letter from Helen Carte, in which she
complained of the *Te Deum* taking precedence over the opera,
Sullivan let out a momentary flash of old humour. He said,

> . . . I couldn't help smiling at the little dig at the *Te Deum*—
> it was so thoroughly womanly. But my dear you are mistaken.
> The 'mistake' of writing the Te Deum, had no more to do with
> the backward state of the opera, than conducting the Leeds
> Festival in 1898, or writing 'The Golden Legend' in 1886 had
> . . . This place has done me much good, & I hope to return home
> on Monday next.

But when he was back in Queens Mansions he relapsed. On 14th
October he noted in his diary that he had done practically nothing
for a month, 'first from illness and physical incapability, secondly
from brooding and nervous terror about myself'. Next day's entry
in the diary, ending, 'I am sorry to leave such a lovely day' was
his last.

On 16th October he wrote to Helen Carte again:

> . . . Forgive me dictating this letter, as I want to save my hand
> for music writing. I need not tell you how grieved I am that
> this last illness of mine should have caused so much delay: if I
> had been well and strong we should now be holding band
> rehearsals, but for nearly five weeks although I have tried to
> work hard, I have not been able to do a note—until last week . . .

Eleven days later he responded manfully to Helen's advice that
he should fulfil his civic responsibilities in the local government
election:

> . . . I will certainly do my municipal duty on Thursday and

vote for Mr. Montagu Smith and any other Unionist or Conservative who holds right views about things generally.

I quite agree with you about its importance, and we ought to try and get a better class of man as representative than the small tradesman, and jerry builder who have hitherto been in such force.

About myself and the opera. I work hard and waste no time knowingly and wilfully, but I am *very slow* at it; the reason being that I am so weak. I cannot get my strength back—the chill I got in Switzerland has pulled me down dreadfully—my voice is still 'absent without leave', and is the result of general debility—and of course my appetite is not worth a brace of shakes . . .

Patience was to be revived eleven days later and the Cartes hoped that Sullivan would be there to take a curtain-call. What is more, Gilbert hoped that he would be there. Having heard of his old partner's declining health he showed concern. As it happened he too was far from well. 'I am plodding on,' Sullivan wrote to Helen on 2nd November,

> but it is very dreary work when the flesh is so weak, however willing the spirit may be. I think that if three such noble wrecks as Gilbert, D'Oyly and myself were to appear on the stage at the same time, it would create something more than a sensation . . .
>
> It wasn't my intention to come to the first night of 'Patience', but if it would really please Gilbert to have me there and go on with him, I will come—not to conduct of course, but to take the call with him (and D'Oyly too) if there should be one. Let us bury the hatchet, and smoke the pipe of peace. I have no doubt we can get both from the property room, and if the result is to relieve G. of some of that awful gout, I shall be well pleased. . . .
>
> P.S. All my men got in for Westminster I see.

But it was not possible after all to go to the Savoy. Writing 'from bed' Sullivan said:

> It's not a question of taking a chill if I come out, but of ever getting out at all again. I am regularly bowled over—kidneys and throat.
>
> Pray tell Gilbert how very much I feel the disappointment.

Good luck to you all. Three invalid chairs would have looked very well from the front.

On the afternoon of 21st November Sullivan's condition underwent a change. It was as though the gradual withdrawal from life suggested by the tone of his diary entries at the deaths of the Duke of Saxe-Coburg and Lord Russell in the summer, and by his references to his work—and of which his loss of voice appeared as a symbol—had taken him to the point of no return. His physician, George Buckston Browne, [18] was not unduly alarmed but promised to call in the Queen's physician, Sir Thomas Barlow, should it seem necessary. Next morning, almost without warning, Sullivan died, the cause of death 'Bronchitis 21 days, cardiac failure'.[19] Herbert Sullivan was in the house at the time. Among the first callers to pay their respects to the dead composer were old John Sullivan, Arthur's uncle, the Dean of the Chapel Royal, and Sir Squire Bancroft, the actor-manager.

On 23rd November *The Times* began a long obituary notice by saying:

> The death of Sir Arthur Sullivan . . . may be said without hyperbole to have plunged the whole of the Empire in gloom; for many years he had ranked with the most distinguished personages, rather than with ordinary nusicians. . . .

The same evening the *Express and Star* of Wolverhampton (where *The Rose of Persia* had just finished playing) paid a less official and more heart-felt tribute in a notable obituary under the heading of 'The People's Singer'. After describing Sullivan's achievements, the writer saw as the greatest the fact that

> . . . His music is still *Volkslied*, the song of the people, free and joyous, but he has set it in a context of artistic workmanship that excites the admiration of the *connoisseurs* and adds to the delight and wonder of the illiterate.

Referring obliquely to those who would have had Sullivan do other than he did the *Express and Star*, after mentioning the composer's long record of ill-health, concluded:

> . . . That under these circumstances he has done so much should be our feeling today, rather than of complaint that he did not do more.

Sullivan's unique place in musical history was recognized in many ways. On the night of his death the Savoy Theatre was closed as a mark of tribute. Sullivan's own instructions regarding his burial were set aside by command of the Queen. He had wished, after having been embalmed, to be buried with his mother in Brompton Cemetery. Instead, what amounted to a State Funeral was ordained, the first part in the Chapel Royal, the second in St Paul's Cathedral, where a burial place in the crypt, near Maurice Greene and William Boyce, was prepared.

The Queen was represented at the funeral by Sir Walter Parratt, the Prince of Wales by Hubert Parry, the German Emperor by Prince Lynar, an attaché at the Embassy who also laid a wreath on behalf of von Hochberg, and the United States Ambassador was among the vast and distinguished company of mourners. The pall-bearers were Sir Squire Bancroft, Sir Frederick Bridge, Organist of Westminster Abbey, François Cellier, Col. Arthur Collins, one of the Royal Equerries, Sir George Lewis, a famous lawyer, Sir Alexander Mackenzie, and Sir George Martin, Organist of St Paul's.

There remained immediately to be dealt with the matter of *The Emerald Isle*. At first it was suggested by the newspapers that Wilfrid Bendall would be empowered to complete the work. On 29th January 1901, however, Carte commissioned Edward German to undertake the task. In his Will Sullivan made many dispositions. Most of the institutions with which he had been connected were remembered; so too were his closest friends. Of these the most significant was Mary Ronalds, whose

> music-room became famous and interesting, for it contained the priceless legacies in manuscripts and instruments which Sir Arthur Sullivan left to the woman whom he was pleased to honor with his especial friendship.[20]

On 27th April 1901, *The Emerald Isle* was performed for the first time. On 2nd June the South African war ended with the announcement of the peace terms by Lord Salisbury in the House of Lords. On 8th June the Public Thanksgiving was held at St Paul's Cathedral. The Duke of Cambridge was present, and observed that 'the new Te Deum composed by the late Sir Arthur Sullivan for such a special occasion is not worthy of his usual good church music'.[21]

On the anniversary of Sullivan's death a Memorial Concert took place at Queen's Hall, the programme being given by the Wolverhampton Festival Choral Society, the Newman Queen's Hall Orchestra, and six distinguished soloists, conducted by Henry Wood. The chosen works were *In Memoriam*, *The Golden Legend*, and a selection from the second act of *Ivanhoe*. This was the last grand flourish to suggest that Sullivan was a great, 'serious', composer.

NOTES TO CHAPTER TWELVE

1. Graves, *Life of Grove*, pp. 243–4.
2. On 14th February 1897, he reported progress on the score to Hermann Klein, from the Villa Mathilde, St Jean-de-Villefranche.
3. 'The application of another musical form to a stage purpose was again tried in the Jubilee ballet, "Victoria and Merrie England"; but from one cause or other the danced fugue was not a great success . . .' Fuller-Maitland, *English Music in the XIXth Century*.
4. *Rule Britannia* is also quoted referentially in the Finale of Act I of *Utopia Ltd.*
5. Sullivan's diary, quoted by Sullivan and Flower, *Sir Arthur Sullivan*, 1950 edn., pp. 242–4. Against these jaundiced views should be set an observation of Hermann Klein: '[In 1891] I saw Sir Arthur Sullivan alone in a pit tier box at Covent Garden, listening to a performance of "Die Meistersinger". After the second act I went to speak to him, and noticed that he had before him a full score of Wagner's work. Presently he pointed to it and remarked: "You see I am taking a lesson. Well, why not? This is not only Wagner's masterpiece, but the greatest comic opera that was ever written."' Klein, *Thirty Years of Musical Life*, p. 196.
6. *See* the Preface to *King Arthur*, in which Wilfrid Bendall refers to Sullivan's early intention to write an opera on the subject of Arthur and Guinevere (*see* p. 59), to the fact that Lionel Lewin once sketched a libretto, and that at the end of his life Sullivan still hoped to accomplish this intention. Thus the incidental music, which was to be used also in the opera, was not published until after Sullivan's death. *See* excerpts from *King Arthur* on p. 244.
7. J. Comyns Carr, *Some Eminent Victorians*, London, 1908, p. 288.
8. See *ibid.* p. 285.
9. '[J. Comyns Carr] was responsible for the lyrics and parts of the plot. But I know that his idea of the man's true love being first awakened after he had become blind was dear to him, and he used it again in his adaptation of Jekyll and Hyde for H. B. Irving; but there it is the wife whose blindness hides from her all but the beautiful side of her husband.' Alice Comyns Carr, *Stray Memories*, p. 105.

10. 'Received of Sir Arthur Sullivan Mus. Doc., by cheque drawn in favour of Messrs. Horn, Son & Co., the sum of ninety five pounds eleven shillings for the purpose of paying the fees on application for the Patents in eight countries for the new Duplex Clarionet according to Messrs. Horn, Son & Co.'s invoice. This sum is a loan to the above company repayable out of the new subscriptions that come in, to this amount or otherwise with five per cent interest.'

11. The full score and orchestral parts to be published without payment, but with royalties on separate items arranged for piano, or any instrumental combination, of 6d. per copy for England, 3d. per copy for America, and 35 Pfennigs for the Continent; the royalty on complete piano solo or short version, one third of the published price.

12. Sullivan signed the agreement on 10th November; he earned 6d. per copy in Great Britain and the colonies, and 3d. per copy in the U.S.A. The sales of this one work were vast.

13. *Bühne und Welt*, 2. Jrg., 1899–1900, Berlin, p. 997.

14. A year later Sullivan's account with the John Church Co. showed $423 in respect of royalties on *Tears, idle tears*, and $352 on *O swallow, swallow*. Sullivan did not complete the set.

15. George Edwardes (1852–1917) was D'Oyly Carte's first business manager at the Savoy and subsequently manager of the Gaiety and Daly's Theatre.

16. First performed at the Opera Comique on 2nd March 1896. The performance was conducted by Henry J. Wood. The stars were Denis O'Sullivan (Shamus) and Joseph O'Mara (Mike Murphy), and Gustav Holst, trombonist, was in the orchestra.

17. Only dated 'Sunday, Sept. 1900', but *c*. 3rd September; cf. diary.

18. George Buckston Browne, M.R.C.S., of University College Hospital, London, a Liston Gold Medallist in Clinical Surgery, was a distinguished surgeon. Browne, who lived to a great age, is remembered by Sir Eric Riches, M.S., F.R.C.S., who testifies to his outstanding skills. His contributions to *Heath's Dictionary of Practical Surgery* included 'Diagnosis of stone in the bladder, and choice of operation'. His consulting-rooms were at 80 Wimpole Street, W.1.

19. Certificate of death, signed by Buckston Browne.

20. *Boston Transcript*, 3rd June 1901. The conclusion of this obituary notice has hitherto escaped comment. It reads: 'Her husband, after separation from Mrs. Ronalds for thirty-three years, filed a petition for divorce in Connecticut courts. He was then seventy-two years of age and his wife was only a few years his junior. Later Mr. Ronalds withdrew his suit.' The Ronalds had separated in 1867.

21. Sheppard, *George, Duke of Cambridge*, II, p. 293.

13
Epilogue

The death of Sullivan afforded his enemies earlier opportunity for denigration than might have been anticipated. Less than three months elapsed before Fuller-Maitland published a long obituary in the *Cornhill Magazine*.[1] After remarking on the genius shown in the *Tempest* music, and contrasting that work with the 'dry, scholastic, uninspired work that represented English music at that time', Fuller-Maitland flayed the oratorios as

> lamentable examples of uninspired and really uncongenial work; [with] choruses that were obviously meant to rival the simple grandeur of Handel, or the narrative force of Mendelssohn, [but which] only succeeded for the most part in being pompous and dull, and [with] solos in which the musical tastes of the multitude were consulted [and which] turned out to be trivial in the last degree.

After bestowing moderate praise on the operettas Fuller-Maitland referred to various of the ballads, in particular *The lost chord* and *The absent-minded beggar*.

> It is not because of the perpetration of such things as these that Sullivan's attainment of a place among the immortal may be doubted. Though the illustrious masters of the past never did write music as vulgar, it would have been forgiven them if they had, in virtue of the beauty and value of the great bulk of their productions. It is because such great natural gifts— gifts greater, perhaps, than fell to any English musician since the time of Purcell,—were so very seldom employed in work worthy of them. The Offenbachs and Lecocqs, the Clays and Celliers, did not degrade their genius for they were incapable of higher things than they accomplished; by temperament and inclination they were fitted for the lightest kinds of music, and failure for them lay in the attempt to produce works of great pretension. . . .

If the author of 'The Golden Legend', the music to 'The Tempest', 'Henry VIII' and 'Macbeth' cannot be classed with these how can the composer of 'Onward Christian Soldiers' and 'The absent-minded beggar' claim a place in the hierarchy of music among the men who would face death rather than smirch their singing-robes for the sake of a fleeting popularity?

The appearance of this article was quoted by Elgar, who was ever conscious of the kindness he had received from Sullivan, as an example of 'the shady side of musical criticism', and as 'that foul unforgettable episode'.[2] Fuller-Maitland's strictures, clearly, were severe. By themselves they could have been passed by, but they represented the views of some who at that time were acting as the arbiters of good taste—a dreary concept that for a long time was to bedevil the progress of English art. A general revival of interest in Victorian culture, and in particular the contemporary trend towards rehabilitation of architects and painters of that era, should at least urge caution in accepting too readily the critical dogmas of a somewhat exclusive and long out-dated circle. In respect of some of those who disapproved of Sullivan's music it may be said that private resentments played their part. Sullivan, it was thought by the envious, had undeservedly won great acclaim. Even posthumously he was signally recognized by the bestowal of an Order by the German Kaiser. The critics and pedagogues of 1901 (despite the appearance of Elgar) were still keen in their expectation of the coming of a new English great master. The danger of forever looking for 'great masters' is that when one appears he is not recognized. Throughout the Victorian period the English musical establishment suffered from an obsession in this respect, which was a by-product of power in other fields. But the same establishment required a great master to behave as one according to its own somewhat limited perspectives. Sullivan was not greatly interested in these perspectives, but with ensuring that he himself should do what he could do best. What he could do best, in the broadest and best sense, was to popularize music. He did this not only through his own works, but also through his selection and direction of music at concerts and festivals throughout Britain, and through his sponsorship of younger men.

He worked hard for the recognition and encouragement of English talent. He believed in it, and his praise was generous and outspoken in discussing the works of his contemporaries.[3]

He also began effectively to dispel the heresy, held abroad, that England was incapable of creative musicianship.

An unusual tribute in this connection appeared in a notice in a French journal published soon after the publication of Fuller-Maitland's article. Reviewing a new piano concerto by Emil Sauer the writer observed of it that

> ... il y a quelque suggestion de Wagner, des souvenirs de la neuvième symphonie de Beethoven et il y a bien aussi un rappel de la gaité d'Arthur Sullivan.[4]

Gaiety, however, was not a virtue highly regarded by the pundits at home at the time of Sullivan's death, and in critical terms it was studiedly ignored. The great composer too often is esteemed for his solemnities.

A year after his death Sullivan had been all but eliminated: partly by the Gilbert and Sullivan synthesis; partly by the propagation of the opinion that he had 'smirched his singing-robes'; and partly by a suspicion that his accumulation of wealth was necessarily a disqualification. He had, in fact, acquired the wrong image. Sullivan, opined the Wolverhampton newspaper reporting the anniversary concert of 1901, had by then

> already become a composer of the past . . . One would have thought that at the Queen's Hall, London, the city where he was born and where he did most of his work, his memory would have been honoured better; but it was not so, and though the popular parts were crowded the highly-priced portions of the auditorium were but poorly filled.

Sullivan's reputation in his lifetime had risen so high that some diminution of it was not only inevitable but necessary. But in so far as justice was done it was justice of a very rough order. Virtually the whole of the one side of his creative output was dropped overboard. The considerable quantity of Shakespeare-inspired music, the symphony, the oratorios, the opera *Ivanhoe*, were as if they had not been. It would be idle to pretend that much of this music is, as is said, of lasting value. Some of it, however, may so be regarded. Sullivan's perceptivity in respect of audio-visual impressions enabled him to transmute the comedy of Shakespeare at least into music that bears marks of authenticity and originality. Sullivan had an instinctive grasp of the significance of sonorities, which enabled him to orchestrate with assurance and brilliance, and as the examples quoted throughout this book demonstrate he was by no means confined to one range of instrumental colours. His methods were inspired most often by verbal references, either implicit or explicit, and in the sense that he was less than happy in the field of 'absolute' music but superlatively gifted in treating verbal concepts he may be seen to some extent to have anticipated the art of Benjamin Britten. Further to this Sullivan's economy both in resources (which circumstance usually enjoined on him) and in musical material may be seen as preludial to latter-day preferences for small forces, particularly of instruments.

All in all Sullivan's 'serious' music bears a Victorian imprint, but its intention sometimes stretched out across the frontiers that were then considered appropriate. Lightness, elegance, emancipation from middle-class values, an eclectic talent that could incorporate impulses from France and Italy as well as from Germany, all tended to open up new vistas. As a composer of oratorio, Sullivan was obviously not uninfluenced by Handel and Mendelssohn, but certainly in *The Prodigal Son* and *The Martyr of Antioch* he attempted definitions of character and of scene that removed their subjects some way from the pulpit interpretations of the period.

In Sullivan's day vulgarity was a vice; it may be now that it is a virtue. At all events an appeal to the suffrages of the many rather than solely to those of the minority is no longer regarded as criminal. In one sense 'Onward Christian Soldiers' is indifferent music; in another, viewed from the standpoint of, say, Charles Ives, it is magnificent. The lesson, which in modern times has taken a long time to re-learn, is that fine music sometimes is inherent in, and often arises from, the commonplace.

Sullivan was no intellectual but an inspired craftsman, and he was torn between his own simple attitudes towards music and the values set on music by the society to which he belonged. An instability which is evident throughout the large body of his compositions was caused to some extent by personal factors—ill-health, the pursuit of achievement as self-justification, and so on—and to some extent by the pressures of the different groups with which he maintained musical and social contact. He did, of course, try to please all the people all the time.

The best of Sullivan stems from those areas in which he could preserve a certain detachment. Because he regarded his collaboration with Gilbert as one part, and not the major part, of his function, he was relieved from the burdens otherwise imposed in England on a serious and official composer. In his introduction to the 'World's Classics' selection of the essays of Matthew Arnold, Noël Annan remarks:

> What is still today irresistible is Arnold's gaiety, his wry astonishment at stupidity, his delighted amusement at folly—and the urbane, self-deprecating inflexion that does not for an instant conceal the hopeful and intense seriousness with which he approached life.

This, surely, is also apposite to the case of Sullivan.

The operettas were a joint production, and the combination of Gilbert and Sullivan is virtually unique in the annals of opera, so unique that it is impossible to separate words from music. Since this end was the objective of all who essayed opera as one art form from the earliest times it may be said that between them, if fortuitously, Gilbert and Sullivan in one particular arrived at one long wished-for end-point. The operettas were devised as entertainment. Progressively they became accepted as an abstract of a philosophy. Collectively they are a criticism of society, couched in the most effective traditional form, caricature. The critical attitudes of Gilbert and Sullivan, if not typically British, are at least an indication of the point of view the British themselves like to imagine as characteristic. The operettas are classics (there is no need for the qualification, 'of their kind'), because they fulfil a permanent need. Scepticism and imagination are necessary ingredients in a civilized society.

While a good deal of this has been accepted it has also been taken for granted, so that Sullivan's genius has been continually underrated. Indifferent performances—supported often by well-meaning amateurs whose capacity for playing and singing the music is severely limited—disguise the superb craftsmanship of the composer. The character of this craftsmanship has been analysed in the earlier parts of this book. For confirmation one may turn to a practising composer of recent times—one of the two or three greatest composers of this century.

Igor Stravinsky heard 'how the Stanislavskys had made "The Mikado" the chic-est thing in Moscow. This knowledge came to me in my teens when I lived in St Petersburg.' The first opportunity to hear the works of Gilbert and Sullivan came to Stravinsky when in

London with Diaghilev in 1912. Since that time Stravinsky claims to have heard all the operas except *The Grand Duke* and *Utopia Limited*. Stravinsky's conclusions may speak for themselves: after referring to the very rare status of unison between librettist and composer, and to *Der Rosenkavalier*, which in comparison with Gilbert and Sullivan he thought 'pretentious', he continued:

> Furthermore, Sullivan has a sense of timing and punctuation which I have never been able to find in Strauss.
> And the British team is never boring. The operas gallop along like happy colts, not like cart horses. They are also moral. The characters are good and bad, and the moral is always clearly drawn, although I do not overlook the sophistication of the satire. They remind me of American Western films or plays when these are of topnotch quality.
> While they depend on conventions, their attack on conventions is always progressive. This is undoubtedly one of the major reasons for the continued popularity of the operas—they will probably last beyond any sunset on the British Empire. I attended a very enjoyable performance of 'The Gondoliers' by the D'Oyly Carte in 1964 at the New York City Center—my most recent connection with Gilbert and Sullivan. Age has not attacked it.
> I might say, in conclusion, that there is one characteristic of Gilbert and Sullivan, apart from the words and music, that has left a lasting impression on me, and that is their pure, remarkable and consistent tact.[5]

The full story of the institution (as it has become) 'Gilbert and Sullivan' lies outside this study, which seeks to present Arthur Sullivan as he was. His was a complex character. Among the greatest of English musicians he was no Englishman, and it was precisely his total lack of English blood that enabled him to become the individual composer that he was. The quality of his music, in its secular facets, was distinctive because uninhibited by extraneous considerations of morality. (It was, indeed, the relative amorality of his approach that led to the particular kind of 'morality' detailed by Stravinsky.) Sullivan was not impelled by convention to sacrifice life to art—a practice much recommended by the well-circumstanced Fuller-Maitland, for instance. He committed the unpardonable crime of accepting the conditions offered by society, of fighting through their frontiers, and acquiring a great wealth. The career of Sullivan—a classic case of the rise from poverty to riches—within the general context of Victorian *mores* was hardly unpraiseworthy. In his achievement in this respect he was able to succour his family as well as others, and also to emancipate his profession. In his insistence on proper material reward he enabled later composers in Britain to lay claim to some sort of economic justice. Nor were his long struggles, together with his partners, without their long-term effect in other parts of the world.

Sullivan, like Wagner and Liszt, though more scrupulous than either, demanded a comfortable, if not luxurious, setting. He was self-indulgent. The conditions on which he insisted were compensation for an inner disequilibrium. He was, despite his apparent gregariousness, a lonely man. To some extent he was strongly homo-erotic, as instanced in his relationship with Grove. This factor, barely disguised in his correspondence, was in large part, no doubt, due to his particular and long dependence on his brother. Not surprisingly this also adversely affected his relationships with women. Apart from the peculiar connection between himself and Mrs Ronalds his adventures usually ended in disaster. Always far from robust, however, he never lived far from pain, and his refusal ever to capitulate betokened qualities little short of heroic.

Sullivan, in short, was many-sided, and the complexities in his character, resolved into a synthesis of musical thought, make him a perpetual source of paradox and fascination. He was, indeed, a rare man.

NOTES TO EPILOGUE

1. March 1901, pp. 300–9.
2. *See* Elgar's lecture on 'Critics', in *A Future for English Music*, London, 1968, p. 187.
3. 'Sir Arthur Seymour Sullivan, As an old Friend knew him', in *The Argosy*, February 1901, pp. 161–7.
4. *L'Art dramatique et musical au XXe siècle*, April 1901, Paris, p. 246.
5. From an interview published in the *New York Times*, 27th October 1968.

Appendix 1

CATALOGUE OF WORKS
WITH INDEX

I *Orchestral Music*

Overture in C minor, *Timon of Athens*, after Shakespeare, 1857, MS.,[1] pp. 12, 71

Overture in D minor, ded. John Goss, 1st perf., Royal Academy of Music, London, 13th July 1858, MS.,[1] p. 12

Overture, *Rosenfest*, after *Lallah Rookh* (Thomas Moore), 1st perf., Leipzig Gewandhaus, 25th May 1860, MS., p. 22

Procession March; arr. for pfte. solo and duet by Franklin Taylor; Cramer (1860)

Princess of Wales' March (based on Danish airs), ded. Prince of Wales, 1st perf., Crystal Palace, 14th March 1863, arr. for pfte. solo and duet; Cramer (1863), p. 43

Symphony in E, the 'Irish',[2] 1st perf., Crystal Palace, 10th March 1866; Novello, 1915, pp. 40–2, 46–7, 48 n. 17, 57, 60, 82, 85–6

Concerto in D major for Violoncello and Orchestra, 1st perf., A. Piatti, Crystal Palace, 24th November 1866, MS., pp. 42, 48 n. 18, 60

Overture in C minor-major, *In memoriam*,[3] 1st perf., Norwich, 30th October 1866; Novello (1885), pp. 43, 46, 47, 57, 80, 88, 208, 261

Concert overture, *Marmion*, after Walter Scott, 1st perf., Philharmonic Society, St James's Hall, London, 3rd June 1867, revised version perf. Crystal Palace, 7th December 1867, MS.,[4] pp. 60, 87–8, 229

---

[1] Detailed by A. C. Mackenzie, 'The Life and Works of Arthur Sullivan', in *Sammelbände der Internationalen Musik-Gesellschaft*, Jahrgang III (1901–1902), Leipzig, 1902, p. 543.

[2] So named by Sullivan in 1893.

[3] MS. (sold at Sotheby's, 13th June 1966) inscribed, 'In memoriam T. S. Obiit 22 Sept., 1866', and annotated, 'Begun 1 Oct: 1866: Finished 10 Oct: 1866. Arthur S. Sullivan'.

[4] Sullivan note on MS. (sold at Sotheby's, 13th June 1966) that the overture was composed in May 1866.

Overture di ballo, 1st perf., Birmingham, 31st August 1870, arr. for pfte. duet by A. O'Leary; Stanley Lucas, Weber (1882); full score, Novello, 1889, pp. 62, 63, 88

March Danois, 'perf. by the Military Bands of England, Denmark, Russia, etc.', ded. Prince of Wales, arr. for pfte.; Weippert (1871)

The Russian Hymn (by Alexis Feodorovich Lvov) arr. for orchestra, MS.[1]

Imperial March, for the Opening of the Imperial Institute on 10th May 1893; arr. for pfte.; Chappell, 1893, p. 196

II *Chamber Music*

Fugue in B flat, in 3 parts, after Mozart (?), R.C.M. MS. 956, no. 6

Romance in G minor, for String Quartet, ded. 'to His Mother', 1st perf., Leipzig, 2nd November 1859; Chappell, 1964, pp. 19, 87

Duo concertante, for violoncello and pfte., Op. 2, ded. Brinley Richards; Lamborn Cock, Addison (1868), pp. 75, 81

III *Music for Pianoforte*

Scherzo, 17th April 1857, and *Capriccio No. 2*, April 1857, MS.[2]

Cadenza for Piano Concerto in A (K. 488), Mozart, MS.,[3] p. 8

Thoughts, Op. 2: No. 1, *Allegretto con grazia*, ded. Lindsay Sloper; No. 2, *Allegro grazioso*, ded. Miss Dunville[4]; Cramer (1862); re-issued for vl. and pfte. as *Reverie in A* and *Melody in D*; Phillips and Page (n.d.)

Allegro risoluto in B flat minor, 8th May 1866, BM. Add. MS. 49977 N, p. 83

---

[1] MS. sold at Sotheby's, 20th July 1965.

[2] Contained in an autograph manuscript book (sold at Sotheby's, 13th June 1966), signed 'Arthur Sullivan May 3rd 1855' and 'A. S. Sullivan, 1857'.

[3] Stated by A. C. Mackenzie (*see* fn. 1, p. 271 above) to have been written for a *Hauptprüfung* in 1859, but of this there is no evidence in the programme of the Leipzig Conservatorium for that year, nor during the time of Sullivan's residence in Leipzig.

[4] Annie Dunville (1841–91), of Holywood, Co. Down, N. Ireland (*see* p. 40), who subsequently married General Evan Gordon.

Day Dreams,[1] (1) *Andante religioso*, (2) *Allegretto grazioso*, (3) *Andante*, (4) *Tempo di Valce* [*sic*], (5) *Andante con molto tenerezza*, (6) *A l'Hongroise, Allegretto*; Boosey (1867); as *Sechs Stücke für das Pianoforte von A. S.*, Op. 14, Kistner, No. 3277, Leipzig, pp. 56, 75–6

Twilight, ded. Miss Rachel Scott Russell; Chappell (1868); as *Klavierstück componirt von A. S.*, Op. 12, Kistner, No. 3276, p. 75

IV *Songs* (*with pfte. accompaniment*)

O Israel, 'sacred song', ded. Mrs C. V. Bridg[e]man; Novello, 1855,[2] pp. 8, 70-1

Various songs (subsequently lost), *c.* 1857

Ich möchte hinaus es jauchzen, ded. Rosamund Barnett, Leipzig, 3rd December 1859, MS.,[3] p. 21

Bride from the north (?), 1st perf., Mrs Harriette Lee, Crystal Palace, 14th March 1863; Cramer, 1863 (No copy extant), p. 43

I heard the nightingale (Rev. C. H. Townsend), ded. Capt. C. J. Ottley; Chappell (1863), p. 74

Sweet day, so cool (George Herbert), ded. Mrs Goldschmidt; Metzler (1864), p. 72

Thou art lost to me (anon.), ded. Mrs Charles Freake; Boosey (1865)

Will he come? (Adelaide A. Procter), ded. Lady Katherine Coke, sung by Mme Sainton-Dolby; Boosey (1865), pp. 52, 59, 74

Orpheus with his lute		ded. Louisa Crampton, pp.44, 71
O mistress mine		„ C. Santley pp. 45, 71
Sigh no more, ladies	(Shakespeare)	„ Sims Reeves
The willow song		„ Mme Sainton-Dolby, p. 71
Rosalind (or *From east to western land*)		„ W. H. Cummings

composed 1863–4; Metzler, 1866

Arabian love song (P. B. Shelley), ded. Fred Clay; Chappell (1866), pp. 44, 73

---

[1] The autographs of nos. 1 and 2 were sold at Sotheby's, 13th June 1966. On 4th March 1915, Boosey's gave permission to H. F. Ellingford to make an organ arrangement of the work, and in 1934 H. Finck issued orchestral arrangements of *Allegretto grazioso, Andante con molto tenerezza* and *Tempo di Valse* (Boosey and Hawkes). The only apparent extant copy of *Day Dreams* in its original form is in the Deutsche Staatsbibliothek, Leipzig.

[2] MS. dated 1st September 1855 (*see* fn. 2, p. 272 above).

[3] Reproduced in Leslie Baily, *The Gilbert and Sullivan Book*, London, 1952, pp. 23–5.

A weary lot is thine, fair maid (Walter Scott), ded. B. Charles Stephenson, sung by Santley; Chappell (1866), p. 46

If doughty deeds (Robert Graham), ded. Mrs Scott Russell; Chappell (1866), p. 47

She is not fair to outward view (Hartley Coleridge), ded. A. D. Coleridge; Boosey (1866)

County Guy (Walter Scott), ded. Lady Alexina Duff; Ashdown (1867)

The maiden's story (Emma Embury); Chappell (1867)

Give (Adelaide A. Procter), ded. Mrs T. Helmore; Boosey (1867)

In the summers long ago (anon.); Metzler (1867); the same music to *My love beyond the sea* (J. P. Douglas), ded. Hon. Mrs Swinton; Metzler (1877)

What does little birdie say? (A. Tennyson); Ashdown (1867), p. 72

The moon in silent brightness (Bishop Reginald Heber); Metzler, 1868, pp. 72, 74

O fair dove, O fond dove (Jean Ingelow), ded. Miss Rachel Scott Russell; Ashdown (1868), p. 59

The snow lies white (Jean Ingelow), sung by Sims Reeves; Boosey (1868), pp. 67 n. 30, 73, 122

O sweet and fair (A.F.C.K.), ded. Mrs Francis Byng; Boosey, 1868, p. 53

I wish to tune my quivering lyre (Anacreon, trans. Lord Byron); Boosey (1868)

The mother's dream (Rev. W. Barnes), ded. Edith Wynne; Boosey, 1868

The troubadour (Walter Scott); Boosey, 1869

Sad memories (C. J. Rowe); Metzler (1869), p. 74

Dove song [W. Brough], comp. expressly for the Prince's Theatre, Manchester, Christmas 1869; Boosey, 1869 [1]

A life that lives for you (Lionel H. Lewin), sung by C. Santley; Boosey, 1870

Village chimes (C. J. Rowe); Boosey, 1870

Looking back (Louisa Gray), ded. Mme Trebelli; Boosey, 1870

---

[1] For the pantomime *Froggee would a wooing go*, libretto by W. Brough. In the 3rd scene, showing the 'Peri Lake', the peris approach: 'As they dance they sing the Dove Polka Song, wherein Mr. A. S. Sullivan has caught and retained the light, airy grace of the scene. The idea was worked out some time ago in that attractive vocal polka, "What the bee says to the flow'ret". Mr. Sullivan has produced quite an original and very pleasing embodiment of the same idea.' *The Manchester Guardian*, 29th December 1869.

The window; or the songs of the wrens (A. Tennyson), 11 songs; Strahan, 1871,[1] pp. 46, 53, 65 n. 8

Venetian Serenade—Nel ciel seren (F. Rizzelli, English words by W. Rainsom), sung by Signor Campassini, 1871; Cramer, 1873,[2] p. 74

Once again (Lionel H. Lewin), for Sims Reeves; Boosey (1872)

Golden days (Lionel H. Lewin), for Janet Patey; Boosey (1872)

None but I can say (Lionel H. Lewin), ded. Mme Cornélie D'Ankara; Boosey (1872), p. 80

Guinevere (Lionel H. Lewin), for Therese Tietjens; Cramer (1872)

The Sailor's grave (H. F. Lyte), ded. Mrs Bourne (Hilderstone Hall); Cramer (1872)

The white plume (J. P. Douglas); Weippert (1872)

Oh! ma charmante (V. Hugo), ded. Mme Conneau; Cramer (1872): Italian version, *Oh! bella mia* (F. Rizzelli); Cramer (1873): English version, *Sweet dreamer* (H. B. Farnie); Cramer (1874), p. 72

Coming home (R. Reece), duet for s. and m.-s.; Boosey (1873)

There sits a bird in yonder tree (G. H. Barham, *Ingoldsby Legends*); Cramer (1873), pp. 72, 91 n. 4

Looking forward (Louisa Gray); Boosey, 1873

The Marquis de Mincepie and *Care is all fiddle-de-dee*; Cramer (1874)[3]

Three Simple Songs—The young mother, ded. Lady Muriel Talbot: (1) 'Cradle song—The days are cold' (anon.), (2) 'Ay de mi, my bird' (George Eliot), (3) 'The first departure' (Rev. E. Monro); Cramer (1874)[4]

---

[1] Preface by Tennyson, dated December 1870: 'Four years ago Mr. Sullivan requested me to write a little song-cycle, German fashion, for him to exercise his art upon. He had been very successful in setting such old songs as "Orpheus with his lute", and I drest up for him, partly in the old style, a puppet, whose almost only merit is, perhaps, that it can dance to Mr. Sullivan's instrument. I am sorry that my four-year-old puppet should have to dance at all in the dark shadow of these days [i.e. of the Franco-Prussian War]; but the music is now completed, and I am bound by my promise.' Of the 12 songs Sullivan set 11.

[2] *Serenata* from *The Merchant of Venice*; see p. 281.

[3] For F. C. Burnand's 'Drawing Room Extravaganza', *The Miller and his man* (1873). This bore the legend: 'with songs by Arthur Sullivan, the Incidental Music composed and arranged James F. Simpson.' From this it would seem that the Serenade, Trio, Duet and Finale were also by Sullivan.

[4] No. 3 was issued as *The chorister* (words by F. E. Weatherley) by Metzler (1873), see p. 80.

Sleep, my love (R. Whyte Melville), for Janet Patey; Boosey
  (1874)

Mary Morison (Robert Burns); Boosey (1874)

The distant shore (W. S. Gilbert); Chappell (1874)

Thou art weary (Adelaide A. Procter); Chappell (1874)

My dearest only love (Marquis of Montrose, 1640), sung by C. Santley;
  Boosey (1874)

Living poems (H. W. Longfellow), for Edith Wynne; Boosey (1874)

Tender and true (unascribed); Chappell (1874)

Love laid his sleepless head (A. C. Swinburne), ded. Hon. Eliot
  Yorke, sung by E. Lloyd; perf. during *The Merry Wives of
  Windsor*, Gaiety Theatre, London, 19th December 1874; Boosey
  (1875)

Christmas bells at sea (C. L. Kenney); Novello, 1875

The love that loves me not (W. S. Gilbert), ded. Mrs D. B. Grant;
  Novello, 1875

Thou'rt passing hence (*The Highland message*) (Felicia Hemans), sung by
  C. Santley; Chappell (1875), pp. 80, 205

Let me dream again (B. C. Stephenson), ded. Mme C. Nilsson;
  Boosey (1875), p. 124

Sweethearts (W. S. Gilbert), sung by E. Lloyd (also in duet form);
  Chappell (1875), pp. 122, 205

The river (anon.) and *We've ploughed our land* (anon.), in *The Sunlight
  of Song*; Routledge/Novello, 1875

My dearest heart (unascribed), ded. Mrs Osgood; Boosey, 1876

The lost chord (anon.); Boosey (1877), pp. 108, 122, 124, 154 n. 13,
  204, 263

Sometimes (Lady Lindsay of Balcarres); Boosey, 1877

When thou art near (W. J. Stewart); Boosey, 1877

I would I were a king (V. Hugo, trans. A. Cockburn), ded. Prince
  Leopold, 'by special desire'; Boosey, 1878

Old love letters (S. K. Cowan), ded. Mrs Ronalds, sung by E. Lloyd;
  Boosey (1879)

St Agnes' Eve (A. Tennyson), ded. Mrs Ronalds, sung by Mme
  Antoinette Sterling; Boosey (1879)

Edward Gray (A. Tennyson); Lucas, Weber (1880)

Dominion Hymn (anon.), ded. 'the people of Canada'; de Zouch &
  Co., Montreal/Chappell, 1880, p. 125

The sisters (A. Tennyson), 'duet for female voices', pub. in *Leisure
  Hour*, 1881; Lucas, Weber (1881)

Life's river (William Boosey) [1]

A shadow (Adelaide A. Procter), sung by Janet Patey; Patey & Willis (1886)

Ever (Mrs Bloomfield Moore); Chappell (1887)

E tu nol sai, Serenata (G. Mazzacato), English version, *You sleep* (B. C. Stephenson), sung in *The Profligate* (A. W. Pinero), 1st perf., Garrick Theatre, London, 24th April 1889; Chappell (1889)

Bid me at least good-bye, sung in *An Old Jew* (Sydney Grundy), 1st perf., Garrick Theatre, London, 6th January 1894; Chappell, 1894,[2] p. 199

The absent-minded beggar (Rudyard Kipling); *The Daily Mail*/Enoch, 1899, pp. 253, 263

O swallow, swallow and *Tears, idle tears* (A. Tennyson, *The Princess*); J. Church Co. (Cincinnati), 1900,[3] pp. 255, 262 n. 14

My child and I (F. E. Weatherley); Boosey, 1901

To one in paradise (Edgar Allan Poe); *Longing for home* (Jean Ingelow); *My heart is like a silent lute* (Benjamin Disraeli, from *Henrietta Temple*); Novello, 1904

V *Part-songs* (*unaccompanied*)

For S.A.T.B. unless otherwise indicated

Madrigal for 4 voices, 1857,[4] p. 8

Seaside thoughts, 1857; Novello, 1904

It was a lover and his lass (Shakespeare), sop. duet and chorus, 1st perf., Royal Academy of Music, London, 14th July 1857, MS.,[5] p. 14 n. 16

---

[1] Although the intended song of this title was never published, payment of one guinea in respect of the words was made to William Boosey on 18th July 1881.

[2] Contract with the Curtis Publishing Co., Philadelphia, Pa., of 29th May 1894, for publication in *The Ladies Home Journal* for £100. (The title of Grundy's *An Old Jew* was changed to *Julius Sterne* in 1905.)

[3] Contract with John Church Co., dated 10th January 1900, was in respect of a 'Set of three songs from Tennyson's *Princess*'.

[4] MS. dated 26th March 1857 (*see* fn. 2, p. 272 above).

[5] On 17th July Cipriani Potter, Principal, wrote to Sir George Smart that Sullivan's recent examination results were excellent, that he had improved in pianoforte playing and harmony, and was industrious. He also observed: 'a Duett and Chorus of his composition was performed at our last concert [14th July] which was much admired.' BM. Add. MS. 41771, f. 133.

The last night of the year (H. F. Chorley); *Musical Times* (Dec.)/
    Novello, 1863
The rainy day (H. W. Longfellow); Novello, 1867/8,[1] p. 66 n. 26
O hush thee, my babie (Walter Scott); Novello, 1867/8, p. 67 n. 28
Evening (Lord Houghton, after Goethe); Novello, 1868
Joy to the victors (Walter Scott); Novello, 1868, p. 76
Parting gleams (Aubrey de Vere); Novello, 1868
Echoes (Thomas Moore); Novello, 1868
I sing the birth (Ben Jonson); Boosey, 1868
The long day closes (H. F. Chorley) and *The beleaguered* (H. F. Chorley),
    for A.T.B.B.; Novello, 1868, pp. 75, 153
All this night, 'an old carol'; Novello, 1870
It came upon the midnight clear (trad.); Boosey, 1871
Lead, kindly light (J. H. Newman); Boosey, 1871
Through sorrow's path (H. Kirke White); Boosey, 1871
Watchman, what of the night; Boosey, 1871
The way is long and drear (Adelaide A. Procter); Boosey, 1871
Upon the snow-clad earth, carol; Metzler, 1876
Morn, happy morn, ded. Mrs John Fairs, trio for the play *Olivia* (W. G.
    Wills), 1st perf., Court Theatre, London, 30th March 1878;
    Metzler, 1878
Hark! what mean those holy voices?, carol, published in *The Lute*, No. 12,
    15th December 1883; Patey & Willis, 1883
Fair daffodils (R. Herrick); *Musical Times* (Oct.)/Novello, 1903

VI *Church music*

Sing unto the Lord and praise His name, anthem sung in the Chapel
    Royal, June (?) 1855, MS.,[2] p. 6
Psalm 103, 4 voices *a cappella*, 1856, MS.,[3] p. 8
Sum sancto spiritu, fugue for chorus and orchestra, MS.[4]
Psalm for chorus and orchestra with German text, 1858, MS.
We have heard with our ears, anthem ded. Sir George Smart, 1st perf.,
    Chapel Royal, January 1860, MS.

[1] This, and the 5 songs that follow, were given the title 'Choral Songs',
dedicated to Otto Goldschmidt, and were published collectively by
Novello in 1868 as *Six Part-songs*.
[2] See *Musical Times*, 1901, p. 167; MS. given by Sullivan to W. H.
Cummings and sold at Sotheby's in 1917 (*see* E. H. Courville, *Autograph Prices Current*, II, 1916–17, London, p. 185).
[3] *See* fn. 2, p. 272 above.
[4] A. C. Mackenzie (*see* fn. 1, p. 271 above).

O love the Lord, ded. John Goss; Novello, 1864

We have heard with our ears, ded. Rev. T. Helmore; Novello (1865),[1] pp. 76, 77

Te Deum, Jubilate, and Kyrie; Novello, 1866/7

O God, Thou art worthy, for wedding of Adrian Hope, 3rd June 1867; Novello (1871)

'Mount Zion', 'Formosa' (or 'Falfield'), 'St Luke' (or 'St Nathaniel'), in *Psalms and Hymns for Divine Worship*; Nisbet, 1867

O taste and see, ded. Rev. C. H. Haweis; Novello (1867), pp. 74-5, 76-7

'Hymn of the Fatherland', pub. in *Good Words*; Strahan/Boosey, 1868

'Thou God of Love' and 'Of Thy Love', pub. in *Book of Praise Hymnal*; Macmillan, 1868

Rejoice in the Lord, for wedding of Rev. Brown-Borthwick,[2] Westminster Abbey, 16th April 1868; Boosey, 1868

'The strain upraise' and 'The Son of God' ('St Anne') in R. Brown-Borthwick, *Supplemental Hymn and Tune Book*, 3rd edn.; Novello, 1868

'Gennesareth' (R. Heber); Aylward, Salisbury, 1869

Sing, O heavens, ded. Rev. F. C. Byng; Boosey, 1869

I will worship towards thy Holy Temple, for 12th Commemoration of St Michael's College, Tenbury, Shropshire, ded. Rev. F. Gore Ouseley; Boosey (1871), p. 78

'Onward, Christian Soldiers' ('St Gertrude'); *Musical Times* (Dec.)/ Novello, 1871,[3] pp. 99, 266

Courage, brother, pub. in *Good Words*; Strahan, 1872

Te Deum laudamus and *Domine salvam fac Reginam*, for the recovery of the Prince of Wales, ded. The Queen, 1st perf., Crystal Palace, 1st May 1872; Novello, 1872, pp. 90-1, 97, 98

---

[1] On internal evidence a different setting from that of 1860, which is lost.

[2] Robert Brown-Borthwick (*b*. Aberdeen, 1840), ordained in 1865, was a curate in Gloucestershire until appointed Assistant Minister of the Quebec Chapel, London, in 1868. During the next year he became Vicar of Holy Trinity, Grange, Keswick, and devoted much of his time in that rural seclusion to the compilation of hymnals.

[3] The words, by Sabine Baring-Gould, were first published in *The Church Times* in 1865, with the following lines from the fourth stanza omitted: 'Kingdoms, nations, empires, / In destruction rolled.'

'Saviour, when in dust' ('St Mary Magdalene'), 'Welcome, happy morning' ('Fortunatus'), 'St Kevin', 'Safe home', 'Gentle shepherd' ('The long home'), 'Angel voices', 'Probior Deo' ('Aspiration'), 'Venite' ('Rest'), 'St Edmund' ('Fatherland'), 'Lacrymas', 'Lux mundi'; contributed to *The Hymnary*, Novello, 1872

'Christus', 'Clarence', 'Coena Domini', 'Coronae', 'Dulci sonantia', 'Ever faithful', 'Evelyn', 'Golden sheaves', 'Hanford',[1] 'Holy City', 'Hushed was the evening hymn', 'Lux eoi', 'Lux in tenebrae', 'Paradise', 'Pilgrimage', 'Resurrexit', 'St Francis', 'St Millicent', 'St Patrick', 'St Theresa', 'Saints of God', 'Ultor omnipotens', 'Valete', 'Veni Creator'; in *Church Hymns*, S.P.C.K., 1874

Litany, nos. 1–3; *Church Hymns*, 2nd edn., S.P.C.K., 1875

'Audite audientes me', 'Constance', 'Ecclesia', 'Promissio Patris'; *New Church Hymn Book*, S.P.C.K., 1875

I will mention Thy loving-kindness, ded. John Stainer; Novello (1875)

'Carrow' ('My God I thank thee'); Hodder & Stoughton, 1875

Hearken unto me; *Musical Times* (Nov.)/Novello, 1877

Turn Thy face; *Musical Times* (Jan.)/Novello, 1878

Who is like unto Thee? ded. Walter Parratt; Novello (1883)

Te Deum Laudamus, A Thanksgiving for Victory, composed 1900, 1st perf. (posthumous), St Paul's Cathedral, 8th June 1902; Novello, 1902, pp. 255, 257, 260

'The roseate hues'; Novello, 1901

'Bolwell' and 'Chapel Royal'; Novello, 1902

I will lay me down in peace; Novello, 1910

VII *Works for chorus and orchestra (cantatas, oratorios, etc.)*

Kenilworth, a Masque (H. F. Chorley), 1st perf., Birmingham, 8th September 1864; Chappell (1865), pp. 38–40, 46, 73, 89, 208

The Prodigal Son (A. S. Sullivan), Oratorio, 1st perf., Worcester, 8th September 1869; Boosey (1869),[2] pp. 60–1, 66 n. 26, 77, 89–90, 116, 222, 266

On shore and sea (Tom Taylor), ded. George Grove, 1st perf., Albert Hall, 1st May 1871; Boosey (1871), pp. 62, 66 n. 26, 73

---

[1] See p. 99.

[2] Prefacing No. 2, 'There is joy', on the autograph score, is Sullivan's signature, followed by the date, 'May 1869'.

The Light of the World (A. S. Sullivan), Oratorio, ded. H. R. H. The
Duchess of Edinburgh, 1st perf., Birmingham, 27th August 1873;
Cramer (1873), pp. 96, 98–9

The Martyr of Antioch (from Dean Henry Hart Milman), Sacred
Musical Drama, 1st perf., Leeds, 15th October 1880; Chappell
(1880), pp. 126, 205–6, 209, 217–21, 266

Ode for the Opening of the Colonial and Indian Exhibition (A. Tennyson),
1st perf., Albert Hall, 4th May 1886; Novello, 1886, p. 146

The Golden Legend (H. W. Longfellow, adapted Joseph Bennett),
Cantata, 1st perf., Leeds, 16th October 1886, R.C.M. MS. 2017;
Novello, 1886, pp. 145–7, 149, 150, 153, 159, 171, 209, 212, 215,
216, 218, 221–6, 227 n. 11, 238, 243, 251, 257, 260, 264

Ode for the Laying of the Foundation Stone of the Imperial Institute (Lewis
Morris), 1st perf. on the site of the Institute, 4th July 1887;
Chappell (1887)

VIII *Music for the theatre*

(1) Incidental music   (3) Operetta
(2) Ballet   (4) Opera

Unless otherwise stated references are to London theatres

(1)

The Tempest (Shakespeare), Introduction, Ariel's song, Entr'acte,
Grotesque dance, Entr'acte and Epilogue, Dance of Nymphs and
Reapers; 1st perf., Leipzig Gewandhaus, 6th April 1861; 1st perf.
in England, with additional numbers, Crystal Palace, 5th April
1862; Novello, 1891, pp. 23, 24, 25, 26, 33–6, 37, 39, 44, 71, 81–5,
159, 160, 215, 229, 263, 264

The Merchant of Venice (Shakespeare), Grotesque dance of Pierrots
and Harlequins, Bourrée, Serenade, Valse; 1st perf., Prince's
Theatre, Manchester, 19th September 1871; pfte. duet, Cramer
(1873); full score, Bosworth, Leipzig (1898),[1] pp. 62, 101, 160, 252

The Merry Wives of Windsor (Shakespeare), Act V, no. 1 'Windsor
Park'; solo and chorus, 'Fairies, black, grey, green and white';
dance; dance with chorus; 1st perf., Theatre Royal, Manchester,
30th August 1874; MS.,[2] pp. 103, 160–2

---

[1] For Serenade, see also *Venetian Serenade*, p. 275.
[2] Note on autograph: 'Bosworth has parts in Leipzig.' Regarding *Love
laid his sleepless head*, see p. 276.

Henry VIII (Shakespeare), March, King Henry's song, Graceful dance, Water music; 1st perf., Theatre Royal, Manchester, 29th August 1877; Metzler (1879–93),[1] pp. 162–3, 208, 264

Macbeth (Shakespeare), Overture, Preludes to 3rd, 5th and 6th Acts, Chorus of Spirits in the air, and 'Over hills and over mountains' (chorus); 1st perf., Lyceum Theatre, 29th December 1888; Overture only, Chappell, 1888, pp. 150, 169, 212–13, 229–31, 264

The Foresters (A. Tennyson), 1st perf., Daly's Theatre, New York, 25th March 1892; Chappell, 1892, p. 194

King Arthur (J. Comyns Carr), Chorus of Lake Spirits (Prologue), Chorus of Unseen Spirits (Prologue), The Chaunt of the Grail (Act I), The May Song (Act II), Funeral March and Final Chorus (Acts III and IV); 1st perf., Lyceum Theatre, 12th January 1895; pfte. score arr. W. Bendall, Novello, 1894, pp. 200, 243–4, 261 n. 6

(2)

L'île enchantée, 1st perf., Covent Garden Theatre, 14th May 1864,[2] pp. 38, 48 n. 11, 103, 160, 161

Victoria and merrie England, for Queen Victoria's Diamond Jubilee: in 8 scenes—(1) Druid period, (2, 3) Elizabethan, (4, 5) vaguely 17th century, centring on 'Herne the Hunter' and 'Arrival of Yule Log', (6) Period of Charles II, (7) Tableau vivant of Coronation of Queen Victoria, (8) English, Irish, Scottish regiments [Welsh soldiery excluded from score on account of contrapuntal incompatibility of Welsh tunes], followed by colonial troops; 1st perf., Alhambra Theatre, 25th May 1897; Metzler, 1897, pp. 248–9

(3)

Cox and Box, *a triumviretta* (F. C. Burnand, based on *Box and Cox*, Maddison Morton), ded. J. W. Davison, 1st perf., Prince's Theatre, Manchester, 17th December 1866; Boosey (1871),[3] pp. 28, 53–5, 63, 64, 66 n. 11, 70, 114, 172

The Contrabandista (F. C. Burnand), 1st perf., St George's Hall, London, 18th December 1867; enlarged and re-titled *The*

---

[1] Original MS. of *Henry VIII* music sold at Sotheby's, *see* fn. 3, p. 271.
[2] Thematic material used in *The Merry Wives of Windsor*, *see* p. 103.
[3] The title on the MS. (sold at Sotheby's, *see* fn. 3, p. 271 above) reads: 'Ouverture à la Triumvirette musicale "Coxe et Boxe" et "Bouncer" composée par Arthur S. Sullivan. Paris. 23 Juillet 1867. Hotel Meurice.'

Chieftain, 1st perf., Savoy Theatre, 12th December 1894; Boosey, 1894,[1] pp. 63, 64, 65, 169, 172, 200

Thespis (W. S. Gilbert), 1st perf., Gaiety Theatre, 23rd December 1871, MS., pp. 102, 104, 106

Trial by Jury (W. S. Gilbert), 1st perf., New Royalty Theatre, 25th March 1875; Chappell (1875), pp. 106, 107, 115, 127, 154 n. 6, 159, 167

The Zoo, Musical Folly (B. Rowe, = B. C. Stephenson), 1st perf., St James's Theatre, 5th June 1875; privately issued (with a note on the libretto by Terence Rees) from 25 Nightingale Square, London, 1969, pp. 106, 173, 187 n. 4

The Sorcerer (W. S. Gilbert), 1st perf., Opera Comique, 17th November 1877; Metzler, 1877, pp. 109, 110, 114, 119 n. 29, 125, 137, 172, 183, 187 n. 10, 251

H.M.S. Pinafore (W. S. Gilbert), 1st perf., Opera Comique, 25th May 1878; Metzler (1878); German version, *Amor am Bord*, in full score, Litolff (1882), pp. 6, 110–12, 114–17, 122–3, 125, 140, 143, 154 n. 6, 157 n. 49, 173, 174, 178, 205

The Pirates of Penzance (W. S. Gilbert), 1st perf., Bijou Theatre, Paignton, Devon, 30th December 1879; 1st American perf., Fifth Avenue Theatre, New York, 31st December 1879; 1st London perf., Opera Comique, 3rd April 1880; Chappell (1880) pp. 103, 117, 120 n. 30, 122–3, 125, 157 n. 49, 173, 184

Patience, Aesthetic Opera (W. S. Gilbert), 1st perf., Opera Comique, 23rd April 1881; Chappell (1881), pp. 105, 126–30 *pass.*, 136, 143, 157 n. 38, 173, 176f., 180–1, 219, 258

Iolanthe, Fairy Opera (W. S. Gilbert), 1st perf., Savoy Theatre, 25th November 1882; Chappell (1883), pp. 3, 104, 105, 129, 134, 136, 142, 172, 173, 182

Princess Ida (W. S. Gilbert), 1st perf., Savoy Theatre, 5th January 1884; Chappell (1884), pp. 137, 172, 173, 183, 185

The Mikado (W. S. Gilbert), 1st perf., Savoy Theatre, 14th March 1885; Chappell (1885), vocal score with German text, Forberg/

---

[1] First title on MS. (sold at Sotheby's, *see* fn. 3, p. 271 above) reads: '"The Contrabandista" or the Law of the Ladrones.' The second title is: '"The Contrabandista" or the Law of the Ladrones. Comic Opera in two Acts . . .' At the foot of p. 1 (Act I) Sullivan wrote, in blue pencil: 'Copy this in D♭ please. I have marked alternatives in blue pencil. If possible send to the St George's Ha[ll] for Miss Franklen to sing tonight. A. S. Sullivan.'

Chappell (1889), pp. 80, 137–45 *pass.*, 147–8, 151, 156–7, 171, 174, 175, 176, 199, 201

Ruddigore (W. S. Gilbert), 1st perf., Savoy Theatre, 22nd January 1887; Chappell (1887), pp. 65, 145, 146, 163, 171, 174, 175, 182–3, 185, 238, 247, 267

The Yeomen of the Guard (W. S. Gilbert), 1st perf., Savoy Theatre, 3rd October 1888; Chappell (1888), pp. 107, 143, 148, 151, 171, 173, 174, 176, 178–9, 181, 182, 184–5

The Gondoliers (W. S. Gilbert), 1st perf., Savoy Theatre, 7th December 1889; Chappell (1890), pp. 153, 159, 165, 171, 172, 173, 174, 187 n. 13, 188f., 251, 268

Haddon Hall (Sydney Grundy), 1st perf., Savoy Theatre, 24th September 1892; Chappell, 1892, pp. 80, 182, 185, 193–4, 195, 214

Utopia Limited (W. S. Gilbert), 1st perf., Savoy Theatre, 7th October 1893; Chappell, 1893, pp. 105, 184, 196–8 *pass.*, 261 n. 4, 268

The Grand Duke (W. S. Gilbert), 1st perf., Savoy Theatre, 7th March 1896; Chappell, 1896, pp. 174, 178, 181, 185, 187 n. 5, 199–201, 268

The Rose of Persia (Basil Hood), 1st perf., Savoy Theatre, 29th November 1899; Chappell, 1900, pp. 253–4, 259

The Emerald Isle (Basil Hood), unfinished by Sullivan, completed by Edward German, 1st perf., Savoy Theatre, 27th April 1901; Chappell, 1901, pp. 256, 260

(4)

The Sapphire Necklace (H. F. Chorley), unfinished; overture perf. St James's Hall, 11th July 1864; song 'Over the Roof' pub. Cramer (1866); madrigal 'When love and beauty' pub. Novello, 1898,[1] pp. 38, 45, 79

Ivanhoe, Romantic Opera (Julian Sturgis from Walter Scott), 1st perf., Royal English Opera House, Cambridge Circus, 31st January 1891; Chappell (1891), pp. 3, 149, 150, 163, 194, 200, 211, 226, 229–44, 261, 265

The Beauty Stone, Romantic Musical Drama (A. W. Pinero and J. Comyns Carr), 1st perf., Savoy Theatre, 28th May 1898; Chappell, 1898, pp. 223, 249–51

---

[1] The opera was assigned to Cramer for £251 10s. as *The False heiress* on 16th July 1868, and, with performing rights, reassigned to Sullivan on 26th May 1880 by Cramer's liquidator for £275.

IX *Miscellaneous*

Additional accompaniments to *Jephtha* (Handel), 1st perf., St James's Hall (Oratorio Concert, cond. J. Barnby), 5th February 1869; unpublished, pp. 61–2

Editor of *Church Hymns* (Sullivan harmonized or arranged 69 tunes and included 38 original tunes, of which 14 had appeared previously) S.P.C.K., 1874

There is none like unto the God of Jeshurun, anthem unfinished by Sir John Goss, completed by Sullivan; Novello (1882)

Turn thee again and *Mercy and truth*, adaptations from Russian liturgical music; Novello (1874)

No. 116 'of a selection of trios ad. to English words', *Hosanna to the Son of David*, after O. Gibbons (a long way), 3 voices and pfte. acc.; Cramer (n.d.)

Speech at the Festival of the Royal Society of Musicians, *The Lute*, No. 4, Vol. I, pp. 77–9 (16th April 1883)

About music, address given at the Birmingham and Midland Institute, 29th October 1888; Birmingham (1888), pp. 135, 136

X *Arrangements of Sullivan's music by other hands*

George Lowell Tracy (1855–1921), *see* pp. 155–6, issued the following Sullivan arrangements in vocal score:

Princess Ida; Stoddart (Philadelphia), 1884

The Mikado; Pond & Co., New York, 1885, p. 139f.

Ruddygore [*sic*]; Pond & Co., New York, 1887

Johann Ernst Perabo (1845–1920), *see* pp. 155–6, issued *Iolanthe*, ten transcriptions for the piano (Op. 14); E. Perabo, Boston, *c.* 1887, p. 156

The music section of the Museum Carolino Augusteum, Salzburg, contains: Potpourri 1–2 from *The Mikado* (pfte.). The arrangement, by an unknown hand, is dated 11th February 1898 (Hs. 352)

Appendix 2

RACING RECORDS

Sullivan's career as race-horse owner effectively covered the years 1894–1896, although the registration of his colours was not discontinued until 1898. He had at one time purposed joining a syndicate with Capt. James Octavius Machell and Ernest Clay Ker Seymer with a view to purchasing the Duchess of Montrose's yearlings for £10,000. Nothing came of this, which, no doubt, was regretted since among the yearlings was La Flêche, which won both the Oaks and the St Leger in 1892 for Baron de Hirsch. When Sullivan took up racing seriously (or half-seriously) he did so on his own account.

Colours: pink, violet belt and cap, registered with the Jockey Club in 1894.

Trainer: J. Jewitt, Bedford Cottage, Newmarket.

Details of entries

Horse	Meeting	Date	Race	Jockey	Finished	Annotations
		1894				
Cranmer, 2 year old bay colt, by Satiety out of Heresy, by Hermit, owned by Sullivan	Newmarket	24 May	Dyke Plate	T. Loates	2	Cranmer (100 to 15 against) finished a length behind the favourite, the Duke of Hamilton's Small Mint
Blue Mark, 2 year old brown filly, by Mark, out of Blue Pennant	Salisbury	1 June	Wilton Park Stakes	C. R. Froude	1	owner, J. Lowe
Cranmer	Ascot	21 June	New Stakes	T. J. Calder	–	
Blue Mark	Newmarket	18 July	A Selling Plate	W. Bradford	2	owner, Capt. J. Orr-Ewing
Cranmer	Great Yarmouth	18 Sept.	A Maiden Two years old Plate	T. Loates	2	favourite at 6 to 4 against; Cranmer finished ¾ length behind C. Howard's John o' Seaham

Horse	Meeting	Date	Race	Jockey	Finished	Annotations
		1894				
Blue Mark	Newmarket	22 Sept.	A Selling Stakes	S. Loates	–	owner, Capt. J. Orr-Ewing
Blue Mark	Newmarket	26 Sept.	A Selling Plate	S. Loates	–	owner, Capt. J. Orr-Ewing
Cranmer	Newmarket	28 Sept.	Scurry Nursery Stakes (a handicap)	G. Barrett	–	
Blue Mark	Newmarket	10 Oct.	A Selling Plate	S. Loates	1	owner, Sir James Miller [1]: favourite at 9 to 4 against
Cranmer	Newmarket	10 Oct.	A Selling Plate	T. Loates	2	5 to 2 against
Blue Mark	Newmarket	11 Oct.	A Selling Plate	F. Allsopp	3	bought by Sullivan on 10 Oct. for 500 guineas; favourite at 5 to 4 against: winner, Lord Ellesmere's Clog-Dance
Cranmer	Gatwick	17 Oct.	Crawter Plate	T. Loates	2	beaten by a head by H. Heasman's Bolero, by Saraband
Blue Mark	Newmarket	24 Oct.	Selling Plate	T. Loates	2	favourite at 4 to 1 against, beaten by a head
Cranmer	Newmarket	26 Oct.	Selling Nursery Handicap	T. Loates	3	5 to 2 against
Cranmer	Warwick	19 Nov.	Kineton Two years old Plate	T. Loates	–	100 to 8 against
Cranmer	Warwick	21 Nov.	Avon Selling Nursery Handicap	T. J. Calder	4	won by Orxema, by Saraband, by 6 lengths; two horses dead heat for 2nd place, Cranmer one length behind
Blue Mark	Manchester	23 Nov.	Eglinton Nursery Handicap	Tilbury	3	owner, Sir J. Blundell Maple, who paid Sullivan 400 guineas
		1895				
Blue Mark	Newmarket	14 May	Visitor's Plate	Bradford	1	won by a neck
Cranmer	Newmarket	14 May	Visitor's Plate	C. Ward	2	100 to 8 against
Cranmer	Newmarket	16 May	Third Welter Handicap	C. Ward	–	100 to 8 against

[1] Winner of the Derby in 1890 with Sainfoin and in 1903 with Rock Sand.

Horse	Meeting	Date	Race	Jockey	Finished	Annotations
		1895				
Cranmer	Newmarket	1 July	A Welter Handicap	C. Ward	–	100 to 8 against
Cranmer	Newmarket	10 Oct.	Flying Welter Handicap	C. Ward	–	100 to 8 against
Cranmer	Derby	15 Nov.	Stainsby Selling Stakes	G. Chalmer	–	100 to 6 against
		1896				
Cranmer	Newmarket	14 May	Third Welter Handicap	T. Loates	2	85 to 40 against, lost by ¾ length
Cranmer	Doncaster	8 Sept.	Champagne Stakes	T. Loates	–	3 to 1 against
Cranmer	Doncaster	10 Sept.	Corporation Selling Handicap	Robinson	–	100 to 12 against
Cranmer	Great Yarmouth	16 Sept.	South Denes Selling Plate	T. Loates	1	4 to 1 against: sold to Mr R. Deptidge for 140 guineas

Bibliography

A Short History of Cheap Music (from the records of Novello, Ewer & Co.), London, 1887.

'Arthur Sullivan', in *Neue Musik-Zeitung*, 22. Jrg., p. 13, Stuttgart/Leipzig, 1901.

Crockford's Clerical Directory, 1852 *seqq.*, London.

Crystal Palace, *Saturday Concerts Programmes*, 1867 *seqq.*

Festschrift zum 75-jährigen Bestehen des Königl-Konservatoriums der Musik zu Leipzig, Leipzig, 1918.

German Reed Repertory of Musical Pieces, London, 1896.

Hochschule für Musik Leipzig, 1843–1968, Leipzig, 1968.

Interview with Fred R. Spark, in *Illustrated London News*, 5th October 1895.

L'Art dramatique et musical au XXe siècle, Paris, 1901 (1º Année), 1902 (2º Année).

Letters to Charles Plumptre Johnson relating to his edition of *Topsyturvydom* (W. S. Gilbert), BM.g. 27.0.132.

Monograph of the Royal English Opera: Proprietor and Manager, R. D'Oyly Carte, London, [1888].

Neue Zeitschrift für Musik, vols. 52–4, Leipzig, 1860–1.

New York [Dramatic] Mirror, 25th July, 26th September and 3rd October 1885.

Obituary of Fanny Carter Ronalds, in *Boston Transcript*, 3rd June 1910.

Obituary of Sullivan, in *Bühne und Welt*, 3. Jrg., pp. 263–4, Berlin, 1901.

Philharmonic Society: *Analytical and Historical Programmes*, 1871 *seqq.*

Prince's Theatre (Manchester), *Programmes*, 1866 *seqq.*

Souvenir of King Arthur, by *J. Comyns Carr* (Lyceum Theatre, 12th January 1895), illustrated by J. Bernard Partridge and Hawes Craven, London, 1895.

Surrey Theatre Playbills, BM. Playbills 311–13 and 389.

The Jewish Year Book, 5657, London, 1896.

The Rogers Memorial Room (*An Account . . . of the Memorabilia presented to Harvard College in 1930 by Clara Kathleen and Henry Munroe Rogers*), privately printed, Cambridge, Massachusetts, 1935.
Theatre Notebook, vol. XV, no. 4, London, 1961.
W. S. Gilbert Collection, BM. Add. MSS. 48289–353 (65 volumes).

ALLEN, REGINALD: *The First Night Gilbert and Sullivan*, New York' 1938.
BACHE, CONSTANCE: *Brother Musicians, Reminiscences of Edward and Walter Bache*, London, 1901. (Sullivan's name appears on the list of subscribers.)
BAILY, LESLIE: *The Gilbert and Sullivan Book*, London, 1952.
BENNETT, JOSEPH, ed.: *The Lute, I*, London, 1883.
—: *Forty Years of Music, 1865–1905*, London, 1908.
BLACKBURN, VERNON: 'Sir Arthur Sullivan' in *The Fortnightly Review*, London, January 1901.
BURNAND, FRANCIS C.: *Records and Reminiscences*, 2 vols., London, 1904.
CARR, ALICE COMYNS: *J. Comyns Carr, Stray Memories, by His Wife*, London, 1920.
CARR, J[OSEPH WILLIAM] COMYNS: *King Arthur, A Drama*, London, 1895.
—: *Some Eminent Victorians*, London, 1908.
CELLIER, FRANÇOIS ARSÈNE and BRIDGEMAN, CUNNINGHAM: *Gilbert, Sullivan, and D'Oyly Carte*, London, 1914.
CERF, B. A. and KLOPFER, D. S.: *The Complete Plays of Gilbert and Sullivan*, New York, 1936.
CLÉMENT, FÉLIX and LAROUSSE, PIERRE: *Dictionnaire lyrique ou Histoire des Opéras*, with second supplement, Paris, 1872.
COURVILLE, E. H., compiler and ed.: *Autograph Prices Current*, vol. i, *1914–16*, London, 1916.
CZECH, STAN: *Das Operettenbuch*, Stuttgart, 1960.
DAVISON, HENRY: *From Mendelssohn to Wagner* (the Memoirs of J. W. Davison), London, 1912.
DELAMOTTE, P. H.: *Photographic Views of the Progress of the Crystal Palace, Sydenham*, London, 1855.
DUNHILL, THOMAS F.: *Sullivan's Comic Operas, A Critical Appreciation*, London, 1928.
DUNN, GEORGE E.: *A Gilbert and Sullivan Dictionary*, London, 1936.
ELKIN, ROBERT: *Royal Philharmonic*, London, [n.d.].
ENGEL, LOUIS: *From Handel to Hallé*, pp. 95–103, London, 1890.

ENGELBRECHT, CHRISTIANE, AND OTHERS: *Theater in Kassel*, Kassel, 1959.

FESCHOTTE, JACQUES: *Histoire du Music-Hall*, Paris, 1965.

FÉTIS, F. J.: *Biographie des musiciens (1835): Supplément II*, Paris, 1880.

FINDON, B. W.: *Sir Arthur Sullivan: His Life and Music*, London, 1904.

FITZ-GERALD, S. J. ADAIR: *The Story of the Savoy Operas* (Introduction by T. P. O'Connor, M.P.), London, 1926.

FITZGERALD, PERCY HETHERINGTON: *The Savoy Operas and the Savoyards*, London, 1894.

FRANCILLON, ROBERT: *Mid-Victorian Memories*, London, [1914].

FULLER-MAITLAND, J. A.: *English Music in the XIXth Century*, London, 1902.

—: *A Door-keeper of Music*, London, 1926.

GILBERT, WILLIAM SCHWENCK: *Original Plays*, 4 vols., London, 1902.

—: *Topsyturvydom*, ed. Charles Plumptre Johnson, private edition of 150 copies, Oxford, 1931.

—: *Plays and Poems of W. S. Gilbert* (Preface by Deems Taylor), New York, 1935.

GODWIN, A. H.: *Gilbert and Sullivan* (Introduction by G. K. Chesterton), London, 1926.

GOLDBERG, ISAAC: *Sir William S. Gilbert. A Study in Modern Satire. A Hand Book on Gilbert and the Gilbert-Sullivan Operas*, Boston, Massachusetts, [1913].

—: *The Story of Gilbert and Sullivan; or the 'Compleat' Savoyard*, London, 1929.

GRAVES, C. L.: *The Life and Letters of Sir George Grove, C.B.*, London, 1903.

GREENE, HARRY PLUNKET: *Charles Villiers Stanford*, London, 1935.

GROSSMITH, GEORGE: *A Society Clown*, Bristol, 1888.

HANSLICK, EDUARD: *Musikalisches Skizzenbuch*, pt. iv, *Moderne Oper*, Berlin, 1888.

—: *Aus dem Concert-Saal, 1848–68*, Vienna/Leipzig, 1897.

HARTNOLL, PHYLLIS, ed.: *Shakespeare in Music*, London, 1964.

HAVERGAL, FRANCIS T.: *Memorials of Frederick Arthur Gore Ouseley*, London, 1889.

HELLBORN, HEINRICH KREISSLE VON: *The Life of Franz Schubert*, translated by A. D. Coleridge, London, 1869.

HOGARTH, GEORGE: *The Philharmonic Society of London*, London, 1862.

HOLLINGSHEAD, JOHN: *Gaiety Chronicles*, London, 1898.

—: *Good Old Gaiety*, London, 1903.

HUGHES, GERVASE: *The Music of Arthur Sullivan*, London, 1960.

JACOBS, ARTHUR: 'Sullivan, Gilbert, and the Victorians' in *The Music Review*, XII, 2, May 1951.

—: *Gilbert and Sullivan*, London, 1951.

JOHNSON, CHARLES PLUMPTRE, ed.: *see under* GILBERT.

JULIAN, JOHN: *Dictionary of Hymnology*, London, 1915.

KAUBISCH, HERMANN: *Operette*, Berlin, 1955.

KEEFER, LUBOV: *Baltimore's Music*, Baltimore, 1962.

KENNEDY, MICHAEL: *The Hallé Tradition*, Manchester, 1960.

KLEIN, HERMANN: *Thirty Years of Musical Life in London, 1870–1900*, London, 1903.

—: *The Golden Age of Opera*, London, 1933.

KNESCHKE, EMIL: *Das Conservatorium der Musik in Leipzig (Festgabe zum 25 jährigen Jubiläum am 2 April 1868)*, Leipzig, 1868.

LANDAUER, BELLA C.: *Gilbert and Sullivan Influence on American Trade Cards*, privately printed, New York, 1931.

LAWRENCE, A.: *Sir Arthur Sullivan*, London, 1899.

LEHMANN, R. C.: *Memories of Half a Century*, London, 1908.

LUBBOCK, MARK: *The Complete Book of Light Opera*, London, 1962.

LYSONS, DANIEL, AND OTHERS: *Origins and Progress of the Meeting of the Three Choirs*, Gloucester, 1895.

MACKENZIE, ALEXANDER C.: 'The Life and Work of Arthur Sullivan' in *Sammelbände der Internationalen Musik-Gesellschaft*, Jrg. III (1901–1902), pp. 539–64, Leipzig, 1902.

MAIR, CARLENE, compiler: *The Chappell Story, 1861–1961*, London, 1961.

[MAPLESON, JAMES HENRY]: *The Mapleson Memoirs, 1848–88*, 3rd edn., 2 vols., London, 1888.

MOSCHELES, CHARLOTTE: *Life of Moscheles, with Selections from his Correspondence*, translated by A. D. Coleridge, 2 vols., London, 1873.

MOSCHELES, F.: *In Bohemia with Du Maurier*, London, 1896.

NICOLL, ALLARDYCE: *A History of English Drama, 1660–1900*, vol. v, *Late Nineteenth Century Drama, 1850–1900*, Cambridge, 1959.

PALADIAN, SIRVART: *Sir Arthur Sullivan: An Index to the Texts of His Vocal Works*, Detroit Studies in Music Bibliography 2, Detroit, 1961.

PEARSON, HESKETH: *Gilbert and Sullivan*, London, 1935.

REES, TERENCE: *Thespis—A Gilbert and Sullivan Enigma*, London, 1964.

ROBINSON, RAY EDWIN: *A History of the Peabody Conservatory of Music* (*Baltimore*), Doctoral dissertation for Indiana University, typescript, 1969.

ROGERS, CLARA KATHLEEN (BARNETT): *My Voice and I*, Chicago, 1910.

—: *Memories of a Musical Career*, Boston, 1919. Also printed in *Clara Kathleen Rogers Memorial Edition*, Norwood, Massachusetts, 1932.

—: 'The Story of Two Lives' in *Clara Kathleen Rogers Memorial Edition*, Norwood, Massachusetts, 1932.

RONALD, LANDON: *Variations on a Personal Theme*, London, 1922.

SCHERING, ARNOLD: *Geschichte des Oratoriums*, pp. 583–5, Leipzig, 1911.

SHAW, GEORGE BERNARD: *Music in London, 1890–4*, 3 vols., London, 1932.

—: *London Music*, London, 1937.

—: *Shaw on Music*, selected by Eric Bentley, New York, 1955.

SHEPPARD, E.: *George, Duke of Cambridge*, 2 vols., London, 1906.

SIMCOE, H. AUGUSTINE: *Sullivan v. Critic, A Study in Press Phenomenon*, London, 1906.

SPARK, FRED R. and BENNETT, JOSEPH: *A Full History of the Leeds Musical Festivals, 1858–89*, Leeds/London, 1892.

SPRITTLES, J.: *Leeds Musical Festivals*, Reprint Thoresby Society Miscellany, vol. xiii, pt. 2, Leeds, [n.d.].

STANFORD, CHARLES VILLIERS: *Studies and Memories*, London, 1908.

—: *Pages from an Unwritten Diary*, London, 1914.

—: *Interludes*, London, 1922.

STEVENS, DENIS, ed.: *A History of Song*, London, 1960.

STRAVINSKY, IGOR: 'How Stravinsky became a Gilbert and Sullivan Fan', in *The New York Times*, 27th October 1968.

SULLIVAN, HERBERT and FLOWER, NEWMAN: *Sir Arthur Sullivan, His Life, Letters and Diaries*, London, 1927. Second edition, 1950.

TENNYSON, CHARLES: *Alfred Tennyson*, London, 1949.

UPTON, GEORGE: *The Standard Cantatas*, Chicago, 1888.

—: *The Standard Oratorios*, Chicago, 1899.

WEATHERLEY, J. E., J. P. and C. T.: *The Racing Calendar, 1894–5*, London.

WELLS, WALTER J.: *Souvenir of Sir Arthur Sullivan, Mus. Doc., M.V.O.*, London, 1901.

WHITE, ERIC WALTER: *The Rise of English Opera*, London, 1951.

WILLEBY, CHARLES: *Masters of English Music*, London, 1893.

WILLIAMSON, AUDREY: *Gilbert and Sullivan Opera: A New Assessment*, New York, 1953.

WOOD, HENRY J.: *My Life of Music*, London, 1938.

WYNDHAM, H. SAXE: *August Manns and the Saturday Concerts*, London, 1909.

—: *Arthur Seymour Sullivan*, London, 1926.

General Index